1988–89 Environmental Law Society Officers

WILLIAM P. KEALEY
President

RANDI B. SILVERMAN
Managing Editor

ANDREW C. DANA
THOMAS F. HAENSLY
WILLIAM P. KEALEY
RANDI B. SILVERMAN
Editors-in-Chief

ELIZABETH R. PULLING
Vice-President, External Affairs

SHARON BUCCINO
Vice-President, Education

PATRICIA M. GREENE
Vice-President, Business Affairs

ALAN N. BICK
PATRICIA M. GREENE
PAMELA S. KELLY
ELIZABETH R. PULLING
JULIETTE M. STEADMAN
JOSEPH M. SULLIVAN
Senior Editors

JANET C. HOEFFEL
JESSICA KAPLAN
Vice-Presidents, Field Studies

The Endangered Species Act

A Guide to Its Protections and Implementation

Contents

ACKNOWLEDGMENTS vii

EDITOR'S PREFACE...................................... viii

FOREWORD 1
      Representative John D. Dingell

CHAPTER 1:   An Introduction to the Extinction Crisis ..   7

CHAPTER 2:   History and Framework of the Endangered
Species Act   19

CHAPTER 3:   Identifying Species to Protect: Listing and
Critical Habitat Designation...............   37

CHAPTER 4:   The Ban on Takings and Other Statutory
Prohibitions.............................   59

CHAPTER 5:   Affirmative Mandates to Conserve Listed
Species   87

CHAPTER 6:   Procedural Aspects of Interagency
Consultation under Section 7   105

CHAPTER 7:   Substantive Protections of Section 7:
Avoiding Jeopardy and Habitat
Destruction   137

CHAPTER 8:   International Aspects   173

CHAPTER 9:   Species Conservation and the Courts:
Judicial Review under the Endangered
Species Act   181

CHAPTER 10: Conclusion   205

Acknowledgments

The Stanford Environmental Law Society (ELS) wishes to thank the Conservation and Research Foundation, whose generosity made publication of this handbook possible. ELS also wishes to thank the Stanford Public Interest Law Foundation, which provided a grant to enable the author to research this handbook in the summer of 1985. A fellowship with the Natural Resources Law Institute, Northwestern School of Law, Lewis and Clark College, enabled the author to make final revisions to the manuscript.

The author would like to thank all of those individuals who took time to answer his questions about the Endangered Species Act and those who provided helpful documents. The author particularly wishes to thank the personnel in the Office of Endangered Species, U.S. Fish and Wildlife Service, Region 6 in Denver, Colorado. The author is also grateful to Andrew Dana, who did excellent editing work under difficult circumstances. Finally, the author wishes to thank his parents and family members for their support and encouragement.

Editor's Preface

Editing this Handbook proved to be an enormous task. Members of the Stanford Environmental Law Society from five Stanford Law School classes contributed precious time and considerable effort to seeing this book through to completion. All deserve praise and thanks for their dedication.

The Stanford Environmental Law Society generally follows standard legal citation conventions set forth in *A Uniform System of Citation.*[1] Nevertheless, several words of clarification are in order. Unless otherwise noted, all citations to the United States Code (U.S.C.) refer to the 1982 Code. Citations to supplementary sections of the Code are identified by year of Supplement. Similarly, all citations to the Code of Federal Regulations (C.F.R.) refer to the 1987 version of the Code, unless specifically noted otherwise.

For purposes of convenience, the Handbook contains several commonly occurring abbreviations for Acts of Congress and for federal agencies. Most of these abbreviations are listed below:

CITES	Convention on International Trade in Endangered Species
ESA	Endangered Species Act
OCSLA	Outer Continental Shelf Leasing Act
FWS	U.S. Fish and Wildlife Service
NMFS	National Marine Fisheries Service
TVA	Tennessee Valley Authority

Other abbreviations occur in places throughout the text, but these are always identified in close proximity to the section where the abbreviations are used.

Although the editorial input of the Stanford Environmental Law Society to this Handbook has been considerable, the Handbook remains solely Dan Rohlf's interpretation of the Endangered Species Act. His dedication to the project has been unswerving, and his patience with the editorial process has been remarkable.

---

1. A Uniform System of Citation (14th ed. 1986).

Foreword

John D. Dingell*

Fifteen years ago, the Endangered Species Act of 1973 (ESA) became law. The goal Congress set then was unparalleled in all of history. Our country resolved to put an end to the decades—indeed, centuries—of neglect that had resulted in the extinction of the passenger pigeon and the Carolina parakeet, and the near extinction of the bison and many other species with which we share this great land. If it were possible to avoid causing the extinction of another species, we resolved to do exactly that. It was my distinct pleasure to serve then as Chairman of the Subcommittee on Fisheries and Wildlife Conservation and Environment of the House Committee on Merchant Marine and Fisheries and to introduce the bill, H.R. 37, that eventually became the Endangered Species Act.

When Congress passed the Endangered Species Act, it set a clear public policy that we would not be indifferent to the destruction of nature's bounty. Our duty to stem that destruction derives from more than ethical considerations, though such considerations would be a sufficient basis for action. Living plants and animals have, through the centuries, developed a means of coping with disease, drought, predation and a myriad of other threats. Understanding how they do so enables us to improve the pest and drought resistance of our crops, discover new medicines for the conquest of disease and make other advances vital to our welfare. Living wild species are like a library of books still unread. Our heedless destruction of them is akin to burning that library without ever having read its books. The Endangered

* Elected to Congress in 1955, Representative John D. Dingell (D-MI) has served as Chairman of the House Energy and Commerce Committee since 1981. He currently serves as a Congressional Board Member of the Migratory Bird Conservation Commission as well as on the Technology Advisory Board of the Office of Technology Assessment (OTA). Representative Dingell is widely recognized as the father of the nation's most important environmental legislation, including the Endangered Species Act, the National Environmental Policy Act, the Marine Mammal Protection Act, the National Wildlife Refuge System, and the Clean Air Act.

1

Species Act is the means by which we seek to avoid complicity in that senseless destruction.

Some people in 1973, and unfortunately still some today, belittled the goals of this great Act by belittling the species it seeks to protect. How easy it is to dismiss the protection of a fish, a mollusk, even a plant, as a frivolity, an example of foolish environmental excess. But who will belittle the lowly mold from which the wonder drug, penicillin, was discovered? Who will belittle the rosy periwinkle, a species of African violet? Had it been allowed to become extinct, we would be without the drug that has made it possible for most victims of childhood leukemia to survive that dreaded disease. Preventing the extinction of our fellow creatures is neither frivolity nor foolish environmental excess; it is the means by which we keep intact the great storehouse of natural treasures that make the progress of medicine, agriculture, science, and human life itself possible.

The Act, like our United States Constitution, was written as a flexible document, but durable enough to withstand the evolutionary alterations that have since occurred. Yet, in 1978, the Endangered Species Act, belittled and nearly eradicated, withstood harsh attacks through negotiations between environmentalists and industry.

The construction of the Tellico Dam project in the Tennessee Valley Authority (TVA) system was near completion, when in 1977 it was halted because of a small, rare fish called the snail darter. Before its construction, the dam had repeatedly been the subject of attack from area property owners concerned about the impact of the dam on property values and actual land possession. The 1973 discovery of the rare snail darter in waters near the Tellico project, and its subsequent listing as an endangered species, resulted in litigation to stop construction. In January 1977, the Sixth Circuit U.S. Court of Appeals upheld the operation of the Act and halted dam construction. Needless to say, the Tellico developers, outraged that their project could be ended because of a conflict with an endangered species, appealed the case to the United States Supreme Court. After much deliberation, the Court upheld the lower court decision in June 1978. The Supreme Court's decision sparked a major assault on the very heart of the Act.

Spearheaded by Congressional leaders from the Tennessee delegation, the industry sought to eliminate section 7 of the Act, which requires Federal agencies to take the necessary steps to prevent any destruction of habitat of an endangered species. The elimination of section 7 would have gutted the effective protective mechanism of the Act. Fortunately, a compromise was reached to create an independent board and an administrative procedure to resolve conflicts between Federal projects and endangered species habitat. The first decision by the board was the Tellico dam project and, once again, the project was put to rest, but not forever.

In 1979, over my objections and those of others intent on preserving the integrity of the ESA, Congress passed a measure to continue the construction of the Tellico Dam. Tellico Dam proponents made an end run around the Act by attaching a rider to a House energy and water appropriations bill. Despite considerable opposition to this legislatively created exception to the Act, the Senate narrowly voted to continue the project after the snail darters were removed to nearby waters.

In fifteen years, we have learned it is possible to reverse the road to extinction. In 1973, the symbol of our Nation, the bald eagle, was en route because the pesticide DDT had so poisoned its environment that the eagle could no longer lay hatchable eggs. When the government proposed to ban DDT, cotton farmers, citrus growers, and countless others rushed to tell us that the sky would surely fall, that they couldn't possibly stay in business without DDT. The sky didn't fall, we still have strong cotton and citrus industries, and the bald eagle is well on the road to recovery, aided by active programs of protection and restoration under the authority of the Endangered Species Act.

Other travelers on the road to extinction have turned around and begun the road to recovery. More whooping cranes fly south across the U.S.-Canadian border each fall and return north each spring than at any time in the past half century. Added insurance for the survival of that species has been purchased in the form of a separate and new population established by the ingenious method of putting whooper eggs into the nests of sandhill cranes. Similar intensive management efforts aided by the Endangered Species Act have made possible the reintroduction of the peregrine falcon into the eastern United States, from which it had once been completely extirpated. The American alligator, once decimated throughout the South by poachers supplying illegal leather markets, has rebounded dramatically. It is no longer classified as endangered. Neither is the brown pelican in the Southeast, where pesticide poisoning once drove it to the brink of extinction.

Behind these success stories and others like them lies a truth too seldom recognized and appreciated. We have learned from fifteen years of experience with the Endangered Species Act that it is almost always possible to conserve endangered species—and thereby promote our long-term welfare—without significantly harming our short-term interests. The number of truly irreconcilable conflicts between endangered species and worthy development projects is astonishingly small. So too is it possible to adjust the ways in which we do business to benefit endangered species without harming our business. The recent example of efforts to reduce the drowning of endangered sea turtles in the shrimp fishery is no exception. Turtle-excluder devices, four of the five varieties of which have been developed by fisherman themselves, offer a means of giving essential protection to several severely imperiled species without harming the shrimp industry. They save turtles and they catch shrimp. They are a positive solution to a serious environmental problem, one that can benefit both the environment and the shrimp industry. All that is needed is the will to make the transition to their use, just as our farmers made the transition from DDT to other, less hazardous pesticides not so many years ago. Farmers, who had used DDT all their lives, were understandably reluctant to give it up when its hazards became known. But once they did, the miraculous recovery of the bald eagle, symbol of the Nation, resulted.

Though many great successes have been achieved under the Endangered Species Act, other efforts have ended in disappointment or failure. A little more than a year ago, that last dusky seaside sparrow, a songbird of Florida's Atlantic coastal marshes, died in captivity. Across the continent, in California, the Palos Verdes blue butterfly has vanished within the past few years. The California condor and the black-footed ferret, two species that have been the targets of rescue efforts since before the Endangered Species Act was passed, now no longer survive in the wild, though captive populations of each may make possible their eventual reintroduction.

Thus, while the Endangered Species Act has enabled us to make great progress in protecting many species, the problem to which the Act is directed remains very much with us. Each day, somewhere in the world, a desperate drama of survival takes place with little notice and little fanfare, but with vital consequences for our future. Despite our efforts, the world continues to experience an alarming, and accelerating, loss of its wild plant and animal species. Scientists believe that never, in all of human history, has the rate of extinction been as rapid as it is today. Human activity may be wiping out another species everyday, whereas perhaps only one a century disappears through natural causes.

The Endangered Species Act commits us to make our very best efforts to stem these unprecedented and irreversible losses. Today, slightly more than a thousand species enjoy the nominal protection of the Endangered Species Act; somewhat more than half of these occur in the United States and its territories, the remainder occur entirely outside our borders. The number of species from within the United States that have been identified as deserving the Act's protection, but are not yet listed for protection, exceeds a thousand—twice the number currently listed. Most of the species in danger of extinction will wait years, perhaps decades, more before they are listed and protected under the Act. In times of deficit reduction, Congress simply has not made available the resources necessary even to list them formally for protection, much less carry out the action necessary to ensure their survival and recovery. For species already listed, the nominal protection afforded by that listing may be all the species receives. Recovery plans have thus far been prepared for less than half the listed species and most of these plans are yet to begin to be implemented.

In the fifteen years since the Endangered Species Act became law, we have learned that the problem it seeks to solve is far more serious and affects far more species than previously understood. At the same time, however, we have also learned that the reasons to prevent the avoidable extinction of other species are even more powerful and compelling. The discovery, within that short period, of the principles of biotechnology have added an urgent new reason to protect the genetic diversity of nature. Suddenly, we have learned how to harness the unique and useful genetic attributes of one organism and implant them in another. This discovery has opened the possibility for advances in agriculture and medicine undreamed of a decade and a half ago. But the raw material for this potential revolution in human welfare is bestowed upon us by nature's great diversity, and is threatened by our mindless destruction of its diversity. Herman Melville's classic observation that "there is no folly of the beasts of the earth which is not infinitely outdone by the madness of men" aptly describes our willingness to countenance the destruction of another peculiar species, while its very peculiarity may hold the key to advances in human welfare. To fulfill the commitment Congress made a decade and a half ago, we need to reinvigorate the nation's endangered species program. In particular, we need to provide it with the resources necessary to carry out its basic objectives. The new Administration that assumed office in January 1989 can make no clearer signal of its commitment to an improved environment than by seeking the expanded resources necessary to carry out the Endangered Species Act.

Chapter 1

An Introduction to the
Extinction Crisis

Every part of the earth is sacred to my people. Every shining pine needle, every sandy shore, every mist in the dark woods, every clearing and humming insect is holy in the memory and experience of my people . . . . I have seen a thousand rotting buffaloes on the prairies left by the white man who shot them from a passing train. What is man without the beasts? If all the beasts were gone, men would die from the great loneliness of spirit, for whatever happens to the beasts also happens to man. All things are connected. Whatever befalls the earth, befalls the sons of the earth.
Chief Sealth of the Duwamish Tribe[1]

. . . [B]y tomorrow morning we shall almost certainly have one less species on Planet Earth than we had this morning. It will not be a charismatic creature like the tiger. It could well be an obscure insect in the depths of some remote rainforest. It may even be a creature that nobody has ever heard of. But it will have gone. A unique form of life will have been driven from the face of the earth forever.
Norman Myers[2]

For millions of years, Earth has been a storehouse of life. First in Precambrian seas and later on more hostile land surfaces, an abundance of life forms appeared and thrived. Creatures capable of adapting to harsh environments not only survived, but diversified and evolved.

This dynamic process of evolution continues today, but with an added twist. Within a relatively tiny fraction of earth's history, humans have acquired the power to determine which organisms survive and which cease to exist. Unfortunately, decisions of life and death—made for eons by the impartial process of natural se-

---

1. Letter to President Franklin Pierce, *quoted in* P. Ehrlich & A. Ehrlich, Extinction: The Causes and Consequences of the Disappearance of Species 239 (1981).
2. N. Myers, The Sinking Ark: A New Look at the Problem of Disappearing Species 3 (1979).

7

lection on the basis of adaptability and efficiency—are increasingly made by humans with indifference or in ignorance.

I. THE EARTH'S SPECIES

Species are generally defined on the basis of similar morphological and behavioral characteristics. Estimates of the number of species existing on earth today vary from five million to twenty million, with the most widely accepted figure pegged at about ten million.[3] Though this figure represents little more than an educated guess, it illustrates that the overwhelming majority of earth's species are as yet unknown to science. Only about 1.5 million species have actually been identified, suggesting that five out of six species remain to be discovered.[4]

Insects make up the majority of all species, with up to six million types. Plants comprise between one-tenth and one-thirtieth of Earth's life forms. The remainder are made up of mammals, other vertebrates and protozoa.

Geographical distribution of species is heavily weighted in favor of the tropics. Between two-thirds and three-fourths of all species live in tropical habitats; tropical moist forests probably support between forty and fifty percent of earth's species. For example, La Amistad National Park in the tropical forests of Costa Rica supports more bird species than the entire North American continent.[5]

Because life on earth is part of a dynamic process of survival and adaptation, few of the species that existed in the geologic past are present today. Scientists estimate that only about two percent of organisms that have ever lived on earth are now alive.[6] Extinctions are thus historically commonplace and represent an important element of natural selection and evolution. Rates of extinction in the distant past were variable. Fossil records contain evidence of several periods of rapid extinction, including the sudden disappearance of most dinosaurs approximately seventy million years ago in the late Cretaceous period.

The natural causes of extinction are numerous. Some theories of extinction, particularly those attempting to explain rapid extinctions, embody elements of catastrophism and are highly

---

3. P. EHRLICH & A. EHRLICH, *supra* note 1, at 17.
4. *Id.*
5. N. MYERS, THE PRIMARY SOURCE 59 (1984).
6. P. EHRLICH & A. EHRLICH, *supra* note 1, at 28.

conjectural. These include many recently proposed explanations for the demise of the dinosaurs, including those which attribute that event to comet strikes or to huge volcanic eruptions. Most causes of extinction, however, are less spectacular. Extirpation of a given species often results from biological succession or ecological relationships with other species. For example, a competitor that appropriates the food source of another species may eliminate that species; disappearance of an insect vital for pollinating a certain plant will likely also result in the disappearance of the plant. Habitat changes also cause extinctions. Climatic upheavals associated with past ice ages, for instance, wiped out many species. Organisms unable to adapt to changing ecosystems were eliminated or succeeded by those that could.

II. MANKIND AND THE EXTINCTION OF SPECIES

In recent history, humans have accelerated the pace of species extinctions. The rate of extinction within the past four hundred years—a minute fraction of the 1.4 billion year history of life on this planet—is unprecedented. For example, during a three thousand year period in the Pleistocene, a period that included the most recent ice ages, North America lost fifty mammalian species and forty birds. In comparison, over five hundred species and subspecies that inhabited the same area have become extinct since the Pilgrims arrived at Plymouth in 1620,[7] a rate of extinction estimated at between five and fifty times greater than in the geologic past.[8] This rate, however, is increasing rapidly. Naturalist Norman Myers predicts that species will be vanishing at a rate of one hundred per day by the turn of the century.[9]

A. *Direct Human-Caused Mortality*

Homo Sapiens have become a sort of super-predator. At our disposal are an incredibly vast array of efficient killing devices, from firearms to poison. Whether killed for food or sport or to make various consumer products, many species have been hunted to extinction or to near extinction. Disappearances of the great auk and the passenger pigeon provide examples of North

---

7. Opler, *The Parade of Passing Species: A Survey of Extinctions in the United States*, 43 SCIENCE TEACHER 30 (Dec. 1976).

8. P. EHRLICH & A. EHRLICH, *supra* note 1, at 8.

9. N. MYERS, *supra* note 2, at 5.

American species that are now extinct due to direct, human-caused mortality.

The well-known demise of the North American bison illustrates the swiftness and scope of human ability to wipe out a species. One conservative estimate places the number of bison inhabiting the North American continent at the time of U. S. westward expansion at approximately thirty million.[10] After an unparalleled twenty years of carnage and slaughter (1865-1885), the entire bison population was reduced to only a few score.[11] By 1894, only about twenty-five bison remained in the wild, the size of the protected herd in Yellowstone National Park.[12] A species whose numbers were thought to be inexhaustible was practically eliminated within thirty years.

B. *Ecological Changes*

Human alteration of the delicate equilibrium between all living organisms in a given environment also plays a large role in eliminating species. Plants serve as an excellent example of how human-caused ecological changes contribute to extinctions. Approximately one-quarter of the flora present today in the northeastern United States was actually introduced from other geographical areas by human action. Competition from these alien species has contributed to the decline of native plants. Imported diseases have also taken a heavy toll on native American plants. Tremendous tree mortality has been caused by Dutch Elm disease of European origin, and by Chestnut Blight, accidentally introduced from Asia.

More subtly, species are endangered when humans adversely affect other organisms on which they depend. For example, the loss or displacement of pollinators threatens many American plants. If a pollinator insect is eliminated by human action or displaced by an introduced competitor, the particular plant species dependent on that pollinator for reproduction may face extinction.[13] The extinction of one plant may also imperil other species in an ecosystem. Extinction of a single plant species may lead to the same fate for other organisms that depend in some way on that plant, further demonstrating that a threat to one con-

---

10. T. McHugh, The Time of the Buffalo 17 (1972).

11. *Id.* at 271-78.

12. *Id.* at 294.

13. N. Myers, *supra* note 5, at 79-82.

stituent of an ecological web is a threat to many others as well.[14]

C. *Habitat Destruction and Modification*

Direct mortality and ecological disruptions are critical problems, but human destruction or alteration of habitats necessary for species survival causes most extinctions. Habitat degradation detrimental to flora and fauna results from many human activities that eliminate, change, or pollute the natural environment.

Humans often simply destroy habitat critical to a species' existence. The most striking example of such destruction is the systematic cutting of tropical forests. Presently, the world's forests are disappearing at the rate of eighteen to twenty million hectares a year—an area approximately one-half the size of California.[15] Most of these losses occur in tropical forests that are cleared for agriculture and stock grazing or that are lumbered for valuable hardwoods. Since up to one-half of all species on earth depend on tropical forest habitats, the implications of the continuing elimination of such areas are frightening.

Modification of habitats, though less noticeable, also threatens many species. For example, to a casual observer in the West or Midwest, miles of unbroken rangelands essentially remain in a "natural" state. But domesticated livestock has changed the ecologically rich tall grass prairie to a much less diverse biota capable of supporting far fewer wild species.

Potentially the most harmful and most difficult to control of all forms of habitat disruption is pollution. Though this problem is often discussed in terms of effects on human health or aesthetic values, pollution and environmental poisons can have devastating effects on all life forms. The precipitous decline of a wide variety of bird species due to a chemical byproduct of the pesticide DDT serves as a particularly notorious example. Use of DDT was finally banned in the United States in 1972, but many more toxins with equally harmful effects are still released into the environment. Recent discoveries in the American west of high levels of selenium, which may be linked to a serious drop in numbers of waterfowl, are yet another example in this dismal litany. Unfortunately, such discoveries may represent only the tip of the

---

14. P. Ehrlich & A. Ehrlich, *supra* note 1, at 78-80.
15. Global 2000: A Report to the President 2 (1980).

proverbial pollution iceberg, as knowledge of the consequences of pollution slowly catches up with the rate at which humans are dumping pollutants into the environment.

III.   WHY PRESERVE ENDANGERED SPECIES?

The Global 2000 Report, commissioned by President Carter in 1977, does not mince words in evaluating future prospects for a great many species. The report bleakly concludes that "[e]xtinctions of plant and animal species will increase dramatically."[16] The study predicts that as many as twenty percent of earth's species will be driven to extinction by the turn of the century—a total of perhaps two million unique life forms.

Immediate preventative action could help avert such an occurrence, but the processes that jeopardize species are increasing rather than diminishing. In less developed countries, where most tropical forests are located, all physically accessible forest will likely be cut within thirty-five years, if present deforestation rates continue. More deserts will be created as more livestock graze fewer acres. Pollution and poisoning may also worsen in an overcrowded world that relies increasingly on "dirty" energy sources, including coal and other fossil fuels, and on a tremendous variety of potentially hazardous agricultural and industrial chemicals.

Modern societies must face many problems—economic stagnation, various social ills, political strife, even hunger and lack of physical necessities. Loss of species is obviously occurring, but should this be a cause for concern? Aren't there more pressing problems? Why should we preserve species?

A.   *Aesthetic and Moral Justifications*

Many people attach aesthetic value to species because of their beauty, their ability to inspire or serve as symbols, or simply because certain unusual characteristics make them interesting. Bald eagles, for example, once carried bounties on their heads and were systematically shot as dangerous predators. Today, however, bald eagles symbolize freedom and the United States itself, and Americans often go to great lengths to protect them. Similarly, conservation of many species enjoys support princi-

---

16. *Id.* at 3.

pally because people find certain species appealing for one reason or another.

Aesthetic justifications for preserving species, however, have little relevance to the fate of obscure plants and animals whose existence, if known at all, is recognized only in the volumes of taxonomic journals. Many people therefore justify conservation of all life forms, no matter how seemingly humble or insignificant, on moral grounds. For example, Professor David Ehrenfeld writes that species should be conserved "because they exist and because this existence is itself but the present expression of a continuing historical process of immense antiquity and majesty. Long-standing existence in Nature is deemed to carry with it the unimpeachable right to continued existence."[17] This type of non-utilitarian, non-homocentric view of conserving species is becoming increasingly prevalent as a justification for preserving endangered species.

B. *Economic Benefits of Species Preservation*

Policy decisions are increasingly made based on quantitative cost-benefit analyses. Some commentators even advocate assigning dollar values to such intangibles as clear views or clean water to assess the cost effectiveness of environmental regulation. Surprisingly, preserving even obscure species can often be justified on this type of economic basis due to their direct benefits or potential benefits to humans.

The medical uses of plants provide an excellent example of an economic argument for species preservation. The overall value of plant-derived drugs and pharmaceuticals sold in the United States tops tens of billions of dollars annually. The value of drugs derived from animals and microbes approaches this figure. The uses of such drugs range from laxatives to cardiovascular regulation. Plant and animal-derived drugs are also used in the battle against cancer. Two compounds derived from alkaloids of the Rosy Periwinkle—a flower found in tropical regions—are vital constituents of a chemotherapy treatment that has increased the remission rate of lymph system cancer in Hodgkin's Disease patients from 19 percent to 80 percent.[18] The same drugs have also increased the remission rates of several other forms of can-

---

17. D. EHRENFELD, THE ARROGANCE OF HUMANISM (1978), *quoted in* P. EHRLICH & A. EHRLICH, *supra* note 1, at 48.

18. N. MYERS, A WEALTH OF WILD SPECIES 106-07 (1983).

cer. In addition to their tremendous life-saving properties, these compounds account for sales of over one hundred million dollars annually. Despite these enormous benefits, less than one percent of the earth's plant species have been thoroughly studied for their possible usefulness to humans.[19] Consequently, preservation of the vast storehouse of potentially life-saving species in the wild may be justified.

Plants and animals are not only useful for directly extracted agents, but as scientific models as well. The cheetah, for example, is a sort of living cardiovascular experiment. It can accelerate to speeds in excess of seventy miles per hour and maintain that pace over several hundred meters. Since the cheetah can obviously withstand sudden and severe oxygen debt, it may harbor vital clues for treatment of heart disease, blood pressure, and circulatory disorders in humans.

Industrial uses of plant and animal derived materials are extensive and wide-ranging. Chemical producers are increasingly looking toward plants as an important source of raw materials for manufactured chemicals due to the increasing scarcity and price of petroleum.[20] Other non-traditional industrial uses of species becoming increasingly prominent include fuel production from conversion of plant biomass, production of rubber from a shrub native to the American Southwest, and use of species as research models for mechanical engineers.[21]

One of the most important utilitarian benefits of species diversity is as a "genetic bank." Industrialized agriculture points to the importance of genetic preservation. Fewer than twenty plants cultivated on a large-scale basis produce the overwhelming majority of the world's current food supply.[22] This situation is attributable to the remarkable gains in the productivity of certain grains during the last half-century. Since 1930, for example, corn production per acre in the United States has increased in certain cases by a factor of ten. Approximately half of this increase stems from selective breeding to alter the corn's genetic codes. Huge plantings of the same type of corn, while extremely productive, are nevertheless highly vulnerable to catastrophe, in-

---

19. G. MILLER, LIVING IN THE ENVIRONMENT: AN INTRODUCTION TO ENVIRONMENTAL SCIENCE 193-94 (4th ed. 1975).

20. N. MYERS, *supra* note 5, at 230-31.

21. For a detailed discussion of the tremendous extent to which humans use materials derived from wild species, see generally N. MYERS, *supra* note 18.

22. P. EHRLICH & A. EHRLICH, *supra* note 1, at 62.

cluding disease or insect infestations. In 1970, an estimated fifteen percent of the entire U.S. corn crop was wiped out by a leaf
blight, causing losses of two billion dollars to farmers and con-
sumers.[23] This epidemic was halted only with the aid of blight-
resistant germ plasm of unique genetic ancestry that originated
in Mexico.

Another recent discovery in Mexico of a wild strain of peren-
nial corn may make possible a commercial hybrid corn that grows
every year without plowing and replanting.[24] The wild corn species survives in three remnant patches covering only four hectares. If nearby settlement and timber cutting had destroyed this
unique strain before it was discovered, a potentially invaluable
genetic property would have been lost.

The genetic resource represented by the ten million species
on earth is of inestimable worth. Losing one-fifth of this resource by the year 2000, before many of its potential benefits are
explored, is a sobering prospect.

C. *Ecological Benefits of Species Preservation*

Species diversity is also important to humans in more subtle
ways. The following events illustrate how human-caused ecological disturbances often have unintended results:

> Malaria once infected nine out of ten people on the island of
> North Borneo, now a state of Indonesia. In 1955, the World
> Health Organization (WHO) began spraying dieldrin (a pesti-
> cide similar to DDT) to kill malaria-carrying mosquitoes. The
> program was very successful, almost eliminating this dreaded
> disease. But other things happened. The dieldrin killed other
> insects besides mosquitoes, including flies and cockroaches in-
> habiting the houses. The islanders applauded. But then small
> lizards that also lived in the houses died after gorging them-
> selves on dead insects. Then cats began dying after feeding on
> the dead lizards. Without cats, rats flourished and began over-
> running the villages. Now people were threatened by sylvatic
> plague carried by fleas on the rats. Fortunately, this situation
> was brought under control when WHO had the Royal Air Force
> parachute cats into Borneo.
>
> On top of everything else, the thatched roofs of some
> houses began to fall in. The dieldrin also killed wasps and
> other insects that fed on a type of caterpillar that either avoided
> or was not affected by the insecticide. With most of their

---

23. N. MYERS, *supra* note 2, at 63-64.
24. P. EHRLICH & A. EHRLICH, *supra* note 1, at 66.

> predators eliminated, the caterpillar population exploded. The
> larvae munched their way through one of their favorite foods,
> the leaves that made up the roofs.[25]

Within an ecosystem, everything is in some way interconnected.
A sudden change in even a seemingly minor constituent can disturb the balance of the entire system, greatly affecting humans as
well.

Ecosystems are structured in a pyramidal fashion, with multi-
tudes of plants at the base and a relatively small number of carnivores at the top. Energy flows along food webs from plant to
herbivore to carnivore, with many interconnections along the
way. Generally, a reduction of species diversity within an ecosystem will lead to increased instability of that system. This trend
occurs within an unpredictable range, however. An ecosystem
may be able to sustain the loss of several species with no noticeable disruption; alternatively, one organism may be the "key-
stone" species in its community, affecting all others. In many
cases the importance of any one species in an ecosystem simply
cannot be accurately foreseen.

Ecosystem stability is important to humans because of a wide
variety of what may be termed ecosystem services. Such services
include maintenance of atmospheric quality, control and amelio-
ration of climate, soil generation and preservation, waste disposal, and pest and disease control. For example, systematic
destruction of tropical forests reduces recycling of water from
plant to atmosphere and increases the reflectivity of the earth's
surface. Such alterations could lead to local or even regional climatic changes to the detriment of the agricultural development
for which the forest was cleared. Devastating chains of events
within ecosystems can also be set in motion by seemingly minor
causes, such as the elimination of a few insect or plant species.
Thus, human-caused extinction of any organism is tantamount to
a planetary game of ecological "Russian Roulette."

This idea has attained perhaps its most compelling expression
in the writings of naturalist Aldo Leopold. Leopold envisioned a
biotic pyramid of which humans are merely a part. He advocated
ecological awareness through development of a "land ethic:"
"[A] land ethic changes the role of Homo Sapiens from con-
queror of the land-community to plain member and citizen of it.
It implies respect for his fellow-members, and also respect for

---

25. G. MILLER, *supra* note 19, at 82-83.

the community as such."[26] Leopold saw all ethics as resting on the premise that the individual is a member of a community of interdependent parts. Within the human community, Leopold argued, an elaborate set of ethics differentiates social from anti-social conduct. Leopold's land ethic simply enlarges the notion of community to include, in his words, "soils, waters, plants, and animals, or collectively: the land."[27] Leopold saw such a community as appropriate and useful, and viewed disturbing this interrelated community, particularly disturbances committed in ignorance, as folly:

> If the land mechanism as a whole is good, then every part is good, whether we understand it or not. If the biota, in the course of aeons, has built something we like but do not understand, then who but a fool would discard seemingly useless parts? To keep every cog and wheel is the first precaution of intelligent tinkering.[28]

IV. DRAWING THE LINE ON EXTINCTION

Most people probably see at least some merit in attempting to slow the rate of human-caused species extinctions. Disputes usually arise, therefore, not over *whether* to conserve species, but over the question of to what *degree* species preservation should be enforced. Few people would likely oppose a ban on shooting whooping cranes, for example. But many may vigorously object to imposition of land-use restrictions over a wide area, even if enacted to protect the habitat of a species threatened with extinction. This Handbook deals with where the United States Congress chose to draw the line when protecting endangered species.

26. A. LEOPOLD, A SAND COUNTY ALMANAC 240 (1949).
27. *Id.* at 239.
28. *Id.* at 190.

Chapter 2

History and Framework of the
Endangered Species Act

The Endangered Species Act of 1973[1] (ESA) has been described as "the most comprehensive legislation for the preservation of endangered species ever enacted by any nation."[2] It represents the culmination of a long history of increasing federal involvement in wildlife management and preservation. The basic framework of the ESA has evolved substantially since 1973, but its far reaching protection for species faced with extinction remains largely intact.

I. The History of Federal Wildlife Law

The Lacey Act,[3] passed in 1900, marked the entry of the federal government into wildlife regulation, an area of law previously left to the states and territories. The Act authorized federal enforcement of state wildlife laws and was based on the federal power to regulate interstate commerce. The Lacey Act was, in part, a direct response to the decimation of passenger pigeons and depletion of a number of other bird species. It authorized the Secretary of Agriculture to take necessary steps to preserve and restore these bird populations. As such, it represents the federal government's first attempt to deal with the problem of species extinctions, albeit on a limited basis.

Federal power over wildlife received a temporary setback in 1912 when the U.S. Supreme Court held that states retained public trust ownership of wildlife within their borders, thus precluding federal regulation.[4] But this doctrine was short lived. The

---

1. Pub. L. No. 93-205, 81 Stat. 884 (Dec. 28, 1973) (current version at 16 U.S.C. §§ 1531-1543 (1982)).
2. Tennessee Valley Authority v. Hill, 437 U.S. 153, 180 (1978) [hereinafter TVA v. Hill].
3. Ch. 553, 31 Stat. 187 (May 25, 1900) (current version at 16 U.S.C. §§ 701, 1540, 3371-78 and 18 U.S.C. § 42).
4. The Abby Dodge, 223 U.S. 166 (1912).

19

Supreme Court upheld the constitutionality of the Migratory Bird Treaty Act[5] of 1918 on the basis of the federal treaty-making power.[6] Other statutes followed, such as the Migratory Bird Conservation Act of 1929[7] and the Fish and Wildlife Coordination Act of 1934,[8] making it clear that the federal government had the authority as well as inclination to regulate wildlife resources.[9]

Meanwhile, sensitivity to the problems of species depletion and extinctions was also increasing. A reshuffling of federal agency jurisdictions in 1939, which brought wildlife management responsibilities under the Interior Department umbrella, was a factor in fostering a broader view of wildlife as something other than simply a game resource. Scientific advancements, including growing development of ecological theory, also contributed to a new outlook on threatened species. The first wide ranging federal recognition of the problem of human-caused species extinctions occurred in 1964 when a Committee on Rare and Endangered Wildlife Species was established within the Department of the Interior. In late 1964, the Committee, made up of nine biologists, published the "Redbook,"[10] the first federal list of fish and wildlife considered to be threatened with extinction.

The public also began to take a greater interest in the issue. National controversy over pesticides and prominent environmental protection litigation in the late 1960's were cornerstones of the growing environmental movement.[11] The image of species being wiped from the face of the earth forever by human activity proved to be a powerful one for environmentalists, and, as a result, endangered species protection became a popular grassroots cause.[12]

---

5. Ch. 128, 40 Stat. 755 (July 3, 1918) (current version at 16 U.S.C. §§ 703-711).

6. Missouri v. Holland, 252 U.S. 416 (1920).

7. Ch. 257, 45 Stat. 1222 (Feb. 18, 1929) (current version at 16 U.S.C. §§ 715-715k and §§ 715n-715r).

8. Ch. 55, § 2, 48 Stat. 401 (1934) (current version at 16 U.S.C. §§ 661-666(c)).

9. For a thorough discussion of the constitutional basis and history of federal wildlife law, see M. BEAN, THE EVOLUTION OF NATIONAL WILDLIFE LAW 9-47 (1983).

10. U.S. DEPARTMENT OF INTERIOR, REDBOOK—RARE AND ENDANGERED FISH AND WILDLIFE OF THE UNITED STATES—PRELIMINARY DRAFT (1964), *cited in* S. YAFFEE, PROHIBITIVE POLICY: IMPLEMENTING THE FEDERAL ENDANGERED SPECIES ACT 35 (1982).

11. *See* R. NASH, WILDERNESS AND THE AMERICAN MIND 253-60 (3d ed. 1982).

12. For a more in-depth discussion of the history of the movement to protect rare species, as well as lengthy legislative histories of the ESA and its predecessors, see generally S. YAFFEE, *supra* note 10 (1982).

A. *The 1966 Endangered Species Preservation Act*

Congress responded to this sentiment for endangered species protection in 1966 with passage of the first federal law that attempted to deal with the issue comprehensively. In many ways, however, the Endangered Species Preservation Act of 1966[13] merely announced a broad but toothless policy. Federal agencies were directed to preserve the habitats of native vertebrate species found by the Secretary of the Interior to be in danger of extinction, but only to the extent "practicable and consistent" with the primary purposes of the federal agencies. Commerce in endangered species or articles made from such organisms was not prohibited. No restrictions were placed on the taking or possessing[14] of species listed as endangered beyond certain very limited geographical areas; that power remained under state jurisdiction. The major operative section of the Act was the creation of the National Wildlife Refuge System. The Department of the Interior was authorized to use existing funding laws to purchase habitat of endangered species for preservation as part of this system. Only on these few parcels was the taking of endangered species prohibited.

Even though the 1966 Act was limited in scope, it reflected a significant national concern with the plight of endangered organisms. The Endangered Species Preservation Act also laid the foundation upon which later legislation was built. Some features within the Act, such as habitat acquisition and protection, taking regulations and affirmative wildlife conservation mandates to federal agencies, were expanded and strengthened in subsequent Acts.

B. *The 1969 Endangered Species Conservation Act*

In 1969, Congress replaced the 1966 legislation with the Endangered Species Conservation Act.[15] The new law expressly extended protection to invertebrates as well as vertebrates, and Congress extended the Lacey Act's prohibitions to cover interstate commerce in illegally taken reptiles, amphibians, and cer-

---

13. Pub. L. No. 89-669, 80 Stat. 926 (Oct. 15, 1966).

14. The Endangered Species Act of 1973 defines "to take" wildlife as to "harass, harm, pursue, hunt, shoot, wound, kill, trap, capture, or collect or attempt to engage in any such conduct." 16 U.S.C. § 1532(19). *See infra* Chapter 4 for an extended discussion of the taking of wildlife under the ESA.

15. Pub. L. No. 91-135, 83 Stat. 275 (Dec. 5, 1969).

tain invertebrates. It also slightly broadened the Department of the Interior's habitat acquisition authority. Other than these relatively minor changes, however, the new Act had little effect on the protection afforded to domestic species.

Significantly, the 1969 Act took a global view of the endangered species problem. It authorized the Secretary of the Interior to make a list of species "threatened with worldwide extinction" and with limited exceptions permitted the Secretary to prohibit imports of such species or their products into the United States. The law also called for an international conference in order to reach a binding international convention on the conservation of endangered species.

The exceptions to the 1969 Act highlighted the fact that by the late 1960's, not everyone wholeheartedly embraced endangered species protection. A blanket prohibition on importation of threatened species, for example, would have directly affected the fur industry, whose last minute lobbying efforts played a key role in delaying the bill's passage. Commercial interests also eventually succeeded in winning concessions that somewhat weakened the language in the original 1969 endangered species bill. These episodes illustrated that serious attempts to conserve endangered species entail costs and served notice that future attempts to protect endangered species would require compromises between foregone economic development opportunities and the benefits derived from endangered species protection.

C.   *Pressure for Stronger Wildlife Protection*

The environmental movement reached a peak in the early 1970's. Events such as the first Earth Day in 1970 heightened public concern over environmental issues, and Congress responded with a host of environmental enactments. In this setting, the Endangered Species Conservation Act of 1969 seemed inadequate. Public sentiment favored extending legal protection to species not facing imminent extinction but whose numbers were quickly being depleted. However, the Department of the Interior read the 1969 Act narrowly, thereby restricting the effectiveness of the Congressionally mandated protection available to rare species under the Act.

Two occurrences were instrumental in prompting Congress to reconsider its stance on endangered species. First, Congress passed the Marine Mammal Protection Act in 1972.[16] This Act included protection for "depleted" wildlife populations in addition to protection for endangered animals, and the Act imposed strong taking restrictions. Second, the international conference on endangered species protection envisioned by the 1969 Act was finally held in early 1973. The Convention on International Trade in Endangered Species of Wild Fauna and Flora resulted in an important international agreement that set up an elaborate scheme of import-export restrictions on species threatened with extinction.[17] A change in the United States' domestic endangered species policy thus became inevitable; President Nixon stated in 1972 that existing United States law "simply does not provide the kind of management tools needed to act early enough to save a vanishing species."[18]

D. *The Endangered Species Act of 1973*

New endangered species legislation was first introduced into both the House and Senate in 1972. Identical bills were introduced by Representative Dingell and twenty-four cosponsors and by Senator Hatfield on behalf of the Interior Department's Bureau of Sport Fisheries and Wildlife (BSFW) and the House Subcommittee on Fisheries and Wildlife Conservation.[19] The bills dropped all previous distinctions between foreign and domestic species and lowered the endangerment threshold to cover species threatened in a significant portion of their range, rather than only those species facing worldwide extinction. The bills proposed a broad prohibition on taking protected species, extending federal power into an area previously left to the states. The bills also classified species into two groups according to the degree of threat species faced. Finally, all federal agencies were directed to use their authority, when practicable, to protect listed species.

The Congressional debates on the 1972 bills centered mainly on technical and administrative matters, rather than on the basic philosophy of the bills. Issues of federalism and agency jurisdiction were discussed, and the Senate added an amendment pro-

---

16. Pub. L. No. 92-552, 86 Stat. 1027 (Oct. 21, 1972) (current version at 16 U.S.C. §§ 1361-1407).

17. Convention on International Trade in Endangered Species of Wild Fauna and Flora, March 3, 1973, 27 U.S.T. 1087, T.I.A.S. No. 8249.

18. *The President's 1972 Environmental Program*, 8 WEEKLY COMP. PRES. DOC. 218, 223-24 (Feb. 8, 1972).

19. *See generally* S. YAFFEE, *supra* note 10, at 49.

viding for suits by private citizens. The substantive issue of whether protection should be extended to plants incited the most controversy and held up final approval of the bills until 1973.[20]

In the meantime, several well-organized environmental groups were pushing hard for passage of a tough bill. Organizations such as the Fund for Animals, Society for Animal Protective Legislation, and the National Parks and Conservation Association made strong showings at committee hearings considering the bills. Commercial interests, on the other hand, did not testify at any of the hearings. As with the 1966 legislation, few seemed opposed to the idea of protecting endangered species. The proposed legislation, while going much further than its predecessors, was not viewed as adverse to any strong economic interests.[21] This lack of controversy was particularly evident when the Ninety-third Congress finally passed the legislation. The Senate bill passed unanimously in July of 1973. The House also approved its version in September by an overwhelming margin.[22]

The bills passed by the two houses differed somewhat from the legislation considered in 1972. Significantly, the legislation approved in 1973 deleted the phrase "where practicable" from the provision dealing with interagency cooperation, thus requiring federal agencies to use their authority to conserve endangered species under all circumstances rather than when merely convenient to do so. The Senate Commerce Committee also inserted language into its version of the bill prohibiting the destruction or adverse modification of habitat determined to be "critical" to an endangered species.

A conference committee quickly ironed out the relatively minor differences between legislation passed by the House and Senate. The committee report was issued in December of 1973, and legislation was almost immediately adopted by both houses with virtually no opposition. The Endangered Species Act of 1973 was signed into law by the President on December 28, 1973.[23]

---

20. *Id.* at 49-54.

21. *Id.*

22. *Id.* at 55.

23. Pub. L. No. 93-205, 81 Stat. 884 (Dec. 28, 1973) (current version at 16 U.S.C. §§ 1531-1543).

II. An Overview of the Endangered Species Act[24]

The Endangered Species Act is an extraordinary piece of legislation. It elevates the goal of conservation of listed species above virtually all other considerations. One might argue that Congress did not really understand the implications of the legislation it enacted, that the legislators were swept up in the environmental movement of the time and enacted broad legislation without actually considering its "real-world" impact. This view may have some validity. Strong pressure from preservation-oriented groups and wide public appeal of endangered species issues likely had significant impact. If commercial interests and government agencies that have subsequently been affected by the Act had presented a vocal opposition in 1973, the legislative outcome may have been altered.

On the other hand, it is more likely that Congress deliberately afforded endangered species extensive protection, mindful of the consequences of the Endangered Species Act. Lawmakers knew from the controversy surrounding the 1969 legislation that protection of endangered species sometimes carried costs. Additionally, a BSFW environmental impact statement addressing the legislation proposed in 1972 acknowledged that "to conserve and protect some endangered species it will be necessary to set aside certain areas and maintain them for the use of the species in question. Generally these areas will not be available for commercial uses such as agriculture."[25] Despite such cautions, lawmakers enacted a far-reaching bill. Most telling, perhaps, is the fact that Congress has subsequently been reluctant to weaken the Act significantly, even in the face of organized opposition to species preservation. In the words of the Supreme Court, "the plain language of the Act, buttressed by its legislative history, shows clearly that Congress viewed the value of endangered species as 'incalculable.' "[26]

A. Species Listing Procedure

The ESA's somewhat complex procedure for identifying or

---

24. Citations in this section are purposely kept to a minimum to emphasize the overall structure of the Endangered Species Act of 1973 and its Amendments. More complete citations are provided in later chapters.

25. U.S. Department of the Interior, Draft Environmental Statement, Proposed Endangered Species Conservation Act of 1972 6 (1972).

26. TVA v. Hill, 437 U.S. at 187.

"listing" imperiled species has changed substantially since the Act was first passed. Two notable features set the ESA apart from previous federal attempts to identify species to receive legal protection. First, the ESA sets forth a two-tiered classification scheme based on the biological health of a species. Endangered species are those in danger of becoming extinct throughout all or a significant portion of their range.[27] Threatened species are those likely to become endangered in the foreseeable future.[28] Environmentalists supported this dual classification system as a means to identify and protect a potentially greater number of species. States and federal agencies advocated the system as a means to provide regulatory flexibility.

Distinct population "segments" of a species may be listed, even if that species is abundant elsewhere in its range.[29] The rationale behind protecting such population groups is that local extirpation may endanger the species on a broader scale. This provision also recognizes the ecological or aesthetic importance of particular species to given areas.

Two Departments share authority to list species. The Secretary of Commerce, acting through the National Marine Fisheries Service (NMFS), is authorized to list marine mammals, and the Secretary of the Interior, acting through the Fish & Wildlife Service (FWS), is empowered to list all other organisms.[30] The Act also allows private individuals to petition to list or change the status of a species.[31] Additions to protected species lists are made by informal agency rulemaking procedures after biological evaluations of candidate species have been completed. In 1973, when the ESA was adopted, 392 species protected under previous federal endangered species laws made up the first list of threatened and endangered species. Another 269 species were added to the rolls by 1978.

In 1978, Congress dramatically changed the listing procedure by requiring designation of a species' critical habitat concurrent with its listing.[32] Though threats to a species' critical habitat was included in the original Act as a relevant factor in the listing decision, it was of little consequence until the 1978 amendments de-

---

27. 16 U.S.C. § 1532(6).
28. *Id.* at § 1532(20).
29. *Id.* at § 1531(a)(3).
30. *Id.* at § 1533(a).
31. *Id.* at § 1533(b)(3)(A).
32. Pub. L. No. 95-632 §§ 11, 13, 92 Stat. 3751 (1978).

fined critical habitat[33] and made listing contingent upon its designation. Additionally, in an apparent attempt to relieve fears that critical habitat designations would impose costly federal land use restrictions, Congress permitted consideration of economic impacts in critical habitat designation decisions.[34]

Linking the listing procedure to critical habitat designation and to economic considerations halted species listing almost entirely. Approximately 2,000 species proposed for listing in 1978 were withdrawn. During the first year of the Reagan Presidency, no species were added to the protected lists.

Congress attempted to remedy this situation with further amendments to the listing process in 1982.[35] These amendments sought to loosen the connection between listing and critical habitat designation. Accordingly, section 4 now requires critical habitat designation concurrent with listing a species only to the "maximum extent prudent and determinable."[36] Congress also stressed that listings themselves should be made solely on the basis of biological criteria,[37] and allowed listings to proceed even if a corresponding critical habitat determination would be delayed for up to a year.[38] Other changes made in 1982 were designed to speed up the listing process, including a requirement that the Secretary make a preliminary finding within ninety days of the receipt of a petition to list a species or to revise critical habitat.[39]

While the pace of species listings accelerated after 1982, a huge backlog of species considered candidates for listing often prevented quick action on listing for many such species. Several species suffered serious population declines or became extinct before they could be added to the protected lists. In an effort to prevent such occurrences, Congress in 1988 again amended the ESA's listing procedure, requiring the Secretary to establish a system which monitors the listing status of candidate species.[40]

---

33. The ESA defines critical habitat as the geographical area essential to the conservation of a species. 16 U.S.C. § 1532(5).

34. 16 U.S.C. § 1533(b)(1)(B)(2).

35. Pub. L. No. 97-304, § 2(a), 96 Stat. 1411 (Oct. 13, 1982).

36. 16 U.S.C. § 1533(a)(3).

37. *Id.* at § 1533(b)(1)(A).

38. *Id.* at § 1533(b)(6)(C).

39. *Id.* at § 1533(b)(3)(A).

40. *See* Endangered Species Act Amendments of 1988, Pub. L. No. 100-478, 102 Stat. 2306 (1988) (to be codified at 16 U.S.C. § 1533(b)(3)(C)(iii)).

Lawmakers also directed the Secretary to make use of his or her emergency listing powers to prevent "a significant risk to the well-being of any [candidate] species."[41]

B.   *Mandates to Conserve Listed Species*

Ultimately, the Endangered Species Act attempts to bring populations of listed species to healthy levels, so that they no longer need special protection. To reach this goal, in addition to prohibiting activities which may harm listed species, the ESA affirmatively requires federal agencies to use their authority to conserve threatened and endangered species.[42] However, the scope of this mandate, while potentially broad, remains somewhat unclear.

In 1978, Congress added a provision to section 4 requiring the Secretary to prepare "recovery plans" for listed species.[43] Such plans set forth steps necessary to bring species' populations to healthy levels, though the legal weight and enforceability of recovery plans are not well defined. Since 1978, Congress has fine-tuned the ESA's recovery plan requirement. In 1982, lawmakers directed that species whose recoveries are or might be in conflict with development or other economic activities receive priority in recovery plan formulation.[44] The 1988 ESA amendments added another qualifier to recovery plan preparation. The 1988 amendments prohibit the Secretary from considering a species' taxonomic classification in establishing recovery plan preparation priorities.[45] In other words, the Secretary may not prepare a recovery plan for a well-known mammal before a recovery plan for an obscure invertebrate solely because of the mammal's greater public visibility. Congress in 1988 also set specific content requirements for recovery plans,[46] provided for public input in plan formulation,[47] and added a provision which requires the Secretary to report to Congress at least once every two years on the status of efforts to develop and implement recovery plans.[48]

---

41. *Id.*
42. *See* 16 U.S.C. §§ 1531(c), 1536(a)(1).
43. 16 U.S.C. § 1533(f).
44. *Id.* at § 1533(f)(1)(A).
45. *Id.*
46. *Id.* at § 1533(f)(1)(B).
47. *Id.* at § 1533(f)(4).
48. *Id.* at § 1533(f)(3).

C.   *Protection of Listed Species: Section 7*

Section 7 of the ESA has proven to be the most significant of
the Act's provisions. It applies exclusively to federal agencies,
directing them to ensure that their actions do not jeopardize the
continued existence of listed species or destroy or adversely
modify species' critical habitats.[49]

In the late 1970s, *TVA v. Hill*[50] tested the effectiveness of section 7 protections. Plaintiffs attempted to enjoin completion of
the multimillion dollar Tellico Dam on the Tennessee River by
arguing that the resulting reservoir would destroy the habitat of a
unique species of minnow, the snail darter, which at the time was
believed to exist only in the doomed river. The U.S. Supreme
Court halted completion of the project, finding defendants in violation of section 7. The court held that the statute admitted no
exception to the policy of protecting endangered species. In a
dissenting opinion, Justice Powell predicted that Congress would
amend the statute to prevent a similar result in the future.[51]

Powell's dissent proved to be prophetic. Congress did amend
the ESA in 1978 in response to *TVA v. Hill*, but, contrary to Justice Powell's prediction, Congress refused to weaken the mandates of section 7. Instead, lawmakers created a high-level
Endangered Species Committee—soon nicknamed the "God
Committee"—authorized to grant exemptions to section 7. To
grant an exemption, the Committee must determine that no reasonable and prudent alternatives to the proposed agency action
exist and that the proposal's benefits clearly outweigh the preservation of the species in question.[52] However, this deliberately
cumbersome exemption process has remained virtually unused
since its creation.

Agencies fulfill their obligations under section 7 through consultation with either FWS or NMFS, the two expert agencies
charged with administering the Act. The consultation procedure
works as follows: If FWS or NMFS advises a federal agency that a
listed species may be present in the area of a proposed agency
action, the agency must conduct a biological assessment to determine whether its proposal is likely to affect any listed species.[53] If

---

49. *Id.* at § 1536(a)(2).
50. 437 U.S. 153 (1977).
51. *Id.* at 210.
52. 16 U.S.C. § 1536(h).
53. *Id.* at § 1536(c).

the assessment concludes that a protected species may be adversely affected, the agency must initiate formal consultation with FWS or NMFS. During formal consultation, the agency must provide FWS or NMFS with the best scientific and commercial data available which permits the expert agency to determine whether the proposed action jeopardizes the continued existence of an endangered or threatened species or destroys or adversely modifies critical habitat. If FWS or NMFS agencies find no adverse impacts on the species in question or its habitat, the agency proposal may proceed to completion. If the wildlife agencies determine that the project may jeopardize a species or adversely affect its critical habitat, FWS or NMFS must suggest "reasonable and prudent alternatives" to the agency's proposal which would avoid this result.[54] If no alternatives to the action exist, the agency risks violating the ESA by carrying out its proposal, unless it receives an exemption from the Endangered Species Committee. In all instances where formal consultation is required, FWS or NMFS must issue a written biological opinion outlining its findings and the information upon which those conclusions are based.[55] Section 7 requires all consultation procedures to be conducted using the best scientific and commercial data available.[56]

Finally, while consultation is still underway, agencies may not make any "irreversible or irretrievable" commitment of resources that would eliminate the feasibility of alternatives to the proposed action.[57] For example, an agency proposing to construct a dam may not begin construction before FWS issues a biological opinion on the project. This requirement is intended to forestall "steamrolling" a project to completion, which occurs when an agency incurs huge sunk costs in a partially completed project, generating pressure to continue the project to completion. Applicants for exemptions from section 7's mandates must demonstrate good faith compliance with these resource commitment restrictions.[58]

---

54. *Id.* at § 1536(b)(3)(A).
55. *Id.*
56. *Id.* at § 1536(a)(2).
57. *Id.* at § 1536(d).
58. *Id.* at § 1536(g)(3)(A).

D. *Prohibition on Takings: Section 9*

Section 9 lists several acts prohibited by the ESA. These include (1) import or export of any endangered species or any products made from endangered species,[59] (2) commerce in listed species or their products,[60] and (3) possession of unlawfully taken endangered species.[61] Unlike section 7, the prohibitions of section 9 apply to all persons within the jurisdiction of the United States. The Secretary may also apply these prohibitions to species listed as threatened, and in most cases has done so.[62]

The central tenet of section 9 is a ban on taking endangered species of fish and wildlife.[63] The term "take" under the ESA means to "harass, harm, pursue, hunt, shoot, wound, kill, trap, capture or collect, or to attempt to engage in any such conduct."[64] Listed plants, however, receive no statutory protection against taking.

Much like section 7, the section 9 taking prohibition was almost absolute when first enacted. Section 9 made illegal any activity—federal, state, or private—that resulted in the taking of an endangered species. Though this provision was not as widely invoked or as controversial as that of section 7, it came under increasing fire in the early 1980's. A conflict involving the last remaining habitat of an endangered northern California butterfly proved to be section 9's version of *TVA v. Hill*.[65] The private owner of a significant percentage of the butterflies' habitat wished to develop a portion of the property, an action that the developer conceded would result in a taking of butterflies. The developer argued that section 9 should not prohibit him from disposing of his own property, and that the development would actually benefit the butterfly on the whole by halting encroaching brush that threatened to render the habitat useless to the species.[66]

---

59. *Id.* at § 1538(a)(1)(A).
60. *Id.* at § 1538(a)(1)(E).
61. *Id.* at § 1538(a)(1)(D).
62. *See* 16 U.S.C. § 1533(d). Unless specifically provided otherwise by special regulations, the Secretary applies all of section 9's prohibitions to species listed as threatened. *See* 50 C.F.R. § 17.21.
63. 16 U.S.C. § 1538(a)(1)(B).
64. *Id.* at § 1532(19).
65. *See* Friends of Endangered Species v. Jantzen, 760 F.2d 976 (9th Cir. 1985).
66. *Id.* at 980.

The debate was eventually taken to Congress, which responded in 1982 by amending the ESA to provide a way around the absolute taking ban of section 9. The amendments set up an elaborate permitting process through which private persons can receive permission to engage in "incidental take." The ESA defines this term as "any taking otherwise prohibited . . . if such taking is incidental to, and not the purpose of, the carrying out of an otherwise lawful activity."[67] Persons who wish to take advantage of this exception must apply to the Secretary for an incidental take permit. As a part of the permit procedure, the applicant must submit a detailed plan to conserve the species to be incidentally taken.[68] The Secretary may issue a permit if he or she considers the conservation plan workable and if the plan contains assurances of adequate funding. Finally, prior to granting the permit, the Secretary must determine that the taking "will not appreciably reduce the likelihood of the survival and recovery of the species in the wild."[69]

Congress also recognized in 1982 that federal agency actions found not to jeopardize the continued existence of a species or destroy or adversely modify critical habitat could nevertheless result in illegal takings of the species. Thus, agency actions in compliance with section 7 could still run afoul of section 9. To reconcile these provisions, Congress amended section 7 to provide for incidental take exceptions similar to those added to exempt private individuals from section 9.[70]

. The 1982 amendments also granted slight protection to endangered plants, forbidding removal and possession of endangered plants from federal land.[71] Under this provision, however, it was not made unlawful to destroy or otherwise to tamper with endangered plants on private lands. Even destruction of such plants on federal land was not illegal so long as the plants were not removed and reduced to possession. In 1988, Congress recognized this situation was unsatisfactory and moved to strengthen statutory protections for endangered plants. Section 9 now forbids acts which maliciously damage or destroy endangered plants found on federal land.[72] Additionally, Congress

---

67. 16 U.S.C. § 1539(a)(1)(B).
68. *Id.* at § 1539(a)(2)(A).
69. *Id.* at § 1539(a)(2)(B)(iv).
70. *Id.* at § 1536(b)(4).
71. *Id.* at § 1538(a)(2)(B).
72. *See* 16 U.S.C. § 1538(a)(2)(B).

prohibited removal or destruction of endangered plants on non-federal land by anyone who in the process of destroying the plants knowingly violates any state law or regulation, including criminal trespass laws.[73] This provision extends some degree of federal protection to plants on non-federal land by subjecting violators to the ESA's stiff criminal and civil penalties.

E. *Trade in Protected Species*

Rare species often have a high market value. The skins, hides, various organs or articles manufactured from these species command high prices in many parts of the world. Some animals and plants are also valued as pets, trophies, or collectors' items. Thus, incentives often exist to kill or capture vanishing species. The ESA contains two major provisions to deal with this problem.

First, section 9 makes it illegal to ship, sell, or offer for sale in interstate or foreign commerce any endangered species, or part thereof, taken in violation of the ESA.[74] A similar prohibition also applies to endangered plants.[75] Mere possession of illegally taken endangered fish or wildlife is also prohibited.[76]

Secondly, ESA section 8 implements[77] the Convention on International Trade in Endangered Species of Wild Fauna and Flora (CITES).[78] The CITES agreement represents a global attempt to regulate international commerce in rare species.

CITES divides protected species into three categories. Those listed in Appendix I are the most vulnerable and include all species threatened with extinction which are or which may be affected by trade. Appendix II consists of organisms which may become threatened with extinction unless strict trade regulations are enacted. Approximately 1,500 species were listed in these two Appendices at the time CITES was drafted, and signatory nations have subsequently made substantial additions through the Convention's listing procedure. Unlike additions to Appendices I and II, a country may unilaterally add species to Appendix III. This category includes species regulated within the jurisdic-

---

73. *Id.*
74. *Id.* at § 1538(a)(1).
75. *Id.* at § 1538(a)(2).
76. *Id.* at § 1538(a)(1)(D).
77. *Id.* at § 1537a.
78. March 3, 1973, 27 U.S.T. 1087, T.I.A.S. No. 8249. *See supra* note 17 and accompanying text.

tion of the individual country whose protection requires cooperation of other nations.

Trade in species listed in Appendix I is subject to the most stringent regulation. These species may not be traded between CITES signatories for primarily commercial purposes. Any other type of trade requires both an import and export permit from the receiving and shipping countries, respectively. Appendix II species may be traded for commercial purposes, but an export permit is required. Finally, export permits are also required for Appendix III organisms if they are being exported from the country responsible for that species' inclusion in Appendix III.

Permits called for by the CITES agreement are issued by each country's Management Authority in consultation with the country's Scientific Authority. These bodies insure that permits are granted only in a manner consistent with the continued survival of the species in question in light of the degree of threat to that species. The Secretary of the Interior, acting through the U.S. Fish & Wildlife Service, serves as both the management and the scientific authority for the United States.[79]

Finally, section 8 of the ESA also requires[80] the Secretary of State to implement a little known but potentially significant international treaty, the Convention on Nature Protection and Wildlife Preservation in the Western Hemisphere.[81]

F.   *Habitat Acquisition*

Section 5 authorizes the Secretary of the Interior and the Secretary of Agriculture to acquire lands to conserve fish, wildlife and plants, including those listed pursuant to the ESA.[82]   To make land purchases, the Secretary of the Interior may use funds available under the Land and Water Conservation Fund Act of 1965.[83]

G.   *Cooperation with States*

Section 6 of the ESA authorizes the Secretary of the Interior to enter into cooperative agreements with states that maintain "an adequate and active program for the conservation of endan-

---

79. 16 U.S.C. § 1537a(a).
80. *Id.* at § 1537a(e).
81. Oct. 12, 1940, 56 Stat. 1354, T.S. No. 981.
82. 16 U.S.C. § 1534(a).
83. *Id.* at § 1534(b).

gered species and threatened species."[84] The statute sets forth a
list of criteria that must be met in order for state programs to be
considered "adequate and active" for the purposes of section 6.[85]
If a state program qualifies, it may receive up to seventy-five percent of the cost of the program in federal funds, a figure that may
increase to ninety percent if two or more states are involved in
joint programs.

Section 6 also contains a supremacy clause which voids all
state laws that allow actions prohibited under the ESA.[86] State
statutes or regulations are valid to the extent that they are more
restrictive than the mandates of the federal ESA.

H. *Enforcement*

The ESA includes criminal penalties of up to $50,000 in fines
and up to one year in prison for violations of the Act.[87] It also
contains a broad citizen's suit provision that grants any person
standing to enjoin violations or to compel the appropriate secretary to perform non-discretionary listing duties under section 4
or to enforce taking prohibitions under section 9.[88] The statute
provides for civil damages of up to $25,000 for each violation,[89]
and allows a court to award attorney's fees when such an award is
deemed appropriate.[90]

84. *Id.* at § 1535(c).
85. *Id.*
86. *Id.* at § 1535(f).
87. *Id.* at § 1540(b).
88. *Id.* at § 1540(g).
89. *Id.* at § 1540(a).
90. *Id.* at § 1540(g)(4).

Chapter 3

Identifying Species to Protect: Listing and Critical Habitat Designation

Federal protection of a rare species and its habitat begins after the Secretary has formally placed it on the official list of endangered and threatened species.[1] Section 4 of the ESA sets forth the procedures and substantive criteria which govern the listing and critical habitat designation processes.

I. CONSIDERATION FOR LISTING: THE DEFINITION OF "SPECIES"

The Secretary may list only groups of organisms which fall into the statutory definition of "species." The ESA defines this term to include "any subspecies of fish or wildlife or plants, and any distinct population segment of any species of vertebrate fish or wildlife which interbreeds when mature."[2] The latter portion of this definition is particularly significant. It allows the Secretary to list distinct vertebrate populations as threatened or endangered even if the species is abundant elsewhere in its range. The Secretary may also list some populations of a species as endangered and others as threatened. For example, the American bald eagle is listed as endangered in some geographical areas, is considered threatened in others, and is not listed at all in still other areas.[3] In testimony before a Senate committee in 1979, General Accounting Office officials criticized this aspect of the listing process.[4] Congress, however, has defended the Secretary's authority to list distinct population segments and declined to make any

---

1. There are minor exceptions to this statement. *See infra* note 63 and accompanying text. *See also* Chapter 7, notes 156-162 and accompanying text. Additionally, under certain circumstances the Secretary must use his or her authority to list a species facing a significant immediate threat to its well being. *See infra* notes 57-62 and accompanying text.

2. 16 U.S.C. § 1532(16).

3. *See* 50 C.F.R. § 17.11.

4. *See* S. REP. No. 151, 96th Cong., 1st Sess. 6-7 (1979).

changes in the statutory definition of species.[5]

Despite Congressional support for listing population segments of vertebrate species, exactly what sort of population can be considered a population segment (and thus a separate species for purposes of the ESA) remains somewhat unclear. The practical implications of this ambiguity are revealed by the plight of grizzly bears in the contiguous United States. Although grizzly bears exist in relative abundance in Alaska and Canada, grizzlies occupy only one percent of their former range in the coterminous United States. The population of grizzlies in the contiguous states has dwindled to less than 1,000 individual bears, and these grizzlies are listed as threatened pursuant to ESA section 4. This grizzly population is in turn made up of six distinct segments, ranging in size from about twenty-five individuals in the Cabinet-Yaak ecosystem to about five hundred individuals in Montana's Northern Continental Divide ecosystem. Each of the six population segments is isolated from the others; bears do not move between the six separate segments. Section 4's ambiguous definition of what constitutes a protectable species poses this question: If a federal action threatens to wipe out the small Cabinet-Yaak bear population, for example, does this action jeopardize the continued existence of grizzly bears in the coterminous United States?[6]

There are two possible answers to this question. If one defines *all* of the grizzly bears living in the coterminous United States as a single population segment of grizzlies, one may conclude that the loss of a small number of that population—for example, the twenty-five bears in the Cabinet-Yaak ecosystem—would not jeopardize the continued existence of grizzlies in the lower 48 states, permitting the hypothetical project to proceed under section 7 of the ESA.[7] On the other hand, if one defines each of the six separate bear populations as distinct population segments, each entitled to ESA protection, any federal action

5. *Id.*

6. 16 U.S.C. § 1536(a)(2) prohibits actions likely to jeopardize the continued existence of listed species. For an extensive discussion of this standard, see *infra* Chapter 7.

7. Note, however, that even under this interpretation of the population segment protected by the ESA, loss of one of the six grizzly populations could jeopardize the existence of the entire lower 48 population in violation of section 7. For example, federal activities significantly affecting the large Northern Continental Divide bear population would likely jeopardize the continued existence of grizzlies in the coterminous states, even if other populations remained unaffected.

threatening to wipe out even one of the separate populations would violate section 7's jeopardy standard. This view essentially defines the six separate grizzly populations as separate species for purposes of section 7, even though the bears in the six separate populations belong to only one taxonomic species. Thus, under this interpretation a federal action could jeopardize the continued existence of a listed "species" of grizzlies even though it imperiled only one of the six grizzly population segments listed as threatened.

The statutory definition of the term "species" supports an interpretation of the ESA which protects distinct, isolated population segments of endangered or threatened species. The definition provides that the term "species" includes distinct population segments *which interbreed when mature.*[8] In the case of grizzlies, bears in each of the six separate populations do not interbreed with those in the other populations; breeding takes place only between individuals of one population. Therefore, the six bear populations taken together arguably do not constitute one "species," as the ESA defines this term. Rather, each separate grizzly population constitutes a distinct listed species entitled to the full substantive protection of the ESA.[9] The same reasoning holds true for distinct population segments of all other listed species.

The Secretaries of Interior and Commerce, however, have tended to adopt the position that distinct population segments of listed species should not receive ESA protection in their own right, but should be considered only in context of projects' impacts on entire taxonomic species. The official view holds that "[j]eopardy opinions cannot be used for individuals or populations unless the loss of such will jeopardize the listed species or listed population throughout its range."[10] In 1986, however, the

---

8. *See* 16 U.S.C. § 1532(16).

9. This distinction makes a great deal of sense biologically. Isolated populations of a species may contain genetic resources crucial to the long term survival of the species as a whole. It therefore is important to safeguard the continued existence of every isolated population segment of a species. Of course, human manipulation would be required to transfer genes from one isolated population to another since no natural interbreeding takes place. For more information on the importance of genetically distinct populations of one taxonomic species, see generally M. SOULE & B. WILCOX, CONSERVATION BIOLOGY (1980); M. SOULE, CONSERVATION BIOLOGY (1984).

10. Memorandum from U.S. Fish and Wildlife Service (FWS) Director to FWS Regional Directors 1 (Mar. 3, 1986) (quoting from another memorandum dated Apr. 26, 1979) (copy in author's files).

Secretary of the Interior began to allow exceptions to this policy. Discussing the need for such exceptions, the Secretary noted:

> While the above policy approach works well in the majority of cases, experience has shown that this standard may not adequately address the needs of certain wide-ranging species. The concern is that such species could face sustained loss of individuals or habitat through actions that do not warrant a jeopardy finding but which, nevertheless, could result in significant cumulative habitat and population losses. Thus, the impact of numerous such actions could accumulate until a jeopardy finding is warranted, but by that time habitat or population size could be reduced to the point where the species' status is much more precarious. . . .
>
> A good example of this problem involves the grizzly bear, which exists in six disjunct populations within the lower 48 states. Under present policy, it seems possible that all but the largest of these populations, that of the Northern Continental Divide, could be lost due to habitat degradation before a jeopardy finding is warranted. A policy which permits such declines in the population of a wide-ranging species like the grizzly is not consistent with the intent of the Endangered Species Act.[11]

The Secretary therefore has identified several listed species whose distinct population segments are entitled to the full ESA protection accorded to separate species.[12] The Secretary has

---

11. *Id.* at 2.
12. These species, as well as their population segments which qualify as separate species for purposes of section 7, include the following:
1. Bald eagle
   a. Chesapeake Bay population
   b. Southeast population
   c. Northern States population
   d. Pacific population
   e. Southwest population.
Endangered and threatened populations can be further subdivided within areas c and d.
2. Peregrine falcon (both subspecies)
   a. Alaska population
   b. Pacific States population
   c. Rocky Mountain-Southwest population
   d. Eastern population.
3. Grizzly bear
   a. Yellowstone population
   b. Northern Continental Divide population
   c. Cabinet-Yaak population
   d. Selkirk population
   e. Selway-Bitterroot population
   f. North Cascades population.
4. Red-cockaded woodpecker
   [distinct population segments to be identified by FWS Region 4 Director].
5. Brown pelican

also noted that other species may qualify for similar treatment if the Secretary determines that a species meets each of the following criteria: (1) the species must be wide-ranging; (2) evidence must exist which shows that the species is, or would be, inadequately protected by strict adherence to the general policy on jeopardy opinions; (3) the species must be composed of discrete population segments that can be dealt with separately when assessing the impact of a given federal action.[13]

The above scheme is arguably flawed. For example, while it gives the Secretary a great deal of discretion in deciding which listed species' population segments will receive recognition as separate entities for purposes of applying section 7 protection, it gives no indication of how the Secretary will decide whether the general policy of looking only at projects' effects on entire taxonomic species "adequately" protects those species. It is difficult to see, moreover, what relevance the size of a species' range has in determining what degree of protection its population segments will receive. The ESA's definition of species, as well as sound biology, suggests that the only factor relevant to whether a population segment of a listed species should be considered a separate species for purposes of section 7 protection is simply whether the population segment interbreeds with other populations of the taxonomic species. The policy of considering population segments separate species only in limited cases at the discretion of the Secretary significantly undercuts the protection available to listed species under the ESA.

In the one reported case in which the definition of a species was at issue, the U.S. district court held that a deer species which was not listed as threatened or endangered was not entitled to endangered species protection merely because it was *possible*, though unheard of, for this type of deer to interbreed with a

---

    a. Gulf Coast population
    b. Pacific Coast population
    c. Puerto Rican-Virgin Islands population.
6. Sea Turtles—In U.S. waters.
7. Ocelot and jaguarundi—U.S. populations.
8. Piping plover
    a. Atlantic Coast population
    b. Great Lakes population
    c. Northern Great Plains population.
Id. at 3-4.
    13. *Id.* at 2.

listed species.[14] This case underscores the importance of inter-breeding in determining what constitutes a species for purposes of the ESA.

II. The Lists

The Secretary may classify a species either as endangered or as threatened. The ESA defines endangered species as any species in danger of extinction throughout all or a significant portion of its range, excluding insects which the Secretary determines to be pests.[15] Threatened species include any species likely to become endangered in the foreseeable future throughout all or a significant portion of its range.[16]

With the exception of experimental populations,[17] the substantive provisions of section 7 apply equally to endangered and threatened species. Whether a species is classified as endangered or threatened, however, may substantially affect the protection it receives under section 9.[18]

A. *The Listing Process*

The following briefly outlines the section 4 listing process:[19] Species become candidates[20] for listing either at the Secretary's initiative or as a result of a petition by any interested person.[21] The Secretary reviews the status of candidate species to determine whether it merits listing in light of specific factors set forth in section 4.[22] When the Secretary finds that a species qualifies for ESA protection, he or she publishes a proposed listing in the

---

14. Fund for Animals v. Florida Game & Fresh Water Fish Comm'n, 550 F. Supp. 1,206, 1,209 (S.D. Fla. 1982).

15. 16 U.S.C. § 1532(6).

16. *Id.* at § 1532(20).

17. Experimental populations are considered threatened species. *See* 16 U.S.C. § 1539(j)(2)(c). Non-essential experimental populations, however, receive no substantive section 7 protection. For further discussion of experimental populations and this exemption, see *infra* Chapter 7, notes 146-153 and accompanying text.

18. For an extensive discussion of this issue, see *infra* Chapter 4.

19. For a more detailed explanation of this process, see M. Bean, The Evolution of National Wildlife Law 334-41 (1983).

20. Section 4 regulations define a candidate species to mean "any species being considered by the Secretary for listing as an endangered or a threatened species, but not yet the subject of a proposed rule." 50 C.F.R. § 424.02(b).

21. 16 U.S.C. § 1533(b)(3)(A).

22. These factors include threats to a species' habitat, overutilization of the species for commercial or recreational purposes, and inadequacies of existing protection for the species. *See* 16 U.S.C. § 1533(a)(1).

Federal Register,[23] gives notice to appropriate groups and individuals,[24] and holds a hearing if requested to do so.[25] A final rule listing the proposed species as endangered or threatened must be published within one year of the proposal, with a possible six month extension to gather more data, or the Secretary must withdraw the proposal.[26] A designation of critical habitat, to the extent prudent and determinable, must accompany final listings.[27] Finally, the Secretary must use the best scientific and commercial data available when making listing decisions.[28]

The Secretary may dispense with most procedural listing requirements in case of any emergency that poses "a significant risk to the well-being of any species of fish or wildlife or plants."[29] In such cases, the Secretary may make an emergency listing, which becomes effective immediately upon publication in the Federal Register.[30] Emergency listings continue in force for 240 days and become permanent only if normal listing procedures are completed within the 240 day period.[31]

Over the last decade, the listing process has encountered substantial difficulties and has been the subject of much criticism. The root of these problems lies in the tremendous backlog of candidate species. The list of candidates includes approximately 4,000 species, prompting one group to estimate that at the historical rate of listing it would take the Secretary over 60 years to make final determinations for each candidate species.[32] In addition to listing delays caused by the tremendous number of species under consideration, critics have charged that listings are

---

23. 16 U.S.C. § 1533(b)(5)(A).

24. *Id.* at §§ 1533(b)(5)(B)-1533(b)(5)(D).

25. *Id.* at § 1533(b)(5)(E).

26. *Id.* at § 1533(b)(6).

27. *Id.* at § 1533(a)(3). For the definition of critical habitat, see *infra* note 76.

28. *Id.* at § 1533(b)(1)(A). Litigation in 1981 upheld the Secretary's general practice of not preparing environmental impact statements, pursuant to NEPA, in conjunction with listing a species. *See* Pacific Legal Found. v. Andrus, 657 F.2d 829, 836 (6th Cir. 1981). An Oklahoma district court reached a contrary result a year earlier. Glover River Org. v. Department of the Interior, Civ. No. 78-202-C (E.D. Okla. 1980). The Tenth Circuit Court reversed on grounds that the plaintiff lacked standing to challenge the listing. Glover River Org. v. Department of the Interior, 675 F.2d 251 (10th Cir. 1982).

29. 16 U.S.C. § 1533(b)(7).

30. *Id.*

31. *Id.*

32. Defenders of Wildlife, Saving Endangered Species: Implementation of the U.S. Endangered Species Act in 1984 12 (1985).

occasionally deliberately delayed or put on indefinite hold for political reasons or to avoid potential conflicts with planned development activities.[33] A 1979 report to Congress prepared by the General Accounting Office concluded that such actions did, in fact, occur.[34]

Congress itself has proven to be sensitive to problems with the listing process. Lawmakers sought to ameliorate listing difficulties by substantially amending section 4 in 1982. One of the 1982 changes added the word "solely" to the statutory directive that the Secretary base listing decisions on the best scientific and commercial data available.[35] Legislative history sets forth this amendment's purpose in no uncertain terms:

> The addition of the word "solely" is intended to remove from the process of the listing or delisting of species any factor not related to the biological status of the species. The Committee strongly believes that economic considerations have no relevance to determinations regarding the status of species and intends that the economic analysis requirements of Executive Order 12291, and such statutes as the Regulatory Flexibility Act and the Paperwork Reduction Act not apply. . . . Applying economic criteria to the analysis of these alternatives and to any phase of the species listing process is applying economics to the determinations made under section 4 of the Act and is specifically rejected by the inclusion of the work "solely" in this legislation.[36]

Also in 1982, Congress tightened the Secretary's duty to respond to listing petitions. Expressing concern that status reviews of species named in petitions had dragged on in some cases for many years, Congress amended section 4 to require the Secretary to determine, within 90 days of receipt of a petition, whether the petition presents "substantial scientific or commercial data that the petitioned action may be warranted."[37] Upon an affirmative finding, the Secretary has one year in which to make a final find-

---

33. *See, e.g.,* S. Yaffee, Prohibitive Policy 86-91 (1982).

34. General Accounting Office, Endangered Species—A Controversial Issue Needing Resolution (1979).

35. Pub. L. No. 97-304; *see* 16 U.S.C. § 1533(b)(1)(A).

36. H.R. Rep. No. 567, 97th Cong., 2d Sess. 20, *reprinted in* 1982 U.S. Code Cong. & Admin. News 2,820.

37. *See* 16 U.S.C. § 1533(b)(3)(A). In keeping with the notion that non-biological factors are irrelevant to the listing process, Congress noted that petitions need not include any information on the economic impacts of listing a species. *See* H.R. Conf. Rep. No. 835, 97th Cong., 2d Sess. 19, *reprinted in* 1982 U.S. Code Cong. & Admin. News 2860.

ing as to whether the petitioned listing is warranted.[38] If listing is warranted, the Secretary must "promptly" publish a proposal to list the species.[39]

The above revisions to the petition process do not guarantee swift action on all petitions, however. Along with the stricter time frame for action on petitions, Congress gave the Secretary a great deal of discretion to avoid these time constraints. The Secretary need only make an initial finding on a petition within 90 days "to the maximum extent practicable."[40] Legislative history indicates that this phrase permits the Secretary to extend this 90-day period if the Secretary's limited resources are needed to work on listing other species in greater need of protection.[41] Congress cautioned that the existence of pending or imminent proposals to list species subject to a greater threat was the only legitimate reason to delay the action on petitions.[42] Even so, the Secretary still has broad discretion to delay given the tremendous number of candidate species, some of which face the threat of immediate extinction. Furthermore, even if the Secretary determines that a petitioned action is warranted, the Secretary need not publish a proposed listing if he or she makes an additional finding that other listing proposals preclude immediate action on the petition and that "expeditious progress" is being made on species' listings in general.[43] Persons whose petitions are delayed on this basis, as well as those whose petitions the Secretary determines are not warranted, may nevertheless seek immediate judicial review.[44]

Recognizing that the vast backlog of candidates for listing, coupled with the Secretary's limited resources, made prompt ac-

---

38. 16 U.S.C. § 1533(b)(3)(B).

39. *Id.* Congress emphasized that the word "promptly" does not authorize the Secretary to delay decisions or actions at this point; Congress inserted the word "promptly" merely to account for the fact that the Secretary does not control the timing of Federal Register notices. *See* H.R. CONF. REP. No. 835, *supra* note 37, at 23-24.

40. 16 U.S.C. § 1533(b)(3)(A).

41. H.R. CONF. REP. No. 835, *supra* note 37, at 21.

42. *Id.*

43. 16 U.S.C. § 1533(b)(3)(B).

44. *Id.* at § 1533(b)(3)(C)(ii). Courts apply the "arbitrary and capricious" standard when reviewing agency listing decisions unless plaintiffs allege a section 4 procedural violation such as the Secretary's failure to use the best scientific and commercial data available. Note that the Secretary's failure to meet the 90-day deadline in responding to petitions is not a procedural violation because section 4 gives the Secretary discretion to exceed the 90-day limit. *See* Note, *A Cause of Action for Agency Delay Under the ESA*, 12 STETSON L. REV. 135 (1982).

tion on all candidate species impossible, Congress amended section 4 in 1979 to require the Secretary to develop a system to identify species which should receive priority for listing.[45] The U.S. Fish and Wildlife Service (FWS) subsequently adopted a ranking system which favored "higher" life forms by assigning priorities in the following order, from highest to lowest: mammals, birds, fish, reptiles, amphibians, vascular plants, insects, mollusks, other plants, and other invertebrates.[46] This scheme, while protecting well-known species of large vertebrates, made little sense from an ecological standpoint. Therefore, in keeping with its drive to eliminate non-biological factors from the listing process, Congress made it clear in 1982 that the Secretary was not to consider distinctions based on whether a species was considered a "higher" or "lower" life form.[47] Instead, lawmakers directed the Secretary to use "a scientifically based priority system to list and delist species, subspecies and populations based on the degree of threat . . . ."[48]

In 1983, the Secretary of the Interior published a listing priority system addressing the concerns expressed by Congress.[49] These guidelines[50] consider three factors in assigning species a priority for listing: magnitude of threat, immediacy of threat, and species taxonomy.[51] The third criterion emphasizes conservation of genetic diversity, giving priority to species representing highly distinctive or isolated gene pools. The Secretary declined to add a fourth factor suggested by comments on the proposed guidelines, namely, the importance of a species to the ecosystem within which it exists.[52] The Secretary noted, however, that such information would be considered on an ad hoc basis outside the for-

---

45. 16 U.S.C. § 1533(h).

46. *See* 48 Fed. Reg. 16,756-57 (1983).

47. *See* H.R. CONF. REP. No. 835, *supra* note 37, at 21.

48. *Id.*

49. 48 Fed. Reg. 43,098 (1983).

50. An explanation accompanying publication of the priority scheme provides: "Inasmuch as such assessments are subjective to some degree, and individual species may not be comparable in terms of all considerations, the priority systems presented must be viewed as guides and should not be looked upon as inflexible frameworks for determining resource allocations." *Id.*

51. *Id.* at 43,103. For discussion of listing priorities' relation to delisting priorities, see *infra* note 73 and accompanying text.

52. *Id.* at 43,101. Legislative history of the 1982 amendments indicates that Congress felt that a species' contribution to its ecosystem should be considered in the listing process: "Biologically, it makes sense to treat all taxonomic groups equally or even to place some special emphasis on protecting plants and invertebrates since they form the

mal guidelines.[53]

B. *Monitoring Candidate Species*

In 1988, Congress again demonstrated its concern over the huge backlog of species awaiting listing. Noting that some of these species had undergone substantial declines in numbers and several had become extinct before being protected, lawmakers enacted a monitoring requirement intended to prevent such occurrences.[54] Congress amended section 4 to require the Secretary to implement a system to monitor species which warranted listing but had not been formally added to the threatened or endangered list or had not been considered as candidate species.[55] Congress indicated that publication of a list of candidate species, based on "a regular review of status surveys," is an "important component" of the monitoring requirement.[56]

The amended version of section 4 also directs the Secretary to make "prompt use" of emergency listing procedures to prevent "a significant risk to the well-being of any [candidate species]."[57] Congress phrased this provision in a mandatory fashion, apparently intending to extend substantive ESA protection to candidate species.[58] This requirement thus could prove to be extremely significant. It extends at least some degree of protection to a huge number of unlisted species. Moreover, since the ESA's citizen suit provision expressly permits any person to file suit to compel the Secretary to perform a non-discretionary duty under section 4,[59] interested parties now may attempt to compel the Secretary to use emergency listing procedures in specific instances. Such cases will turn upon whether the species involved faces a significant risk to its well-being, a phrase the ESA does not define. This ambiguity notwithstanding, an activity which jeopardizes the continued existence of a candidate species, or which would destroy or adversely modify its critical habitat,

---

bases of ecosystems and food chains upon which all other life depends." S. REP. No. 418, 97th Cong., 2d Sess. 14 (1982).

53. 48 Fed. Reg. 43,098, 43,101 (1983).

54. S. REP. No. 240, 100th Cong., 1st Sess. 8 (1988).

55. *See* 16 U.S.C. § 1533(b)(3)(c)(iii).

56. S. REP. No. 240, *supra* note 54, at 7-8.

57. 16 U.S.C. § 1533(b)(3)(c)(iii).

58. *See* S. REP. No. 240, *supra* note 54, at 8 ("Under current law [candidate] species receive no protection until they are formally proposed for listing. This amendment will correct this shortcoming.").

59. *See* 16 U.S.C. § 1540(g)(1)(C).

would almost certainly trigger the emergency listing mandate. These effects are flatly prohibited by section 7 with respect to species already listed.[60] A more difficult question is whether an adverse impact on a candidate species' chances of recovery constitutes a significant risk to its well-being. Arguably it does because the ESA's ultimate goal is to foster species recovery.[61] However, in light of the Secretary's narrow interpretations of the ESA's conservation mandate and substantive protection of species recovery,[62] it seems likely that the Secretary will also attempt to take a restrictive view of circumstances which amount to a significant risk to the well-being of a candidate species.

C. *Protection of Non-Listed Species*

Under very limited circumstances, section 4 allows the Secretary to treat a species as threatened or endangered despite the fact that it is not officially listed. If an unlisted species so closely resembles a listed species as to confuse identification of the listed species and therefore poses a threat to its protection, the Secretary may promulgate regulations protecting the look-alike species as if it were listed as threatened or endangered.[63] Additionally, agencies must "confer" with the Secretary when an action is likely to jeopardize a species proposed for listing or adversely modify proposed critical habitat.[64]

D. *Reclassification and Delisting*

Occasionally, biological evidence may indicate that a species listed as threatened should be listed as endangered, or vice-versa. The Secretary may reclassify such species using the same criteria and procedures as are used in the listing process.[65] Petitions to reclassify species are treated in the same way as petitions to list species.[66] The listing priority guidelines discussed above apply to proposals to reclassify a threatened species as endangered. A separate priority system applies to proposals to relist an

---

60. *See* 16 U.S.C. § 1536(a)(2).
61. *See* 16 U.S.C. § 1531(b) ("The purposes of this chapter are to provide . . . a program for the conservation of . . . endangered species and threatened species . . . .").
62. *See generally* chapters 5 and 7.
63. 16 U.S.C. § 1533(e).
64. *See infra* Chapter 7, notes 156-162 and accompanying text.
65. *See* 50 C.F.R. § 424.11.
66. *See* 16 U.S.C. § 1533(b)(3)(A).

endangered species as threatened.[67]

In 1982, Congress expressed concern that the endangered and threatened species lists "harbor a number of improperly listed species."[68] Lawmakers thus amended section 4 to apply the same procedures and time frame to delisting as those which apply to listing.[69] The Secretary may delist a species only if one of the following criteria applies: (1) the species has become extinct; (2) the species has recovered; or (3) the original data upon which the species' listing was originally based is in error.[70] When deciding which species eligible for delisting should receive priority, the Secretary employs a ranking system which takes into account the "management burden" required by the species being listed.[71] Among species presenting equal "management burdens," those species which are the subject of delisting petitions receive first consideration.[72] However, the Secretary has indicated that listing of species facing immediate, critical threats will generally take precedence over competing delisting proposals.[73]

E. *Periodic Review of Lists*

The Secretary must review the status of every listed species once every five years to determine whether any species should be reclassified or delisted.[74] Any change in the endangered and threatened lists as a result of this review must be made according to the regular section 4 listing and delisting process.[75]

III. CRITICAL HABITAT DESIGNATION

Section 7 prohibits the destruction or adverse modification of

---

67. This system is also used for determining delisting priorities. *See infra* notes 71-73 and accompanying text.

68. H.R. REP. No. 567, 97th Cong., 2d Sess. 22, *reprinted in* 1982 U.S. CODE CONG. & ADMIN. NEWS 2822.

69. Pub. L. No. 97-304 (1982); *see* 16 U.S.C. § 1533(b)(3).

70. 50 C.F.R. § 424.11(d).

71. 48 Fed. Reg. 43,098, 43,103 (1983). The "management burden" required by a species being listed refers to the quantity of resources expended on that species which could be diverted to more urgent conservation efforts.

72. *Id.*

73. *Id.* at 43,100. The Secretary also noted that delisting of a recovered species that would eliminate significant unwarranted restrictions on identifiable activities may prevail over listing of species not facing severe, imminent threats. In all other circumstances, the Secretary reserved discretion to determine the "complex mesh" between listing and delisting priorities. *Id.*

74. 16 U.S.C. § 1533(c)(2).

75. *Id.*

critical habitat.[76] Though it is unsettled whether this provision protects species with no formally identified critical habitat,[77] section 7's restrictions clearly apply to areas designated by the Secretary as critical habitat of a listed species.

In 1978, Congress amended section 4 to require the Secretary to designate critical habitat concurrently with listing a species.[78] Also in 1978, Congress authorized—but did not require—the Secretary to designate critical habitat for species already listed at the time of the 1978 amendments.[79] These legislative actions created a dichotomy with respect to designation of species' critical habitats. The Secretary's responsibility to designate critical habitat for species listed prior to the 1978 ESA amendments, as well as the applicability of section 7's critical habitat provisions to these species, remain unsettled.[80] On the other hand, the Secretary now may refrain from designating critical habitat when adding a species to the endangered or threatened lists only in the limited circumstances discussed below.

Section 4 requires the Secretary to designate critical habitat "to the maximum extent prudent and determinable" at the time a species is listed.[81] Though section 4 is broadly phrased, the legislative history and the statutory listing process indicate that Congress intended the "prudent and determinable" exception to be narrowly construed. Congress has noted that critical habitat designation would not be prudent if it would disclose the location of a listed species commonly sought by unscrupulous collec-

---

76. 16 U.S.C. § 1536(a)(2). The ESA defines critical habitat as:

(i)   the specific areas within the geographic area occupied by the species, at the time it is listed . . . , on which are found those physical or biological features (I) essential to the conservation of the species and (II) which may require special management considerations or protection; and

(ii)   specific areas outside the geographical area occupied by the species at the time it is listed . . . upon a determination by the Secretary that such areas are essential for the conservation of the species.

Id. at § 1532(5)(A).

77. For a discussion of this issue, see *infra* Chapter 7, notes 77-88 and accompanying text.

78. Pub. L. No. 95-632 (1978) (codified at 16 U.S.C. § 1532(a)(3)). This requirement arguably also applies to listed species which the Secretary reclassifies from threatened to endangered or even vice-versa. The Secretary has apparently adopted this interpretation of section 4 as evidenced by recent rules reclassifying previously listed species.

79. *Id.*

80. *See infra* Chapter 7, notes 77-95 and accompanying text.

81. 16 U.S.C. § 1533(a)(3).

tors.[82] Congress has not cited any other instances, however, where critical habitat designation would be imprudent. Discussing the requirement to designate critical habitat to the extent prudent, a 1978 House report concluded that "[i]t is only in *rare circumstances* where the specification of critical habitat concurrently with the listing would not be beneficial to the species."[83] Additionally, though section 4 permits the Secretary to list species whose critical habitats are undeterminable at the time of listing, within one year of listing the Secretary must designate critical habitat for such species to the extent prudent on the basis of whatever data is available at that time.[84]

The Secretary, however, has apparently expanded the circumstances under which critical habitat designation is not considered prudent beyond the mandates of Congress. In calendar year 1986, for example, the Secretary determined in 41 cases out of a total of 45 final listings that critical habitat designation was not prudent.[85] This statistic, clearly at odds with Congressional intent that non-designation of critical habitat during the listing process should occur only rarely,[86] results from broad discretion accorded to the Secretary in making critical habitat determinations by regulations implementing section 4. Section 4 regulations permit the Secretary to avoid designating critical habitat concurrently with listing whenever such designation "would not be beneficial to the species."[87] An official explanation of this provision indicates that the Secretary performs an informal balancing test on a case-by-case basis to determine whether critical habitat designation benefits a species:

> [T]he Services will examine the balance between risk to a species that might be a consequence of designating its critical habitat and benefits that the species might derive from such designation. . . . In those cases in which the possible adverse consequences would outweigh the benefits of designation of critical habitat, the Services may forego such designation as a

---

82. *See* H.R. Rep. No. 1625, 95th Cong., 2d Sess. 15 (1978); H.R. Rep. No. 567, 97th Cong., 2d Sess. 20, *reprinted in* 1982 U.S. Code Cong. & Admin. News 2820; H.R. Conf. Rep. No. 835, 97th Cong., 2d Sess. 24, *reprinted in* 1982 U.S. Code Cong. & Admin. News 2865.

83. H.R. Rep. No. 1625, 95th Cong., 2d Sess. 17, *reprinted in* 1978 U.S. Code Cong. & Admin. News 9453, 9467 (emphasis added).

84. 16 U.S.C. § 1533(b)(6)(C).

85. Telephone interview with Laverne Smith, FWS Office of Endangered Species, (Sept. 1, 1987).

86. *See supra* notes 83-84 and accompanying text.

87. 50 C.F.R. § 424.12(a)(1)(ii).

matter of prudence.[88]

This procedure affords the Secretary broader discretion over designation of critical habitat than Congress intended. By allowing the Secretary to identify what he or she feels are the benefits of critical habitat designation and to weigh these perceived benefits against the drawbacks of critical habitat designation, the section 4 regulations in effect grant the Secretary complete discretion in deciding whether to designate critical habitat when adding a species to the protected list. This scheme conflicts with section 4's mandate to designate critical habitat concurrently with species listings. The fact that the language and history of section 4 require the Secretary to designate critical habitat along with listing indicates that Congress *presumed* that critical habitat designation benefits listed species. It is not appropriate, therefore, for the Secretary to attempt to identify critical habitat benefits and to weigh them against the adverse consequences of critical habitat designation. In so doing, the Secretary usurps Congressional authority by upsetting a Congressional presumption favoring critical habitat designation. Though Congress also recognized that critical habitat designation could in fact harm listed species, it emphasized that such cases would be rare exceptions to section 4's mandate to designate critical habitat with listing.[89] Section 4, therefore, merely gives the Secretary discretion to identify these few exceptions. As the regulations erroneously interpret this section, the exception swallows the general rule.

A.   *Critical Habitat Designation Criteria*

When the Secretary decides to designate critical habitat concurrently with listing, or when the Secretary designates critical habitat for a species which was listed prior to 1978, he or she must consider several factors. The Secretary first takes into account whether the area under consideration for designation fits the multi-part statutory definition of critical habitat.

Critical habitat in part consists of a geographical area containing physical or biological features essential to the conservation of a listed species.[90] As the ESA and implementing regulations define key terms, an area essential to the conservation of a listed species means that the species needs the area to make a success-

---

88.   49 Fed. Reg. 38,900, 38,903 (1984).
89.   *See supra* note 82-83 and accompanying text.
90.   16 U.S.C. § 1532(5)(A)(i).

ful recovery.[91] Section 4 regulations list some of the physical and biological features a species may require for recovery which the Secretary considers when designating critical habitat.[92]

The ESA further defines critical habitat as an area which "may require special management considerations or protection."[93] In at least one instance, the Secretary cited this provision in refusing to designate an area as critical habitat. That case involved proposed critical habitat designation for waters in the northwest Hawaiian Islands to protect endangered monk seals.[94] The Secretary asserted that portions of a large area recommended by the monk seal recovery plan for critical habitat designation did not require special management considerations or protection.[95] The Secretary made this finding despite implicitly acknowledging that two types of human activities, deep seabed mining and commercial fishing operations, could affect monk seals and their habitat.[96] The Secretary noted, however, that a seabed mining industry was "likely years away," and also that fishery management plans provided protection for monk seals.[97] On this basis, the Secretary concluded that much of the area recommended by the recovery plan for critical habitat designation did not require special management and thus did not qualify as critical habitat within the statutory meaning of the term.[98]

This interpretation of "special management considerations and protection" within the statutory definition of critical habitat contains serious practical and legal flaws. It makes little sense to wait until a threat to essential habitat of a listed species is imminent before according the habitat protected status. One of the

---

91. *See infra* Chapter 7, notes 71-72 and accompanying text.

92. *See* 50 C.F.R. § 424.12(b).

93. 16 U.S.C. § 1532(5)(A)(i).

94. *See* 51 Fed. Reg. 16,047-53 (1986).

95. *Id.* at 16,048.

96. *Id.* at 16,051.

97. *Id.*

98. *Id.* at 16,048, 16,051. However, the Secretary reversed this decision two years later. *See* 53 Fed. Reg. 18,988-90 (1988). The explanation accompanying this reversal implicitly concludes that the entire area recommended for critical habitat designation requires special management considerations and protection, but it does not clearly specify why the Secretary abandoned his earlier conclusion that much of the area did not require special considerations. Although not mentioned in the rulemaking record, a lawsuit filed by environmental organizations likely played a role in prompting the Secretary to reconsider this issue. The Secretary's decision to accept the recovery plan's critical habitat recommendation came before the district court ruled on the environmentalists' claims. *See infra* Chapter 5, note 15.

benefits of specifying critical habitat is notification to federal
agencies that a certain area is crucial to a listed species, permitting agencies to plan projects which may affect the area while
cognizant of the species' needs. Early designation of critical
habitat may thus prevent conflicts between federal projects and
conservation of listed species, whereas attempting to specify critical habitat in the face of ongoing federal actions would undoubtedly create difficulties. The former approach is also more
consistent with the statute itself; a recurring theme within the
ESA is the resolution of conflicts at the earliest possible time.[99]

Additionally, the existence of other laws, regulations, or
guidelines which address imminent or potential threats to essential habitat of listed species should be irrelevant to critical habitat
designation. Declaring an area critical habitat does not preempt
any other regulation of federal activities in a given land area. It
simply provides the Secretary authority to insure that federal actions do not destroy or adversely modify physical and biological
features needed for the recovery of a listed species. Other forms
of regulation may also accomplish this task, but the Secretary
would have to spend time and money analyzing any non-ESA
regulations to insure that they provided species' habitat with adequate protection. Even if the Secretary concludes that non-ESA
regulations offer sufficient protection, the Secretary may have no
control over enforcement or subsequent modification of such
regulations.[100] Thus, whenever any restrictions are needed to
protect habitat essential for recovery of a listed species, critical
habitat designation is appropriate, regardless of whether such restrictions are already in place independent of the ESA.[101]

The statutory definition of critical habitat also contains two

---

99. For example, section 7(d), which prohibits federal agencies from making irreversible commitments of resources while a project's effects on listed species are still
being studied, reflects this principle. *See infra* Chapter 7, notes 1-8 and accompanying
text. *See also* 124 CONG. REC. 21,132-34 (1978) (remarks of Senator Culver advocating
early resolution of conflicts between federal projects and species conservation).

100. Similarly, citizens may not have standing under non-ESA regulatory schemes
to seek a court injunction against activities harming the essential habitat of listed species. The ESA, on the other hand, encourages private enforcement of habitat protection
by permitting citizens to sue to enjoin the destruction or adverse modification of critical
habitat. *See* 16 U.S.C. § 1540(g)(1)(A).

101. Section 4 regulations support this interpretation. The regulations define
"special management considerations or protection" as "*any* methods or procedures useful in protecting physical and biological features of the environment for the conservation of listed species." 50 C.F.R. § 424.02(j) (emphasis added). Under this definition,
therefore, the existence of non-ESA restrictions on a species' habitat demonstrates that

references to the area which can be considered critical habitat of a listed species. First, the ESA authorizes the Secretary to designate as critical habitat geographical areas outside those occupied by a species at the time it is listed provided that such areas are essential to the conservation of the species.[102] This is the same standard as applied by the Secretary in determining critical habitat within the area occupied by a species at listing. In addition, the ESA specifies that critical habitat for a listed species does not include all areas which the species could potentially occupy, except under circumstances at the Secretary's discretion.[103] The Secretary has apparently determined that the only circumstances justifying designation of a species' entire potential range as critical habitat occur when the *entire* potential range is essential to the species' conservation.[104]

Unfortunately, Congress itself has demonstrated confusion over how the Secretary should apply the statutory definition of critical habitat to determine critical habitat boundaries. A 1978 Senate report discussing a then-proposed critical habitat designation for grizzly bears covering approximately 10 million acres contains the following passage:

> Much of the land involved in this proposed designation is not habitat that is necessary for the continued survival of the bear. It instead is being designated so that the present population within the true critical habitat can expand. The goal of expanding existing populations of endangered species in order that they might be delisted is understandable. This process does, however, substantially increase the amount of area involved in critical habitat designation and therefore increases proportionately the area that is subject to the regulations and prohibitions which apply to critical habitats.[105]

While this discussion indicates Congressional concern over the politically sensitive issue of subjecting large land areas to increased federal regulation, it also reveals an apparent fundamental misunderstanding of critical habitat. Under the statutory definition of the term, critical habitat does not describe an area

---

the area is in need of special management considerations or protection and, thus, is within the statutory definition of critical habitat.

102. 16 U.S.C. § 1532(5)(A)(ii).

103. *Id.* at § 1532(5)(C).

104. *See* 50 C.F.R. § 424.12(e).

105. S. Rep. No. 874, 95th Cong., 2nd Sess. 10 (1978). This proposed critical habitat designation was withdrawn a year later.

"necessary for the continued survival" of a listed species.[106] Critical habitat is an area essential to the *conservation* of a listed species.[107] Conservation of listed species—recovery to the point at which species may be removed from the protected lists—is not, as the Senate report observes, merely "understandable;" it is the purpose and mandate of the ESA itself. The protection provided to listed species by critical habitat designation is specifically designed to facilitate species' recovery.[108] Therefore, a designation of critical habitat is not only appropriate under the ESA, it is required by the statute itself.

A final paradox in the critical habitat designation process involves consideration of economic factors. Even assuming the Secretary determines during the listing process that an area meets the statutory definition of critical habitat, and assuming further the Secretary finds that critical habitat designation is prudent, the Secretary still has discretion to exclude any or all of the area from designation as critical habitat. This was not true prior to 1978, when the Secretary made critical habitat determinations solely on the basis of biological criteria. In 1978, however, Congress amended section 4 to require the Secretary to designate critical habitat "after taking into consideration the economic impact, and any other relevant impact, of specifying any particular area as critical habitat."[109] A House report explaining this provision[110] noted that "[t]he consideration and weight given to any particular impact is completely within the Secretary's discretion."[111] The report went on to express lawmakers' expectations that the consideration of economic and other impacts would probably result in instances where the Secretary would designate smaller areas as critical habitat than he or she would have designated if relying solely on biological criteria. The lawmakers also

---

106. The section 7 jeopardy standard, rather than the section 7 provisions dealing with critical habitat, insures the continued survival of listed species. *See infra* Chapter 7, notes 57-59 and accompanying text.

107. 16 U.S.C. § 1532(5)(A)(i).

108. *See infra* Chapter 7, notes 70-76 and accompanying text.

109. 16 U.S.C. § 1532(b)(2).

110. H.R. REP. No. 1625, 95th Cong., 2d Sess. 17, *reprinted in* 1978 U. S. CODE CONG. & ADMIN. NEWS 9453, 9467. Actually, under the House version of the 1978 amendments, the Secretary could consider non-biological criteria only when designating critical habitat for invertebrate species. When the final version of the amended ESA emerged from committee, however, the limitation to invertebrate species had been dropped.

111. *Id.*

noted other situations in which the Secretary would simply decline to specify critical habitat if economic and other criteria were considered.[112] The House report emphasized, however, that even in areas where the Secretary expressly refuses to designate critical habitat, federal projects remain subject to the jeopardy standard of section 7.[113]

Consideration of non-biological criteria in designating critical habitat as required under section 4 is a statutory aberration at odds with the purpose and structure of the remainder of the ESA. This procedure allows the Secretary to deny species statutory protection designed to further their recovery. The "Additional Views" section of the 1978 House report on the ESA amendments succinctly describes the incongruities between the section 4 critical habitat designation procedure and the rest of the ESA:

> By definition, the designation of critical habitat requires an objective, scientific assessment on the part of the Secretary of [the] Interior. The committee bill, unfortunately, ignores this fact by requiring the Secretary to consider economic impacts when designating critical habitat for invertebrate species, and by empowering him to exclude all or part of a biologically critical area on purely economic grounds.
>
> In effect, then, the Secretary is given broad power to grant exemptions to the Endangered Species Act through a simple, unilateral administrative determination of his or her own. This is a process which stands in sharp contrast to the laboriously constructed exemption process, with its clear standards and procedural safeguards . . . .
>
> We want to emphasize that we do believe that economic considerations should be considered when weighing the desirability of granting an exemption to the Endangered Species Act. We simply believe that such consideration should be included in the basic exemption process, rather than singled out in a separate procedure where it does not logically belong.
>
> As currently written, the critical habitat provision is a startling section which is wholly inconsistent with the rest of the legislation. It constitutes a loophole which could readily be abused by any Secretary of the Interior who is vulnerable to political pressure, or who is not sympathetic to the basic purposes of the Endangered Species Act.[114]

112. *Id.*

113. *Id.*

114. H.R. REP. No. 1625, 95th Cong., 2d Sess. 69, *reprinted in* 1978 U.S. CODE CONG. & ADMIN. NEWS 9453, 9483.

This analysis has been echoed by other commentators.[115]

By its terms, the provision of section 4 directing the Secretary to consider non-biological criteria in designating critical habitat applies only to critical habitat designations made concurrently with listing a species.[116] The ESA is unclear as to whether the Secretary must consider non-biological factors when designating critical habitat for species listed prior to 1978 for which no critical habitat has yet been designated.

B.   *Revision of Critical Habitat Designation*

Finally, any person may petition the Secretary to revise a critical habitat petition.[117] To the maximum extent practicable, the Secretary must make a finding within 90 days of receipt of the petition as to whether such a petition presents substantial scientific information indicating that the petitioned action may be warranted.[118] Upon an affirmative finding, the Secretary has one year to determine whether to act on the petition.[119] These requirements do not apply to petitions requesting designation of critical habitat for species which presently have no designated critical habitats. Upon receipt of this type of petition, the Secretary merely must conduct a review of the requested action in accordance with the Administrative Procedure Act.[120]

---

115. *See, e.g.*, M. BEAN, THE EVOLUTION OF NATIONAL WILDLIFE LAW at 339 n.95 (1983).

116. *See* 16 U.S.C. § 1533(b)(2).

117. *Id.* at § 1533(b)(3)(D) (referring to the Administrative Procedure Act, 5 U.S.C. § 553(e) (1982) ("Each agency shall give an interested person the right to petition for the issuance, amendment, or repeal of a rule")). A petition to revise critical habitat need not contain economic information relevant to the revision. *See* H.R. CONF. REP. No. 835, 97th Cong., 2d Sess. 22, *reprinted in* 1982 U.S. CODE CONG. & ADMIN. NEWS 2860, 2863.

118. 16 U.S.C. § 1533(b)(3)(D)(i); 50 C.F.R. § 424.14(c)(1).

119. 16 U.S.C. § 1533(b)(3)(D)(ii); 50 C.F.R. § 424.14(c)(3).

120. 50 C.F.R. § 424.14(d)

Chapter 4

The Ban on Takings and Other Statutory Prohibitions

ESA section 9 forbids specified acts which directly or indirectly harm listed species. These prohibitions have two particularly notable aspects. First, unlike other major ESA provisions, section 9's restrictions apply not only to federal agencies and permittees, but to all persons subject to United States' jurisdiction. Second, the protection accorded to plants differs from the protection extended to wildlife and fish; similarly, the section 9 provisions applicable to endangered species differ from those applied to threatened species.

I. PROHIBITED ACTS: ENDANGERED FAUNA

A. *Prohibition on Takings*

Section 9 prohibits all persons[1] subject to United States' jurisdiction from "taking"[2] any species of wildlife or fish *listed as endangered*.[3] This prohibition applies within the United States and

---

1. The ESA defines "persons" broadly. 16 U.S.C. § 1532(13).

2. For a discussion of the historical development of the taking concept in the context of wildlife protection, see Field, *The Evolution of the Wildlife Taking Concept From Its Beginning to Its Culmination in the Endangered Species Act*, 21 HOUS. L. REV. 457 (1984).

3. 16 U.S.C. § 1538(a)(1)(B-C). Occasionally, federal statutes which prohibit all persons from taking or harming certain wildlife have come under indirect attack by allegations that damage to private property caused by protected wildlife constitutes an unconstitutional taking of property unless the federal government compensates the aggrieved property holder. Courts have generally rejected such arguments. *See, e.g.*, Mountain States Legal Found. v. Hodel, 799 F.2d 1423 (10th Cir. 1986) (damage to grazing lands by protected wild horses and burros not a taking of property).

The United States Supreme Court unanimously held that the Bald and Golden Eagle Protection Act, 16 U.S.C. § 668, abrogated Indian treaty rights to hunt eagles. United States v. Dion, 476 U.S. 734, 745 (1986). Though the Court did not reach the question of whether the ESA also abrogated Indian hunting rights, it observed that the Eagle Protection Act and ESA prohibit the same conduct with respect to eagles for the same reasons. *Id.* at 746. *See also* Reynolds, *Indian Hunting and Fishing Rights: The Role of Tribal Sovereignty and Preemption*, 62 N.C.L. REV. 743 (1984); Comment, *Eagles and Indians: The Law and the Survival of a Species*, 5 PUB. LAND L. REV. 100 (1984).

its territorial waters as well as on the high seas. The ESA provides that the term "take" means to "harass, harm, pursue, hunt, shoot, wound, kill, trap, capture, or collect, or attempt to engage in any such conduct."[4]

Despite this expansive statutory definition, several limitations exist on the actual application of section 9's takings prohibition. Plaintiffs or prosecutors attempting to invoke section 9 have the burden of establishing that a taking has occurred or will occur.[5] Thus, when data on how an activity affects endangered species is unavailable, or is difficult or expensive to obtain, section 9 may offer species little protection.[6] Moreover, to carry the burden of proving a taking, it is insufficient for a litigant to demonstrate that a taking may have occurred or might occur in the future. In *North Slope Borough v. Andrus*,[7] plaintiffs argued that offshore oil leasing constituted an unlawful taking of endangered bowhead whales. Despite admissions by the federal defendants that future activities stemming from the leases could harm whales, the court refused to grant injunctive relief under section 9 because the plaintiffs failed to demonstrate that danger to the whales was "sufficiently imminent or certain."[8] This reasoning was echoed by another court facing a similar set of facts. In *California v. Watt*,[9] the court examined ESA takings prohibitions, as well as those under the Marine Mammal Protection Act, and concluded:

> Assuming arguendo that the proposed leasing activities do constitute a threat to the continued survival of species protected by these statutes, such a threat would still not constitute a "taking" under the statutes . . . . [I]n prohibiting "taking," the draftsmen of the statutes envisioned a more immediate injury. . . . A review of the record reveals no clear showing of such harm . . . .[10]

These decisions apparently set forth two predicates to establish-

---

4. 16 U.S.C. § 1532(19).

5. *See infra* Chapter 9, note 105 and accompanying text.

6. When a federal entity or any other person seeks permission from the Secretary to incidentally take a listed species, however, the Secretary must comply with all of section 7's substantive and procedural mandates in making this decision, including the statutory requirement to use the best scientific and commercial data available. *See infra* notes 83-85 and 113-114 accompanying text. *See also* 16 U.S.C. § 1536(a)(2).

7. 486 F. Supp. 326 (D.D.C. 1979), *aff'd & rev'd*, 642 F.2d 610 (1980).

8. *Id.* at 362. The court did not indicate the degree of proof "sufficient" to prove immediate or certain harm.

9. 520 F. Supp. 1359, 1387-88 (C.D. Cal. 1981), *aff'd & rev'd on other grounds*, 683 F.2d 1254 (9th Cir. 1982), *rev'd on other grounds*, 464 U.S. 312 (1984).

10. *Id.*

ing a taking: first, that a taking is relatively certain, and second, that the taking is imminent.

The first of the above requirements is defensible within the context of the ESA. It is often difficult to quantify risks in fields as technically complex as biology. Even assuming that the Secretary or a reviewing court could accurately assess the risk that taking of a listed species would occur if an action was carried out, the ESA provides no guidance as to how much risk is too much. Section 9 prohibits takings rather than actions posing risks that takings will occur.[11] This structure suggests that Congress viewed takings as essentially an "all-or-nothing" proposition—actions which result in takings of listed species are unlawful under section 9 while all other actions are not affected by section 9's taking prohibitions, even if they pose risks of future takings.[12]

No arguments support a view that section 9 prohibits only takings which are "imminent." While likely to occur infrequently, instances where a taking is relatively certain but unlikely to take place immediately are not inconceivable. For example, the activities that the court in *National Wildlife Federation v. Coleman*[13] determined would affect whooping cranes were not planned at the time of the court's decision, but were inevitable with completion of the challenged highway. Given such an instance, there is no rational reason to consider future adverse impacts to endangered species as not constituting takings merely because they do not affect the species immediately. On the contrary, it makes much sense to halt or modify activities as early as possible before takings occur, both to benefit endangered species and to avoid the potential waste of resources on an activity which may be enjoined in the future when a taking becomes

---

11. Compare the unqualified section 9 takings prohibition with the basic mandate of section 7. The latter, which requires federal agencies to "insure" that their actions are not "likely to" jeopardize listed species or destroy critical habitat, calls for a risk analysis procedure. Section 9 flatly bans specified actions.

12. However, persons who proceed with actions which may result in takings of listed species run the risk that their activities may be halted in the future if in fact a taking occurs. Unfortunately, in some cases, such as when an area is permanently altered by construction, the activity which eventually causes a taking may be irreversible. In such instances, civil penalties could still be assessed against the party responsible for the activity which causes a taking. While this remedy would not benefit the affected species, it could serve to deter others from carrying out activities which risk a section 9 violation.

13. 529 F.2d 359 (1976).

imminent.[14]

Despite the decisions in *North Slope* and *California v. Watt*, the question of whether harm to a protected species must be imminent to constitute a taking is not settled. Neither court squarely faced the immediacy issue because future takings as a result of the disputed oil and gas leasing activities were found to be merely speculative. Therefore, the courts' discussions of a time element in relation to a taking could have been meant simply to emphasize the uncertainty over whether a taking would ever occur. At most, the decisions' requirement that harm be "imminent" to constitute a taking is dictum. Moreover, another federal district court expressly declined to read an immediacy requirement into section 9's taking prohibition. In *Palila v. Hawaii Department of Land & Natural Resources ("Palila II")*,[15] defendants admitted that an activity then underway could harm a protected species in the future. Nevertheless, defendants argued that the activity did not constitute a taking because it was not *presently* harming the species. Calling this view "shortsighted," the court enjoined the challenged activity as a taking.[16]

B.   *The Definition of "Harm"*

Substantial controversy surrounds the meaning of the term "harm" within the statutory definition of a taking.[17] In *Palila v. Hawaii Department of Land & Natural Resources ("Palila I")*,[18] plaintiffs argued that an activity which significantly degrades the habitat of a protected species constitutes a taking under section 9. Specifically, plaintiffs argued that populations of feral goats

---

14. Congress clearly intended that the ESA promote resolving conflicts between species conservation and human activities at the earliest possible time. In an oft-quoted remark, Senator Culver stated: "The earlier in the progress of a project a conflict [between a species and the project] is recognized, the easier it is to design an alternative consistent with the requirements of the act, or to abandon the proposed action." 124 CONG. REC. 21,134 (July 17, 1978). ESA section 7(d) encourages early resolution of such conflicts by prohibiting "irreversible and irretrievable" commitments of resources while consultation is underway on a federal proposal.

15. Palila v. Hawaii Dep't of Land & Natural Resources, 649 F. Supp. 1070 (D. Hawaii 1986), *aff'd*, 852 F.2d 1106 (9th Cir. 1988).

16. *Id.* at 1075.

17. Regulations provide: " 'Harm' in the definition of 'take' in the Act means an act which actually kills or injures wildlife. Such acts may include significant habitat modification or degradation where it actually kills or injures wildlife by significantly impairing essential behavioral patterns, including breeding, feeding or sheltering." 50 C.F.R. § 17.3

18. 471 F. Supp. 985 (D. Hawaii 1979), *aff'd*, 639 F.2d 495 (1981).

and sheep maintained by the State of Hawaii for sport hunting illegally harmed an endangered bird species, the palila, by destroying the vegetation upon which the birds exclusively depend. It was undisputed that the goats and sheep did in fact destroy palilas' habitat. The regulatory definition of harm in effect at the time *Palila I* was initiated, which included the phrase "significant environmental modification or degradation," bolstered the plaintiffs' case.[19] The district court found that the state-maintained feral animals constituted an unlawful taking of the endangered palila, a holding upheld by the Ninth Circuit.[20]

Palila I is a far-reaching decision because it enjoined habitat modification detrimental to a protected species on non-federal land when no federal agency or federal permits were involved. FWS reaction to the decision was swift. An Interior Department Solicitor's Opinion concluded that the *Palila I* decision "demonstrates fundamental confusion over the distinction between habitat modifications and takings."[21] The Opinion argued that *Palila I* erroneously found that habitat modification alone could constitute a taking. The Solicitor interpreted section 9 as proscribing habitat modification only when that modification was shown actually to kill or injure wildlife.[22] Accordingly, in an attempt to essentially overrule what it believed to be the holding of *Palila I*, FWS redefined the term harm to its present form.[23]

Whether the redefinition of harm effected any change over the previous regulatory definition of the term became a major

---

19. The regulatory definition of harm in effect during the *Palila I* litigation provided that:

"Harm" in the definition of "take" in the Act means an act or omission which actually injures or kills wildlife, including acts which annoy it to such an extent as to significantly disrupt essential behavioral patterns, which include, but are not limited to, breeding, feeding or sheltering: significant environmental modification or degradation which has such effects is included within the meaning of "harm."

50 C.F.R. § 17.3 (superceded).

20. 639 F.2d 495 (9th Cir. 1981). For further discussions of *Palila I*, see Smith, *The Endangered Species Act and Biological Conservation*, 57 S.C.L. Rev. 361 (1984); Note, *Palila v. Hawaii: A New Interpretation of Taking Under the Endangered Species Act of 1973*, 19 Idaho L. Rev. 157 (1983); Note, *Palila v. Hawaii: Taking Under Section 9 of the Endangered Species Act of 1973* 4 U. Hawaii L. Rev. 181 (1982). *See also* Comment, *Palila v. Hawaii: State Governments Fall Prey to the Endangered Species Act of 1973* 10 Ecology L. Q. 281 (1982) (emphasizing procedural aspects of the case, as well as federalism issues).

21. 46 Fed. Reg. 29,492 (1981).

22. *Id.* at 29,491.

23. For further discussion of FWS's rationale for redefining "harm," see the explanation accompanying the final agency rulemaking. 46 Fed. Reg. 54,748 (1981).

issue in *Palila II*.[24] The case was factually identical to *Palila I* except that it involved a different species of feral sheep whose destructive habits had only recently been scientifically documented. In *Palila II*, however, defendants argued that the Secretary's redefinition of harm, with its emphasis on actual injury or death to protected species, precluded the result reached by the courts in *Palila I*. The State of Hawaii stressed that plaintiffs had failed to show that any endangered palilas had actually died as a result of the presence of feral sheep. Implicitly, this argument substantially relied on the Solicitor's Opinion issued after *Palila I*. When plaintiffs in *Palila II* made no attempt to document the demise of individual birds, the State of Hawaii, citing census data on the palila population which indicated that the total number of birds had remained constant or had even increased slightly in the years following the *Palila I* decision, argued that this information demonstrated that no birds had actually died as a result of the presence of feral sheep and hence no taking of palilas had demonstrably occurred.

After trial on the merits, the district court in *Palila II* flatly rejected defendants' contentions. Reaffirming a determination it had made at an earlier stage of the proceedings in *Palila II*,[25] the court held that the amended regulatory definition of harm did not embody a substantial change in the definition of harm upon which the same court partially relied in its *Palila I* decision. The *Palila II* court also rejected the notion that section 9 requires evidence of death or injury to specific individual members of a protected species as a prerequisite to finding that a taking had occurred. Instead, the court found that the concept of harm should be applied to a species as a whole. It went on to find that presence of the feral sheep was in fact harming the Palila population as a whole despite population figures suggesting that the numbers of birds had not recently declined. The court held that habitat destruction or modification that prevents an endangered population from *recovering* causes harm to the species as a whole and is thus proscribed by section 9.[26]

In a relatively brief opinion, the Ninth Circuit affirmed the findings and conclusions of the district court.[27]

---

24. 649 F. Supp. at 1075-77.
25. Denial of plaintiffs' motion for summary judgement, 631 F. Supp. 787 (1985).
26. 649 F. Supp. at 1082.
27. 852 F.2d 1106 (9th Cir. 1988).

Palila II's emphasis on how an activity affects species recovery as the standard to determine whether a taking has occurred breaks new legal ground with respect to section 9. The district court's *Palila II* decision interpreted the ESA's prohibition on taking as protecting not only individual members of endangered species, but also such individuals' opportunity to increase their collective numbers to the point where an entire population can be said to have recovered. This notion of a taking links section 9 with the stated purposes of the ESA itself. Since Congress expressly listed conservation (i.e., recovery) of listed species as well as conservation of the ecosystems upon which such species depend as primary aims of the statute, the court reasoned that activities which frustrate these goals harm protected species within the meaning of section 9.

Ironically, the *Palila II* court deliberately fit its expansive view of takings within the revised regulatory definition of harm promulgated by the Secretary in an attempt to narrow the category of activities considered to be a taking. To do so, the court focused on an activity's impact on a species as a whole rather than individual species members, and construed foreclosure of a species' eventual recovery as constituting an actual and present injury to the species. The court's application of the concept of harm to a species' population as a whole rather than individual members of a species will likely make it easier to establish unlawful takings. Data documenting actual deaths or injuries of specific individuals of a species is often difficult to obtain, as is information conclusively linking such deaths and injuries to the challenged activity. On the other hand, information documenting more generalized population trends and information on how an activity affects a species as a whole is often more readily available.

In *Palila II*, the district court determined that the controversial feral sheep would *prevent* recovery of the palila population and thus concluded their presence in the palilas' habitat constituted an illegal taking. The court's opinion, however, does not address whether an activity which assertedly only *delays* a species' recovery or otherwise adversely affects a species, short of precluding its recovery altogether, also constitutes a taking. The Ninth Circuit's opinion mentioned but expressly declined to address this question. Nevertheless, it is important because information will seldom exist to allow biologists—much less courts—

to find that a specified activity will actually preclude recovery of a given species.

There are several reasons to conclude that actions which adversely affect species recovery constitute takings. The express goal of Congress in enacting the ESA was to conserve populations of vanishing species.[28] It seems inconsistent with this goal to allow actions which partially frustrate this conservation purpose as long as those actions do not completely eliminate a species' chances for recovery. Additionally, as a practical matter it is often difficult to pinpoint when impacts merely impair recovery and when impacts completely foreclose recovery. Finally, many activities often affect a protected species incrementally. Assuming that takings were defined to occur only when species' recovery is completely precluded, at some point the cumulative effect of several separate activities could become takings. Would all of the separate activities affecting a species then constitute an unlawful taking of the species? Alternatively, would only the activity which finally pushes species' recovery over the brink constitute an unlawful taking?[29] Neither of these approaches seems satisfactory. On one hand, an activity which was legal when first initiated could be rendered an illegal taking by the subsequent activities of others. In the second alternative, only the person who carries out the final activity would suffer, despite the fact that many contributed to the species' decline.

On the other hand, broadly construing harm within the statutory definition of takings to include all actions which adversely impact species recovery presents serious problems. Interpreting section 9's taking restrictions to prohibit all actions which adversely impact or preclude species recovery would render the jeopardy standard of section 7 virtually meaningless. A federal action found to harm a species under a broad interpretation of harm would be prohibited regardless of whether the action jeopardized the species' continued existence, thereby obviating the need for section 7's prohibition against placing species in jeopardy of extinction.[30] In addition, since section 9 applies to all person subject to United States jurisdiction, an expansive read-

---

28. 16 U.S.C. § 1531(b).

29. The federal government adopts this approach with respect to cumulative effects in the context of section 7.

30. All actions which jeopardize the continued existence of a listed species also obviously adversely affect that species' recovery, but the converse is not necessarily true. Actions which jeopardize a species are therefore a subset of actions which adversely

ing of section 9's taking restrictions carries tremendous implications for private land use. A wide array of activities on non-federal land could adversely impact the recovery of endangered species and thus be illegal under a broad interpretation of harm. The ESA's legislative history, however, gives no indication that Congress intended the statute to create sweeping controls on non-federal land use. On the contrary, the 1982 ESA amendments suggest that Congress was sympathetic to non-federal landowners whose actions may be restricted by section 9.[31]

The above discussion demonstrates the difficulties in resolving the question of whether the term harm within the ESA's definition of taking includes delay of species' recovery. While it makes little sense to conclude that impairment of recovery does not harm a species, the structure of the ESA itself, as well as the broad reach of section 9, may not justify an expansive reading of harm. How courts may resolve this tension is not clear.

In general, however, two principles relating to the meaning of harm have emerged from the *Palila* decisions. First, an activity which indirectly causes a decline in the population of an endangered species[32] harms that species within the meaning of section 9 and its implementing regulations. A population decline can be shown either by evidence that the activity has killed or injured specific individuals within the population *or* by demonstrating that the activity in question has caused a decrease in the population as a whole. This principle is not likely to be subject to dispute. Indeed, the defendants in *Palila II* argued strenuously in favor of this interpretation of harm. The holding of the district court in *Palila II* embodies the other clear interpretation of harm. Activities that *preclude* recovery of an endangered species fall within the meaning of harm and are thus prohibited by section 9. Though evidence must show that the challenged activity will in

---

affect species recovery. If the taking prohibition of section 9 prohibits the latter, section 7's jeopardy prohibition becomes largely superfluous.

31. The 1982 ESA amendments created a permit process whereby actions by non-federal entities may be exempted from section 9's taking restrictions. With this process, Congress sought to "address[ ] the concerns of private landowners who are faced with having otherwise lawful actions not requiring federal permits prevented by section 9 prohibitions against taking." H.R. CONF. REP. 835, 97th Cong., 2d Sess., *reprinted in* 1982 U.S. CODE CONG. & ADMIN. NEWS 2870.

32. Indirect impacts on endangered species are caused by some form of habitat modification. Habitat modification itself can be direct, such as constructing roads in grizzly habitat, or indirect, such as was the case in the Palila litigation where humans introduced a non-native species which in turn destroyed the Palilas' habitat.

fact preclude species recovery, whether the activity causes death or injury to individual species members or causes a decline in the species' overall population is irrelevant. In *Palila II* the district court determined that the State of Hawaii was harming palilas even though the state produced studies suggesting that the birds' population had increased in recent years. However, whether impacts on species recovery short of complete elimination of a species' chances of increasing its population to healthy levels also constitute harm is an open—and difficult—question.

Despite fears expressed by FWS and the Solicitor's Office, the *Palila* decisions are unlikely to lead to an explosion of litigation under section 9. Nor are the decisions likely to cause substantial interference with private land use. The Solicitor's Office primarily criticized *Palila I* on grounds that the decision condemned habitat modification alone, without attendant death or injury to an endangered species, as a violation of section 9.[33] In *Palila II*, however, the court stressed that this view misinterpreted its decision in *Palila I*. The decision in *Palila II* notes that "overwhelming" evidence produced by plaintiffs in *Palila I* demonstrated that the presence of feral goats and sheep injured the palila population. Thus the *Palila I* decision made it clear that plaintiffs bear the burden of demonstrating that habitat modification kills or injures members of a protected species before such modification constitutes harm under section 9. *Palila II* simply clarified this burden by demonstrating that death or injury to a species may be shown by reference to the species as a whole, and that preclusion of recovery constitutes injury to a species.

The factual circumstances of the *Palila* cases made it relatively easy for the plaintiffs to carry their burden of linking the challenged habitat modification to injury or death of endangered species. Palilas are confined to a small, easily defined habitat. Further, parties in the *Palila* litigation did not dispute that palilas depend exclusively on mamane-naio forest for their existence, and that the controversial feral animals destroyed that type of vegetation. However, for wider-ranging species dependent upon more diverse ecosystems and for species whose habits are not well understood, establishment of a causal connection between habitat modification and injury or death to protected species may be more difficult.

---

33. 46 Fed. Reg. 29,490 (1981).

However, in *Sierra Club v. Lyng*,[34] plaintiffs succeeded in show-ing that clearcutting in national forests located in Texas had caused a dramatic decline in the population of endangered red-cockaded woodpeckers. The federal district court found that the birds would become extinct in Texas national forests by 1995 if current management practices continued,[35] and concluded that clearcutting resulted in "significant habitat modification" which harmed the woodpeckers.[36] Citing the *Palila* decisions, the court held that the U. S. Forest Service's management practices consti-tuted a taking of the species.[37] Significantly, due to its conclusion that continued clearcutting would lead to the red-cockaded woodpecker's extinction—thus obviously precluding their recov-ery—the court did not consider whether management practices that merely delayed or somewhat lessened the birds' chances for recovery would also constitute a taking.

The link between habitat disturbance and the takings prohibi-tion of section 9 was at issue in two other cases subsequent to *Palila I*. In *Fund For Animals v. Florida Game and Fresh Water Fish Commission*,[38] the court found that any habitat degradation likely to result from a proposed one-time, four-day deer hunt would not be "significant" and thus would not effect a taking of endan-gered species in the area. The court's opinion stresses the tem-porary nature of the challenged hunt, as well as the fact that hunting on an annual basis—not challenged by plaintiffs in the case—was common in the affected area. The *Fund For Animals* decision illustrates that in order to demonstrate that habitat dis-turbance illegally harms endangered species, in addition to link-ing habitat disruption with injury to a protected species, plaintiffs must show that the species' habitat will in fact suffer due to the challenged activity.[39]

In *National Wildlife Federation v. Hodel*,[40] the court determined that FWS had taken bald eagles by permitting hunters to use lead shot in areas where eagles were present. The parties in the case did not dispute that lead shot poisons eagles when the birds in-gest lead present in their prey. The federal defendants even con-

34. 694 F. Supp. 1260 (E.D. Texas 1988).
35. *Id.* at 1266.
36. *Id.* at 1271.
37. *Id.* at 1270-72.
38. 550 F. Supp. 1206 (1982).
39. 550 F. Supp. at 1207.
40. 23 Env't Rep. Cas. (BNA) 1089 (1985).

ceded that their action was a taking of eagles.[41] Thus, this case merely serves as an example of *Palila*-type harm to an endangered species: degradation of a species' habitat (e.g., introduction of lead shot into eagles' prey) resulted in injury or death to the protected species (e.g., eagles poisoned by eating lead-contaminated waterfowl).

C. *The Definition of "Harass"*

Like the term harm, the word harass within the ESA's definition of take could be subject to broad interpretations. Regulations define harassment to mean:

> "Harass" in the definition of "take" in the Act means an intentional or negligent act or omission which creates the likelihood of injury to wildlife by annoying it to such an extent as to significantly disrupt normal behavioral patterns which include, but are not limited to, breeding, feeding or sheltering.[42]

No cases have relied on this definition alone to find a taking of an endangered species. However, ongoing controversies involving human interactions with listed species, such as those surrounding whale-watching boats in Hawaii and helicopters flying low over high density grizzly areas in Montana, could spawn litigation over whether these activities harass protected wildlife.

D. *Other Prohibitions*

In addition to prohibiting takings of endangered wildlife and fish, section 9 forbids possession, sale, and transport of illegally taken species.[43] Section 9 also outlaws importation of endangered species into the United States, as well as export of such species from the United States.[44] Sales of endangered species in interstate or foreign commerce and shipment of endangered species in interstate and foreign commerce for commercial purposes are also illegal.[45]

---

41. The Secretary attempted to justify his actions as an incidental taking of eagles. The court rejected this contention, finding that the defendants did not comply with the ESA's incidental taking requirements. *Id.* at 1092.

42. 50 C.F.R. § 17.3.

43. *See* 16 U.S.C. § 1538(a)(1)(D).

44. *See id.* at § 1538(a)(1)(A); *see also* United States v. 3,210 Crusted Sides of Caimen Crocodilus Yacare, 636 F. Supp. 1281, 1284 (S.D. Fla. 1986) (holding that hides shipped from Bolivia to Paris on a flight which made an unscheduled landing in Miami were imported into the United States within the meaning of the ESA's definition of "import").

45. *See* 16 U.S.C. § 1538(a)(1)(E)-(F).

Several judicial decisions have applied these section 9 restrictions. The court in *Man Hing Ivory & Imports v. Deukmejian*[46] found that section 9's import restrictions preempt state law.[47] In *Cayman Turtle Farms v. Andrus*,[48] the court found that extending the ESA's ban on importing protected species to commercially "farmed" specimens of protected species was consistent with the purposes of the ESA. Courts have also held that section 9's prohibitions do not effect an unconstitutional taking of property,[49] that endangered species en route to a foreign country mistakenly shipped to the United States are not subject to seizure,[50] and that Congress desired the broadest possible applications of section 9's prohibitions.[51]

II. Prohibited Acts: Endangered Flora

Prohibited acts set forth in section 9 involving endangered plants differ from restrictions applicable to endangered wildlife and fish. In particular, section 9 does not extend its takings proscription to plants. It also differentiates between plants found in areas under federal jurisdiction and those that occur on state or private land. On federal land, section 9(a)(2) makes it illegal for any person to "remove and reduce [any endangered plant] to possession" or "maliciously damage or destroy" any endangered plant.[52] On land not under federal jurisdiction, it is unlawful to "remove, cut, dig up, or damage or destroy any [endangered plant] . . . in knowing violation of any law or regulation of any

---

46. 702 F.2d 760 (9th Cir. 1982).

47. A California statute prohibited importation of elephant parts or products for commercial purposes. Though African elephants are listed as threatened pursuant to the ESA, federal regulations allow limited commercial imports of ivory. *See* 50 C.F.R. § 17.40(e). The Ninth Circuit held that federal regulations preempt the California statute, despite the court's recognition that elephants would receive less protection as a result. *Man Hing Ivory*, 702 F.2d at 765 n.4. For further discussion of actions which the Secretary may permit with respect to threatened species, see *infra* notes 60-76 and accompanying text. *See also* Note, *Federal Preemption of State Commerce Bans Under the Endangered Species Act* 34 STAN. L. REV. 1323 (1982) (arguing that the ESA preempts state law only under narrow circumstances).

48. Cayman Turtle Farms v. Andrus, 478 F. Supp. 125 (D.D.C. 1979) (upholding regulatory ban on importation of threatened sea turtles raised in captivity abroad).

49. United States v. Kepler, 531 F.2d 796 (6th Cir. 1976) (upholding defendant's conviction for illegally transporting species in interstate commerce).

50. Carpenter v. Andrus, 485 F. Supp. 320 (D. Del. 1980). Congress amended the ESA in 1982 to codify this holding. 16 U.S.C. § 1549(i).

51. Delbay Pharmaceuticals v. Department of Commerce, 409 F. Supp. 637 (D.D.C. 1976) (upholding seizure of sperm whale products).

52. 16 U.S.C. § 1538(a)(2)(B).

state or in the course of any violation of a state criminal trespass law."[53]

With respect to section 9's protection of endangered plants on federal land, the Secretary interprets the prohibition on removing plants and reducing them to possession as applying to "a person who removes an endangered plant from its location . . . and holds it as his/her own."[54] However, the Secretary construes this provision as not applicable to development activities on federal land that physically displace endangered plants.[55] Similarly, the House of Representatives report accompanying the 1988 ESA amendments, which outlawed maliciously damaging or destroying endangered plants on federal land, notes that this prohibition was intended only to stop "willful acts of vandalism," and not to "interfere with otherwise lawfully permitted land use operations such as mining, logging, or grazing . . . ."[56]

Legislative history also indicates how the provision relating to endangered plants on state or private land should be interpreted. Generally, lawmakers emphasized that this provision was not intended to interfere with rights traditionally accorded landowners; it was simply designed to boost the deterrent effect of state plant protection and trespass statutes.[57] More specifically, a House report notes that the term "criminal trespass laws" in the context of section 9's plant provisions refers to laws that apply to the general public rather than special trespass laws aimed at a specific group.[58]

Section 9 also prohibits imports and exports of endangered plants into or out of the United States. Interstate and foreign commerce in such species is also outlawed. Unlike restrictions applied to wildlife and fish, however, section 9 does not make mere possession of illegally obtained plants unlawful. Technically, therefore, a person within the United States who receives a plant which someone else has illegally reduced to possession does not violate the ESA unless the specimen was obtained in interstate commerce.[59]

---

53. *Id.*
54. 50 Fed. Reg. 39,686 (1985).
55. *Id.*
56. H.R. REP. No. 467, 100th Cong., 1st Sess. 15 (1988).
57. S. REP. No. 240, 100th Cong., 1st Sess. 12 (1987).
58. H.R. REP. No. 467, *supra* note 56, at 14-15.
59. However, receiving a plant taken in violation of the ESA would violate the Lacey Act, which makes it unlawful for any person to "import, export, transport, sell,

III. PROHIBITED ACTS: THREATENED SPECIES

The prohibitions set forth in section 9 apply only to species listed as endangered. ESA section 4(d), however, requires the Secretary to issue regulations deemed "necessary and advisable to provide for the conservation of [threatened] species."[60] With this regulatory power, the Secretary may prohibit any or all acts involving threatened wildlife and fish which section 9 proscribes for endangered wildlife and fish. Similarly, the Secretary may enact regulations covering threatened plant species that include any or all of section 9's prohibitions involving endangered plants. Violation of such regulations by any person is statutorily proscribed by section 9.[61]

Section 4(d)'s directive contains two components. First, this section directs the Secretary to issue regulations which he or she deems "necessary and advisable." Secondly, the regulations issued pursuant to this directive must conserve threatened species. The phrase "necessary and advisable" in the context of section 4(d), however, is arguably meaningless. Whenever an action is necessary to bring a threatened species to the point where the ESA's protection are no longer needed, that action must also be advisable. Although one could argue that inclusion of the word "advisable" within section 4(d) gives the Secretary discretion to omit a regulation necessary for a threatened species' recovery, it seems extremely unlikely that Congress intended to grant the Secretary discretion not to take action determined to be necessary to protect threatened species.[62] Such an interpretation of section 4(d) conflicts with the basic purpose of the ESA, as well as specific statutory directives to conserve listed species.[63] Thus, the word "advisable" in section 4(b) appears to be superfluous. Even the word "necessary" in this section is redundant. The ESA defines conservation in part as "the use of all methods and procedures which are *necessary* to bring any . . . threatened species

---

receive, acquire, or purchase any fish or wildlife or plant taken or possessed in violation of any law, treaty, or regulation of the United States . . . ." 16 U.S.C. § 3372(a)(1).

60. 16 U.S.C. § 1533(d).

61. 16 U.S.C. §§ 1538(a)(1)(G), 1538(a)(2)(E).

62. Congress intended to give protection and conservation of listed species highest priority by enacting the ESA. *See* TVA v. Hill, 437 U.S. 153, 174 (1978). Therefore, subordinating conservation of a threatened species to other considerations could never be "advisable."

63. 16 U.S.C. § 1531(b) (purpose of ESA to conserve listed species); 16 U.S.C. §§ 1531(c), 1536(a)(1) (directing federal agencies to conserve listed species).

to the point at which the measures provided pursuant to this chapter are no longer necessary."[64] Since only those actions necessary to bring about species recovery fall within the definition of conservation, it is repetitive to say that an action is necessary to conserve a listed species. Therefore, section 4(d) simply directs the Secretary to issue regulations to conserve threatened species.

Regulations issued by the Secretary pursuant to section 4(d) clearly must be evaluated on the basis of whether or not they in fact promote the recovery of threatened species within the statutory meaning of conservation. How to perform such an evaluation was at issue in *Sierra Club v. Clark*.[65] There, plaintiffs challenged FWS regulations which expressly permitted limited sport trapping of eastern timber wolves, listed as threatened under the ESA. The Secretary defended his regulations by arguing that sport trapping would reduce the level of wolf-human conflict, thus enhancing the value of wolves in the eyes of the public and leading to a reduction in illegal wolf killings. Defendants emphasized that section 4(d) provides that the Secretary *may* prohibit any act with respect to threatened species that section 9 forbids with respect to endangered species. Hence, the Secretary argued that he had discretion to ban takings of timber wolves, but was not obligated to do so. The district court rejected this position. The court stressed that regulations promulgated under section 4(d) must conserve threatened species, and ruled that the statutory definition of conservation authorized takings only "in the extraordinary case where population pressures within a given ecosystem cannot otherwise be relieved."[66] Since the government made no attempt to show any population pressures existed with respect to wolves, the court struck down the challenged regulations.

On appeal, the Secretary argued that in depriving him of discretion to permit taking of wolves "pursuant to regulatory measures which address the problems contributing to the species' decline," the district court erred by destroying the statutory distinction between threatened and endangered species.[67] Over a dissent, the Eighth circuit rejected this view. It held that the dis-

---

64. 16 U.S.C. § 1532(3) (emphasis added).
65. 577 F. Supp. 783 (D. Minn. 1984), *aff'd & rev'd*, 755 F.2d 608 (8th Cir. 1985). For a more in-depth discussion of the case, see Halleland, *Sierra Club v. Clark: The Government Cries Wolf*, 11 WM. MITCHELL L. REV. 968 (1985).
66. 577 F. Supp. at 788.
67. 755 F.2d at 612.

trict court's opinion correctly outlined the statutory distinction between threatened and endangered species, namely that section 9 forbids taking of endangered species altogether, whereas section 4(d), read in conjunction with the statutory definition of conservation, allows the Secretary to permit takings of threatened species in extraordinary circumstances where population pressures cannot otherwise be relieved. The appellate court emphasized that the Secretary's discretion to issue regulations under section 4(d) is constrained by the requirement that such regulations must conserve threatened species.[68]

The *Sierra Club v. Clark* decisions did not reach the issue of whether the Secretary *must* prohibit takings of threatened species absent extraordinary circumstances of population pressure. The decisions held that the Secretary may not explicitly permit takings of threatened species absent extraordinary circumstances of population pressure. However, the courts did not address the question of whether government *inaction, i.e.,* failure to issue regulations banning taking of timber wolves, would also violate section 4(d). It is unclear, therefore, whether any relevant statutory distinction exists between circumstances where the Secretary explicitly permits takings or other actions proscribed by section 9 with respect to endangered species, and instances where the Secretary merely refuses to ban such actions. This issue carries significant implications for the scope of section 4(d)'s mandate. Even though section 4(d) provides that the Secretary *may* prohibit by regulation with respect to threatened species any of the actions prohibited by section 9 with respect to endangered species, if one equates the Secretary's failure to ban an activity with explicit authorization of the activity, this seemingly permissive clause actually gives the Secretary very little discretion in promulgating regulations. Since it is unlikely that any activity prohibited by section 9 with respect to endangered species will benefit a threatened species, the Secretary will almost always be required to apply all of section 9's restrictions to threatened species as well.[69] For example, if a court equated the Secretary's failure to

---

68. *Id.* For a discussion of the legislative history of the ESA's definition of conservation, as well as the relationship between conservation and section 4(d), see Goldman-Carter, *Federal Conservation of Threatened Species: By Administrative Discretion or Legislative Standard?*, 11 Bost. C. Envtl. L. Rev. 63 (1983).

69. Current regulations promulgated pursuant to section 4(d) essentially adopt this approach. Save a minor exception involving states with cooperative agreements with the federal government, 50 C.F.R. § 17.31(a) applies all of section 9's prohibitions

ban imports and exports of a certain threatened species with explicit authorization of imports and exports of the species, the Secretary's regulatory inaction would violate the conservation mandate of section 4(d) unless he or she could show that imports or exports were necessary to conserve the species.

The statutory distinction between threatened species and endangered species under the above reading of section 4(d) thus becomes very narrow. It can be summarized as follows: section 9 absolutely prohibits any person from carrying out a number of activities involving endangered species; section 4(d) requires the Secretary to similarly prohibit all of these activities by regulation with respect to threatened species, unless the Secretary determines that an otherwise prohibited activity is necessary to bring a threatened species to the point where it no longer needs the protection of the ESA (i.e., the activity conserves the threatened species).

The final point above deserves particular emphasis. Regulations promulgated under section 4(d) which allow an activity prohibited by section 9 are valid only to the extent that they promote the recovery of specific threatened species. The following example illustrates this concept. Section 9 prohibits all interstate commerce in endangered species or parts thereof.[70] However, in proposed amendments to regulations dealing with threatened grizzly bears in the lower 48 states, the Secretary included a provision which would have allowed limited commercial disposal of illegally taken bears confiscated by federal authorities.[71] The Secretary justified this proposal on the basis that it would not have detrimental impacts on wild grizzly populations. Even assuming the truth of this statement, however, the proposed regulation allowing commercial sales would not satisfy the standard of section 4(d). Since regulations enacted pursuant to this section must conserve threatened species, i.e., further their recovery, promulgation of regulations that permit an activity prohibited by section 9 with respect to endangered species yet confer no benefits on a threatened species exceeds the Secretary's authority under section 4(d).[72] Regulations which actually harm rather

---

to all threatened species. None of these restrictions, however, applies to species covered by a special rule. Note that the Secretary must justify such special rules on the basis that they conserve species. *See infra* notes 70-71 and accompanying text.

70. *See* 16 U.S.C. § 1538(a)(1)(F).

71. 51 Fed. Reg. 25,914 (1986).

72. The proposal to allow commercial disposal of illegally taken bears confiscated

than benefit a threatened species are of course similarly unlawful.

In *Sierra Club v. Clark*, defendants attempted to fit their arguments into the above framework by asserting that the limited takings permitted by regulation would conserve wolves, making the regulations a valid exercise of the Secretary's authority under section 4(d). Both the district and appellate courts rejected this reasoning, holding that takings of threatened species fall within the ESA's definition of conservation only when population pressures cannot otherwise be relieved.[73]

State of Louisiana v. Verity[74] presented the court with a situation opposite to that in *Sierra Club v. Clark*. Rather than permitting takings, the Secretary issued regulations pursuant to section 7(d) which were designed to limit unintentional takings of endangered sea turtles by regulating the actions of commercial shrimpers. The shrimpers argued that the regulations were arbitrary because the Secretary did not demonstrate that the regulations would conserve the turtles. The Fifth Circuit rejected this contention, holding that the Secretary need only show that the regulations would prevent takings of sea turtles, a burden the court noted that the Secretary had amply satisfied.[75] The court reasoned that Congress presumed takings deplete a species: therefore, the Secretary need not show a link between regulations designed to limit takings of threatened species and conservation of the species.[76]

The *Sierra Club v. Clark* and *Verity* decisions apparently establish the following dichotomy: when the Secretary uses his or her regulatory authority under section 4(d) to outlaw any act with respect to a threatened species that section 9 bans with respect to endangered species, a court will presume that the regulation conserves the threatened species. On the other hand, when the Secretary uses his or her section 4(d) authority to permit an act with respect to a threatened species which section 9 bans with respect to endangered species, a reviewing court will inquire into whether the regulation will in fact conserve the threatened species.

---

by federal authorities was dropped in the final regulations. *See* 51 Fed. Reg. 33,753 (1986).

73. 577 F. Supp. at 789; 755 F.2d at 614-15, 618. *See also* Saxe, *Regulated Taking of Threatened Species Under the Endangered Species Act*, 39 HASTINGS L.J. 399 (1988).

74. 853 F.2d 322 (5th Cir. 1988).

75. *Id.*

76. *Id.*

IV. Exceptions to Section 9's Ban on Takings

A. *Threats to Humans*

Regulations allow any person to take an endangered species or threatened species in defense of his or her own life or the lives of others.[77] In addition, certain federal and state employees may take individual members of a protected species which constitute "a demonstrable but nonimmediate threat to human safety."[78] The latter provision, however, authorizes killing or injuring the animal only when it is not "reasonably possible" to alleviate threats to human safety by capturing the animal and transporting it to a remote location.[79]

B. *Exceptions for Federal Agency "Incidentals" Takings*

In 1982, Congress amended the ESA to create broad statutory exceptions to the Act's taking prohibitions.[80] These exceptions allow federal agencies and permittees, as well as all other persons, to take listed species under certain conditions when the "taking is incidental to, and not the purpose of, the carrying out of an otherwise lawful activity."[81]

Through the 1982 amendments, Congress sought to remedy what it termed the "dilemma" where a proposed federal action satisfies the mandate of section 7(a)(2) but would nonetheless run afoul of section 9's taking restrictions.[82] Lawmakers added provisions to section 7 whereby the Secretary, after section 7 consultation, can formulate a plan to exempt agency actions from the ban on takings in section 9.[83] To qualify for such an exemption, federal actions must meet two criteria. First, takings likely to occur as a result of the proposed action must be incidental to the action, rather than the purpose of the action.[84] Second and more generally, the activities must satisfy the mandates of section 7(a)(2).[85] In other words, the proposed action, or reasonable

---

77. 50 C.F.R. § 17.21(c)(2) (endangered species); 50 C.F.R. § 17.31(a) (threatened species).

78. 50 C.F.R. § 17.21 (c)(3)(iv); 50 C.F.R. § 17.31 (a).

79. *Id.*

80. Pub. L. No. 97-304 (1982).

81. 16 U.S.C. § 1539(a)(1)(B).

82. *See* H.R. Rep. No. 567, 97th Cong., 2d Sess. 26, *reprinted in* 1982 U.S. Code Cong. & Admin. News 2826 [hereinafter H.R. Rep. No. 97-567].

83. 16 U.S.C. §§ 1536(b)(4), 1536(o).

84. *Id.* at § 1536(b)(4)(B).

85. *Id.* at § 1536(b)(4)(A).

and prudent alternatives to the action identified by the Secretary pursuant to section 7(b)(3), may not jeopardize the continued existence of a listed species or destroy or adversely modify critical habitat. The Secretary makes a determination of whether the proposed activity meets these standards *prior* to imposing conditions on the activity to reduce incidental takings.[86]

When an action satisfies the above criteria, the Secretary issues an incidental take statement. This statement is usually included with the biological opinion issued for the proposal.[87] The statement must specify how incidental taking as a result of the proposed activity will affect the species.[88] When possible, this requires the Secretary to produce a numerical estimate of the number of individuals likely to be taken.[89] When precise data are not available, however, the Secretary may merely describe the likely incidental takings in terms of the land or marine areas which the activity in question will likely affect.[90] The incidental take statement must also identify "reasonable and prudent measures which the Secretary considers necessary or appropriate to minimize [the] impact" of incidental takings on the species as a whole.[91] The statement must set forth "terms and conditions" to implement these measures.[92] If at any time the actual takings exceed the level of takings contemplated by the statement, the federal agency involved in the activity must immediately reinitiate section 7 consultation.[93]

The exact level of incidental take permitted by the incidental taking exemption scheme is somewhat ambiguous. The statutory framework outlined above seems to contemplate two distinct levels of species mortality. The incidental take caused by a project as proposed (or as modified by reasonable and prudent alternatives so as to satisfy section 7(a)(2)) is the first relevant level.

---

86. *Id.* at § 1536(b)(4). For a discussion of reasonable and prudent measures to reduce impacts of incidental taking, see *infra* notes 98-102 and accompanying text.

87. 51 Fed. Reg. 19,925, 19,953 (1986) (description of amendments to section 7 regulations).

88. 16 U.S.C. § 1536(b)(4)(i).

89. H.R. REP. No. 97-567, *supra* note 82, at 27; *see also* 51 Fed. Reg. 19,953-54.

90. H.R. REP. No. 97-567, *supra* note 82, at 27.

91. 16 U.S.C. § 1536(b)(4)(ii).

92. *Id.* at § 1536(b)(4)(iii).

93. 50 C.F.R. § 402.14(i)(4). While renewed consultation is underway, the federal agency or permittee need not cease all activities in question unless the "impact of the additional taking would cause an irreversible and adverse impact on the species." H.R. REP. No. 97-567, *supra* note 82, at 27.

The incidental take statement must identify this level numerically if possible or at least descriptively.[94] A second and distinct level of incidental taking is the estimated number of incidental takings which occur once the federal agency or applicant implements the reasonable and prudent measures specified by the Secretary to minimize such takings. This number should be lower than the expected takings level for a project as originally proposed. It is unclear, however, which level of incidental takings is the maximum permitted by section 7, i.e., what is the point beyond which further takings trigger reinitiation of section 7 consultation.

Federal regulations implementing section 7 provide that the first, or higher, level of incidental take must be exceeded before renewed consultation is required.[95] This position arguably misinterprets the 1982 amendments. The report accompanying the House version of the 1982 amendments, which included the section 7 incidental take scheme eventually enacted, provides that "[t]he Committee intends that . . . incidental takings be allowed provided that the terms and conditions specified by the Secretary to minimize the impact of the taking are complied with."[96] Further, section 7(o) exempts from section 9 only takings which occur in compliance with the terms and conditions set forth in the incidental take statement designed to minimize incidental takings.[97] Clearly, Congress did not favor takings above those which estimates predict are likely to occur when an agency complies with the terms and conditions identified in an incidental take statement as necessary to minimize the impact of the agency's activity on a listed species. Therefore, takings above this minimal level should trigger reinitiation of section 7 consultation.

It is unclear what burdens the Secretary may impose on a proposed activity in order to minimize incidental takings caused by the activity. Section 7(b)(4) requires the Secretary to impose "reasonable and prudent *measures*" to accomplish this goal.[98] FWS holds a narrow view of what these measures may entail and sharply differentiates them from "reasonable and prudent *alternatives*" to a proposed activity:

---

94. *See supra* note 89 and accompanying text.
95. 50 C.F.R. § 402.14(i)(1)-(i)(4).
96. H.R. Rep. No. 97-567, *supra* note 82, at 26.
97. 16 U.S.C. § 1536(o).
98. *Id.* at § 1536(b)(4)(ii) (emphasis added).

The Service agrees with several commentators that reasonable and prudent measures are not the same as reasonable and prudent alternatives. Substantial design and routing changes—appropriate only for alternatives to avoid jeopardy—are inappropriate in the context of incidental take statements because the action already complies with section 7(a)(2). . . . Reasonable and prudent measures were intended to minimize the level of incidental taking, but Congress also intended that the action go forward essentially as planned. Therefore, the Service believes that they should be minor changes that do not alter the basic design, location, duration, or timing of the action.[99]

This reasoning is not compelling. Nothing in the legislative history of the 1982 amendments suggests that Congress intended actions to go forward "essentially as planned" when they involve incidental takings.[100] The fact that activities considered in incidental take statements already comply with section 7(a)(2) has no relevance to the scope of reasonable and prudent measures, which attempt to narrow the exceptions made to *section 9's* taking prohibitions. By adopting a very narrow reading of reasonable and prudent measures, FWS creates two widely divergent meanings for the statutory phrase "reasonable and prudent," depending on whether the phrase modifies "measures" or "alternatives." According to FWS, a reasonable and prudent *alternative* which avoids violating section 7(a)(2)[101] is generally one that "can be implemented consistent with the intended purpose of the action, . . . can be implemented consistent with the scope of the Federal agency's legal authority and jurisdiction, [and] . . . is economically and technologically feasible . . . ."[102] In contrast, with respect to measures to reduce incidental takings, FWS considers only minor changes in a proposed agency action to be reasonable and prudent.

There appears to be little justification for this dichotomy. Prior to the 1982 amendments, federal actions which would result in takings of endangered species, as well as threatened species except in extraordinary circumstances, were unlawful under

99. 51 Fed. Reg. 19,937 (1986).

100. Congress made it clear that it intended that activities involving incidental takings proceed only provided that the activities complied with reasonable and prudent measures specified by the Secretary to reduce incidental takings. *See* 16 U.S.C. § 1536(b)(4)(B)(iii). Congress, however, did not specify any limits on the Secretary's discretion to alter projects by imposing such measures.

101. *See* 16 U.S.C. § 1536(b)(3)(A).

102. 50 C.F.R. § 402.02 (definition of reasonable and prudent alternatives).

section 9. However, FWS now interprets the ESA's incidental take provisions to virtually eliminate statutory concerns over takings save for requiring only minor project modifications. It seems more likely, particularly given the statutory procedure to minimize incidental takings, that Congress intended to allow only those activities which require the smallest possible exception to section 9, i.e., activities modified by measures which mitigate incidental takings to the maximum extent possible without rendering the activity infeasible. This view also allows for a consistent definition of the phrase "reasonable and prudent" throughout section 7.

C.   *Exceptions for Non-Federal "Incidental" Takings*

Also in 1982, Congress recognized that the ESA's absolute ban on taking endangered species and severe restrictions on taking threatened species could substantially affect private and state land-use decisions. It therefore created a permit process analogous to the section 7(b)(4) scheme whereby nonfederal entities may apply for permission to incidentally take listed species in the course of an otherwise lawful activity.[103] This permit process, set forth in section 10, is quite demanding.[104] The permit applicant must submit a conservation plan to the Secretary which specifies (1) how the proposed activity will affect listed species, (2) what steps the applicant will take to monitor, minimize, and mitigate such impacts, what funding will be available to carry out these steps, and how the applicant will deal with unforeseen circumstances, (3) what alternatives which would not result in takings were considered by the applicant and why these alternatives were abandoned, and (4) other measures specified by the Secretary as necessary or appropriate for purposes of the plan.[105] In addition to these statutorily mandated elements of conservation plans, Congress voiced a strong desire that section 10 plans address conservation of unlisted as well as listed species.[106] Lawmakers cited two reasons why conservation plans should also cover unlisted species. First, if a plan considers unlisted as well as listed species, subsequent listings of species in the area would require

---

103.   16 U.S.C. § 1539(a)(1)(B).

104.   *Id.* at § 1539(a)(2); *see also* Webster, *Habitat Conservation Plans under the Endangered Species Act,* 24 SAN DIEGO L. REV. 243 (1987).

105.   50 C.F.R. § 17.32(b)(1)(iii)(C) (implementing 16 U.S.C. § 1539(a)(2)(A)).

106.   H.R. CONF. REP. No. 835, 97th Cong., 2d Sess. 30, *reprinted in* 1982 U.S. CODE CONG. & ADMIN. NEWS 2860, 2871 [hereinafter H.R. CONF. REP. No. 97-835].

few or no changes to the plan, enabling the activity in question to continue without interruption. In addition, plans not limited to listed species would more closely conform to the broad conservation policies Congress sought to further by enacting the ESA, particularly that "individual species should not be viewed in isolation, but must be viewed in terms of their relationship to the ecosystem of which they form a constituent element."[107]

Despite strong Congressional support for broad conservation plans, FWS interprets treatment of unlisted species in section 10 plans as optional.[108] Regulations implementing section 10 reflect this view.[109] Nevertheless, FWS concedes that an applicant who does not submit a comprehensive conservation plan runs the risk that activities covered by the plan may have to be halted to assess the activities' impacts on species subsequently listed.[110] This view, however, fails to take into account that some ongoing activities which adversely affect newly listed species may not be easily halted. For example, a housing development constructed after its builders obtain a section 10 permit to take a certain species incidentally cannot be "halted" if the development constitutes a taking of a species listed *after* the development is completed. Arguably, therefore, consideration of unlisted species[111] in a conservation plan should be required, particularly when the activity covered by a section 10 permit is essentially irreversible.

After opportunity for public comment on conservation plans, section 10 requires the Secretary to issue an incidental take permit if, in addition to other assurances that the Secretary may require, the Secretary finds that:

    (i)   the taking will be incidental;

---

107. *Id.*

108. *See* 50 Fed. Reg. 39,681-83 (1985) (explanation accompanying final regulations implementing incidental taking exceptions).

109. 50 C.F.R. § 17.32.

110. 50 Fed. Reg. 39,683.

111. Conservation plans need not consider every type of flora and fauna which occurs in the area affected by the plan. The Secretary has identified several thousand species considered candidates for addition to the threatened and endangered list. In addition, at any given time the Secretary has proposed to list several species, though final action has not yet taken place to formally add these species to the protected lists. Given expressed Congressional concern over species listed after issuance of a section 10 permit for a specific project, the Secretary should at least require that conservation plans address species considered by the Secretary to be candidates for listing, as well as species proposed for listing, which may be affected by projects covered by such plans.

(ii)   the applicant will, to the maximum extent practicable, minimize and mitigate the impacts of such taking;
(iii)   the applicant will ensure that adequate funding for the plan will be provided;
(iv)   the taking will not appreciably reduce the likelihood of the survival and recovery of the species in the wild; and
(v)   the measures, if any, required under subparagraph (A)(iv) will be met . . . .[112]

The fourth requirement is of particular significance. Congress included this provision to emphasize that granting a permit pursuant to section 10 is a federal action subject to section 7's consultation requirements and substantive mandates.[113] This in effect sets an absolute limit on the Secretary's authority to grant section 10 permits: if granting a permit would allow an activity which jeopardizes the continued existence of a listed species or destroys or adversely modifies critical habitat, the Secretary must deny the incidental taking permit.[114] This scheme thus essentially imposes the requirements of section 7 on nonfederal entities that apply for an incidental take permit. Because section 10 also requires the Secretary to determine that the applicant will minimize and mitigate incidental takings of listed species to the maximum extent practicable before granting a permit,[115] the substantive standards set forth in section 7 represent the absolute minimum standards a nonfederal permit applicant must satisfy.

Some elements of the section 10 incidental take permit process—for example the meaning of "to the maximum extent practicable"[116]—are not altogether clear. Few nonfederal entities have used the incidental take exemption process.[117] Only one dispute involving section 10 has resulted in litigation.[118] That case ironically involved the conservation plan Congress used as

---

112.   16 U.S.C. § 1539(a)(2)(B).

113.   H.R. CONF. REP. No. 97-835, *supra* note 106, at 29-30. *See also* 50 Fed. Reg. 59,683 (1985).

114.   An action that jeopardizes the continued existence of a listed species or destroys or adversely modifies critical habitat by definition reduces the likelihood of that species' survival and recovery. *See* 50 C.F.R. § 402.02 (definitions of "jeopardize the continued existence of" and "destruction or adverse modification"). Therefore, granting of an incidental take permit in the face of such effects would violate 16 U.S.C. § 1539(a)(2)(B)(iv).

115.   16 U.S.C. § 1539(a)(2)(B)(ii).

116.   *Id.*

117.   As of April, 1987, the Secretary had issued only three Section 10 incidental take permits. Interview with Larry LaRochelle, Endangered Species Office, U.S. Fish and Wildlife Service, Washington, D.C. (Apr. 3, 1987).

118.   Friends of Endangered Species v. Jantzen, 596 F. Supp. 518 (N.D. Cal. 1984)

its model for writing section 10.[119] Due to the close link between
the conservation plan involved in the case and the 1982 ESA
amendments, the plaintiff did not seriously contend that any of
section 10's procedural requirements were violated. Instead, the
plaintiff argued that FWS erroneously concluded that the conservation plan minimized the impact of taking on the endangered
Mission Blue butterfly and thus erred in granting a permit authorizing incidental taking.[120] Both district court opinions rejected this position, finding that implementation of the
conservation plan would actually enhance the butterfly's survival.[121] Significantly, the district court opinions noted that in order to prevail on a claim alleging that a conservation plan does
not minimize and mitigate incidental taking, a plaintiff must
demonstrate that the Secretary acted arbitrarily and capriciously
by finding otherwise and approving an incidental take permit.[122]
This demonstrates that the relevant issue under section 10 is not
whether the conservation plan minimizes and mitigates incidental takings as a matter of fact, but rather whether as a matter of
law the Secretary has abused his or her discretion in making a
finding on whether a conservation plan fulfills this section 10 requirement. In addition, the plaintiff contended that FWS approval of the incidental take permit violated section 7(a)(2) by
failing to consider the best scientific data available. Noting that
the plaintiff failed to point to any information not considered by
the Secretary, the Ninth Circuit found plaintiff's argument
groundless.[123] This finding demonstrates once again the difficulties plaintiffs face in successfully challenging the conclusions of a
biological opinion on substantive, rather than procedural,
grounds.[124]

In addition to exceptions for incidental takings of listed species, the ESA and its implementing regulations also contain several relatively narrow exceptions to the prohibitions set forth in

---

(denying plaintiff's motion for preliminary injunction); 589 F. Supp. 113 (granting defendant's motion for summary judgment), *aff'd*, 760 F.2d 976 (9th Cir. 1985).

For a more extensive discussion of this case, see Note, *Where Have All the Butterflies
Gone? Ninth Circuit Upholds Decision to Allow Incidental Taking*, 16 GOLDEN GATE U. L. REV.
93 (1986).

119. *See* 596 F. Supp. at 552; 589 F. Supp. at 119-20.
120. 596 F. Supp. at 522; 589 F. Supp. at 119.
121. 596 F. Supp. at 522-23; 589 F. Supp. at 120.
122. 596 F. Supp. at 522; 589 F. Supp. at 117-18.
123. 760 F.2d at 985.
124. *See infra* Chapter 9, notes 79-85 and accompanying text.

section 9. These include provisions allowing authorized state officials to take members of listed species when acting pursuant to a state-federal cooperative agreement,[125] exceptions governing members of listed species held in captivity or controlled environment,[126] hardship exemptions (including subsistence hunting and native craft manufacture by Alaskan natives),[127] exceptions dealing with parts of endangered species lawfully held prior to passage of the ESA,[128] provisions covering noncommercial transshipments and species mistakenly imported to the United States,[129] and exceptions for antiques.[130] Persons claiming the benefit of an exemption from the prohibitions of section 9 have the burden of proving that their actions fit into an exempt category.[131]

---

125. 16 U.S.C. §§ 1538(a)(1) and 1535(g)(2) (cooperative agreements are outlined at 16 U.S.C. § 1535(c)); 50 C.F.R. §§ 17.21(c)(5) and 17.31(b).
126. 16 U.S.C. § 1538(b).
127. *Id.* at §§ 1539(b) and (e).
128. *Id.* at § 1539(f).
129. *Id.* at § 1539(i).
130. *Id.* at § 1539(h).
131. *Id.* at § 1539(g).

Chapter 5

Affirmative Mandates to Conserve Listed Species

The ESA strives not only to prevent endangered and threatened species from becoming extinct, but also to restore these species to the point where they no longer require special legal protection.

Much of section 7, as well as section 9, attempts to insure that listed species do not become worse off by prohibiting various activities. The ESA provisions discussed in this chapter, however, require or encourage federal agencies to take affirmative actions to better the position of listed species.

I. RECOVERY PLANS

Section 4(f) requires the Secretary to develop and implement "recovery plans."[1] Neither the ESA nor its implementing regulations specify procedures to be used in developing recovery plans or outline required contents of recovery plans. Such plans, however, must be prepared for all listed species unless the Secretary finds that a recovery plan would not promote the conservation of a certain species.[2]

Recovery plans generally include a discussion of species biology, past and present distribution, and the reasons for a species' listing as threatened or endangered. Plans also often include description of a target population, representing the point at which a species would be considered recovered.[3] An outline or narrative within recovery plans details actions or conditions necessary to promote species recovery. This portion of a recovery plan also

---

1. 16 U.S.C. § 1533(f).
2. *Id.*
3. Section 7 regulations define the term "recovery" as "improvement in the status of listed species to the point at which listing is no longer appropriate under the criteria set out in section 4(a)(1) of the Act." 50 C.F.R. § 402.02. For further discussion of the concept of recovery, see *infra* notes 67-70 and accompanying text.

may identify federal agencies responsible for carrying out activities to implement species' recovery.

A priority system guides recovery plan development. Section 4(f) directs the Secretary to give priority to species most likely to benefit from having recovery plans, particularly species facing pressure from construction or other developmental or economic activities.[4] The U. S. Fish and Wildlife Service (FWS) published recovery priority guidelines in 1983.[5] The guidelines set recovery plan development and implementation priorities by combining immediacy of threats to a species' survival with the species' "recovery potential." The latter term represents an estimate of a species' chances for recovery, based on how well the threats to its existence are understood and how much management is necessary to remedy those threats. The recovery priority guidelines also consider genetic distinctiveness of listed species, with monotypic genera taking precedence over subspecies and population segments. Finally, among species with equal recovery priorities, those faced with conflict from economic activities, such as construction, are considered first. Species in the conflict category are identified principally in jeopardy biological opinions conducted by federal agencies under section 7 of the ESA.[6]

The recovery priority guidelines also set forth a system to prioritize activities identified in individual recovery plans as necessary for species' recovery. This priority system divides recovery activities into three categories. Priority 1 tasks include actions necessary to prevent extinction or irreversible decline of a species.[7] Priority 2 actions are necessary to prevent significant population decline or habitat degradation, while priority 3 tasks include everything necessary for full recovery of a given species.[8]

Recovery plans are prepared using one of two methods: (1) FWS or National Marine Fisheries Service (NMFS) personnel supervise preparation of the plan, which is actually written by an outside group or individual under contract, or (2) FWS or NMFS

---

4. 16 U.S.C. § 1533(f).

5. 48 Fed. Reg. 43,098 (1983).

6. 48 Fed. Reg. 43,104 (1983).

7. Aside from agencies' duties to implement recovery plans, discussed *infra*, section 7(a)(2) arguably obligates federal agencies to carry out priority 1 recovery tasks. Since these tasks are by definition necessary to prevent the extinction of listed species, agencies' failure to carry out priority 1 activities would jeopardize the continued existence of listed species in violation of section 7(a)(2).

8. *Id.*

establishes its own "recovery team" to prepare the plan. In the latter method, the recovery team usually consists of representatives from agencies that will be charged with implementing the plan, scientists with expertise about the species involved, representatives from industries that may be affected by the plan, and FWS/NMFS personnel.

Federal agencies do not consider recovery plans to be "decision documents."[9] Thus, before 1988 the public was not given an opportunity to provide input into the plan formulation process or to comment on proposed recovery plans. In 1988, Congress amended section 4(f) to require that the Secretary provide the public with notice and an opportunity to comment on recovery plans before approving new or revised plans.[10] The Secretary must "consider" all information presented during this comment period.[11] Lawmakers made it clear, however, that the requirement to consider public comments imposed an additional procedural requirement on the Secretary.[12] Congress also directed that "the development and content of recovery plans will continue to be based solely on biological considerations."[13]

Section 4(f) provides that "[t]he Secretary shall develop *and implement* [recovery] plans . . . ."[14] This clearly frames recovery plan implementation as a mandatory duty and suggests the Secretary must undertake activities identified in plans to conserve listed species. Courts have yet to interpret this duty, however.[15]

---

9. In other words, the Secretary and other federal agencies view recovery plans as internal government blueprints for conserving listed species as opposed to public documents such as formal records of decision and NEPA documents. Interview with Jane Royball, U. S. Fish & Wildlife Service, Region 6 (July 17, 1985).

10. 16 U.S.C. § 1533(f)(4).

11. *Id.*

12. H.R. CONF. REP. No. 928, 100th Cong., 2d Sess. 21 (1988).

13. *Id.*

14. 16 U.S.C. § 1533(f) (emphasis added).

15. In 1986, environmental organizations relied on section 4(f)'s mandate to implement recovery plans in a lawsuit which attempted to force the Secretary of Commerce to designate critical habitat for endangered Hawaiian monk seals. The Secretary had declined to follow the monk seal recovery plan's recommendation that critical habitat be designated around several islands to a depth of 20 fathoms. Instead the Secretary designated waters to a depth of 10 fathoms as critical habitat for monk seals. *See* 51 Fed. Reg. 16,047-48 (1986). Two years later, however, the Secretary reversed himself and designated critical habitat to 20 fathoms. *See* 53 Fed. Reg. 18,988-90 (1988). This action rendered the environmental groups' suit moot prior to any ruling on the merits. *See* Greenpeace International, Inc. v. Baldridge, No. 86-0129 (D. Hawaii 1988).

But cf. National Wildlife Federation v. National Park Service, 669 F. Supp. 384, 388-89 (D. Wyo. 1987) (holding that implementation of grizzly bear recovery plan should be

A. Limitations on Recovery Plan Implementation

Recovery plans drafted prior to 1988 identified activities necessary to conserve species only in very general terms. For example, the Northern Rocky Mountain Wolf Recovery Plan directed federal agencies to "minimize direct, man-caused mortality."[16] To achieve this goal, the plan required agencies to "[m]ake provisions for minimizing or resolving conflicts between wolf recovery objectives and man."[17] This directive obviously did not provide field level guidance on exactly how to minimize wolf-human conflicts. Recovery plans containing only broadly stated goals and vague directives thus do little to implement uniform, comprehensive conservation programs to benefit listed species. Additionally, without specifics recovery plans are difficult to enforce or evaluate.

Recognizing these problems, Congress in 1988 added provisions to section 4(d) which set forth required contents for recovery plans. Plans must contain "site-specific management actions" necessary to achieve the recovery of listed species,[18] a mandate lawmakers noted "should be interpreted broadly as delineation of discrete measures to be taken for species, subspecies, populations, geographic subpopulations, or individuals."[19] This requirement was designed to make recovery plans "as explicit as possible."[20] Furthermore, to assist interested parties in judging the progress being made toward the recovery of listed species,[21] plans must contain "objective measurable criteria" to determine when species can be said to have recovered and thus be removed from the protected list.[22] Finally, recovery plans must include estimates of the time and money needed to achieve the plans' ultimate goals, as well as estimates of the resources needed to reach intermediate steps toward those goals.[23] Every two years the Secretary must issue a report outlining the status of efforts to

---

stayed pending new information to be developed by the environmental impact study process).

16. U.S. FISH & WILDLIFE SERVICE, NORTHERN ROCKY MOUNTAIN WOLF RECOVERY PLAN (1985).

17. *Id.*

18. 16 U.S.C. § 1533(f)(1)(B)(i).

19. S. REP. No. 240, 100th Cong., 1st Sess. 9 (1987).

20. *Id.*

21. *Id.*

22. 16 U.S.C. § 1533(f)(1)(B)(ii).

23. *Id.* at § 1533(f)(1)(B)(iii).

develop and implement recovery plans for all listed species.[24]

However, even recovery plans containing specific directives may not be fully implemented in all cases. The mandate to implement recovery plans applies only to the Secretaries of the Interior and Commerce.[25] Therefore, section 4(f) standing alone apparently does not legally obligate federal agencies outside the Departments of the Interior and Commerce to implement recovery plan directives, even if a plan indicates that such an agency's cooperation is necessary to achieve recovery. Several agencies commonly involved in endangered species conflicts, such as the U.S. Forest Service and Army Corps of Engineers, therefore are probably not directly affected by the mandate to implement recovery plans.[26]

Feasibility may also limit agencies' abilities to carry out recovery plans. Insufficient knowledge of a species' biological requirements or inadequacy of known management techniques may hinder recovery actions.

The final limitation on recovery plan implementation is funding. Affirmative actions and programs to conserve species often require substantial amounts of money and resources. The ESA implicitly recognizes that funding may limit recovery plan implementation by directing the Secretary to give recovery plan development and implementation priority to species most likely to benefit from these actions.[27] An agency may therefore be able to justify not implementing recovery plans by citing insufficient funding. Clearly, however, an agency cannot arbitrarily allocate its resources. For instance, if an agency allocates funds to recovery plan implementation but ignores the recovery priority guidelines, the agency likely could not claim lack of funding as a reason for not implementing recovery plans of higher priority species.

Congress in 1988 expressed concern that the Secretary was

---

24. *Id.* at § 1533(f)(3).

25. Even though FWS and NMFS are responsible for preparing and approving recovery plans, the responsibility for implementing plans arguably includes *all* agencies under control of the Interior and Commerce Secretaries because section 7(a)(1) directs these Secretaries to utilize all programs they administer to further conservation of listed species. Since recovery plans are designed to conserve listed species, it follows that all Interior and Commerce Department agencies must implement the plans. *See* 16 U.S.C. § 1536(a)(1).

26. Nevertheless, agencies' duties to conserve listed species under section 7(a)(1) may require *all* federal agencies to follow recovery plan directives. *See infra* discussion of this section, notes 32-56 and accompanying text.

27. *See* 16 U.S.C. § 1533(f).

disproportionately allocating funds expended on species recovery efforts. A senate report accompanying the 1988 ESA amendments noted that during a five year period ending in 1986, approximately 45 percent of the funds available for development and implementation of recovery plans was spent on only five percent of listed U.S. species.[28] The report also noted that the Secretary earmarked little money for recovery of listed insects, mollusks, crustaceans, and plants.[29] Congress thus inserted into section 4(f) a requirement that recovery plans be developed and implemented "without regard to taxonomic classification,"[30] a provision intended to force the Secretary to allocate recovery resources more evenly among listed species.[31]

II. OTHER AFFIRMATIVE CONSERVATION DUTIES

The first section of the ESA provides that "[i]t is further declared to be the policy of Congress that all Federal departments and agencies shall seek to conserve endangered species and threatened species . . . ."[32] Read in conjunction with the statutory definition of "conserve,"[33] the legislature made it clear that all Federal agencies should promote the recovery[34] of listed species. Section 7(a)(1) echoes this mandate, requiring all Federal agencies to carry out programs aimed at recovery.[35] Section 7(a)(1) also directs the Secretaries of the Interior and Commerce to review all programs they administer and to use such programs to further conservation of listed species.[36]

Courts have infrequently examined the scope of section

28. S. REP. No. 240, 100th Cong., 1st Sess. 9 (1987).
29. *Id.*
30. 16 U.S.C. § 1533(f)(1)(A).
31. S. REP. No. 240, 100th Cong., 1st Sess. 9 (1987).
32. 16 U.S.C. § 1531(c).
33. The ESA provides that:
The terms "conserve", "conserving", and "conservation" mean to use and the use of all methods and procedures which are necessary to bring an endangered species or threatened species to the point at which the measures provided pursuant to this chapter are no longer necessary. Such measures include, but are not limited to, all activities associated with scientific resources management such as research, census, habitat acquisition and maintenance, propagation, live trapping, and transplantation, and, in the extraordinary case . . . may include regulatory taking.
16 U.S.C. § 1532(3).
34. *See supra* note 3 for the regulatory definition of the term "recovery."
35. 16 U.S.C. § 1536(a)(1).
36. *Id.*

7(a)(1)'s affirmative duties. The first case to consider these provisions was *Defenders of Wildlife v. Andrus.*[37] There, plaintiffs challenged FWS regulations governing duck hunting. Plaintiffs contended that regulations which permitted hunting one-half hour before sunrise and one-half hour after sunset would cause misidentification of birds and thereby imperil non-game, endangered birds. The D.C. district court set aside the regulations, holding:

> [the FWS] must do far more than merely avoid the elimination of protected species. It must bring these species back from the brink so that they may be removed from the protected class, and it must use all methods necessary to do so. The Service cannot limit its focus to the most important management tool available to it . . . to accomplish this end."[38]

Significantly, this conclusion rejected the argument that section 7(a)(1) permits federal agencies to choose which available conservation measures to implement. The court emphasized that an agency must use *all* methods at its disposal to promote recovery of listed species.[39]

In *Enos v. Marsh,*[40] plaintiff argued that by refusing to designate critical habitat for an endangered plant threatened by a naval harbor, the federal defendants violated section 7(a)(1) by not using "all" methods to conserve the plants. The court rejected this position, finding that critical habitat designation was not "necessary" for recovery of the species and thus was not a conservation measure under the statutory definition of "conservation."[41] Plaintiff did not press this argument on appeal.

Evidentiary showings played an important role in the outcomes of the cases discussed above. In *Defenders of Wildlife,* the court's opinion cites "numerous well prepared affidavits" that present "a substantial argument that the destruction of protected

---

37. 428 F. Supp. 167 (D.D.C. 1977).
38. *Id.* at 170.
39. In National Wildlife Federation v. Hodel, 23 Env't Rep. Cas. (BNA) 1089 (E.D. Cal. 1985), defendants again argued that section 7(a)(1) permits federal agencies to pick and choose between a number of different conservation measures. The court, however, did not reach the question of whether section 7(a)(1) requires agencies to use all possible conservation measures or allows agencies to make their own choices because it found the defendant's chosen conservation program arbitrary. *Id.* at 1092. *But see* National Wildlife Federation v. National Park Service, 669 F. Supp. 384, 387-88 (D. Wyo. 1987) ("[a] mere cursory reading . . . supports the Secretary's discretion as to methods of conservation.").
40. 616 F. Supp. 32 (D. Hawaii 1985), *aff'd*, 769 F.2d 1363 (9th Cir. 1985).
41. 616 F. Supp. at 59.

species may be considerable."[42] In *Enos v. Marsh*, on the other hand, the court observed that the overwhelming number of plants in question thrived outside the area in dispute.[43] These rulings suggest that as a prerequisite to ordering agencies to take affirmative actions to conserve listed species, plaintiffs must clearly indicate that such actions are necessary to species recovery.[44]

The most significant decision to date which examines the scope of section 7(a)(1)'s mandate to conserve listed species is *Carson-Truckee Water Conservation District v. Watt*.[45] The case centered on the Stampede Reservoir and two endangered fishes living downstream. Plaintiff argued that defendant Bureau of Reclamation[46] was obligated by the ESA only to release the amount of water from the reservoir necessary to insure the bare survival of the fishes, leaving additional water available for sale to the plaintiffs. The district court rejected this position, citing *Defenders of Wildlife*[47] and *Connor v. Andrus*[48] for the proposition that the ESA required the Secretary to give endangered species priority over all other water uses until fish recovery was achieved. The court upheld the Secretary's plan to use all reservoir water releases to conserve the species, rejecting an alternative plan proposed by plaintiffs due to lack of evidence that the alternative was feasible or cost effective.[49]

After the district court's decision, a federal Solicitor's Opinion denounced the court's conclusions.[50] The opinion argued that section 7(a)(1) authorizes federal agencies to incorporate species conservation into their planning processes but does not

---

42. 428 F. Supp. at 168, 170.

43. 616 F. Supp. at 62.

44. This follows from the statutory definition of conservation, which notes that this term means the use of methods *necessary* to bring species to the point at which ESA protection is no longer necessary. *See supra* note 19. Thus, section 7(a)(1)'s directive to agencies to conserve species requires the use of necessary measures to enhance species' recovery.

45. 549 F. Supp. 704 (E.D. Cal. 1983), *aff'd*, 741 F.2d 257 (9th Cir. 1984).

46. Though the Secretary of the Interior and the Bureau of Reclamation were named as defendants, the Pyramid Lake Paiute Indian Tribe clearly represented the interests of the endangered species as defendant-intervenors.

47. 428 F. Supp. at 167.

48. 453 F. Supp. 1037 (W.D. Tex. 1978).

49. 549 F. Supp. at 712.

50. Memorandum to the Director, U.S. Fish and Wildlife Service, from the Associate Solicitor, Conservation and Wildlife, U.S. Department of the Interior (Sept. 7, 1983) (copy in author's files).

mandate agencies to accord endangered species conservation the highest priority in planning efforts. The Solicitor maintained that the district court's interpretation of section 7(a)(1) subsumed the ESA's section 7(a)(2) mandate. In other words, the Solicitor argued that federal agencies, in light of the ruling in *Carson-Truckee*, would have to show that all proposed or ongoing agency actions would benefit listed species before the action passed muster under section 7(a)(1). This requirement, the Solicitor argued, would "swallow up" the section 7(a)(2) mandate, which prohibits only agency actions which jeopardize the continued existence of listed species or adversely modify critical habitat.

On appeal, the Ninth Circuit opinion in *Carson-Truckee* dodged the Solicitor's argument by distinguishing between agency actions principally aimed at goals other than species conservation (i.e., building a dam or highway), and programs specifically designed to promote species recovery. The court found that the jeopardy and critical habitat standards of section 7(a)(2) apply to the former, while the ESA's conservation mandates apply to the latter. Reasoning that the Secretary's plan to operate Stampede Reservoir exclusively for the benefit of endangered fishes was a program designed to conserve those species, the Court of Appeals held that the lower court properly applied ESA section 7(a)(1) and related sections rather than section 7(a)(2) standards.[51]

The *Carson-Truckee* decisions merit careful analysis. The district court sweepingly concluded that the various ESA conservation mandates "required [the Secretary] to give the Pyramid Lake fishery priority over all other purposes of Stampede until the cui-ui fish and the Lahontan cutthroat trout are no longer classified as endangered or threatened."[52] This broad language carries enormous potential ramifications, as the Solicitor's Opinion pointed out. Liberally construed, the district court holding would require all federal agencies to give endangered species recovery top priority in carrying out all activities.

The Ninth Circuit significantly limited the scope of the lower court ruling. The appellate opinion made it clear that agencies must give recovery of listed species first priority only when agen-

---

51. 741 F.2d at 262.
52. 549 F. Supp. at 710.

cies "actively seek[] to conserve endangered species."[53] In implementing other actions that "incidentally jeopardize" listed species, the court implied that agencies need only insure that their activities do not jeopardize the continued existence of such species or adversely modify critical habitat.[54]

The two *Carson-Truckee* decisions are difficult to reconcile. The ESA "requirement" cited by the district court, mandating that agencies accord species recovery highest priority in all activities they carry out, becomes illusory under the Ninth Circuit's interpretation of section 7. If an agency takes an action designed to "actively conserve" a listed species, the appellate court found that the ESA requires that the action is undertaken with the species' recovery as its first priority. This "requirement," however, simply states a truism since programs designed to actively conserve listed species are by definition primarily aimed at bringing about species' recovery.[55] The Ninth Circuit opinion provides no indication of *when* section 7(a)(1) obligates agencies to seek to actively conserve listed species. Had the Secretary wished to sell water to plaintiffs in the *Carson-Truckee* case, for example, he merely could have asserted that operation of the Stampede Reservoir constituted an agency action that incidentally affected the endangered fish. Therefore, under the Ninth Circuit's rationale, the sale of water from the reservoir could have proceeded unless it jeopardized the fish or modified critical habitat.

In the actual case, the Secretary wished to carry out a plan to speed the recovery of the fish by refusing to divert reservoir water to other uses. Though the *Carson-Truckee* decisions conclude that the Secretary was "required" to follow through with this plan, the only reason behind this conclusion is that the Secretary decided to operate the reservoir to conserve these species in the first place.

The *Carson-Truckee* cases thus bring up a difficult problem in interpreting the conservation mandates of the ESA. Sections 7(a)(1) and 2(c) affirmatively direct agencies to use all methods necessary to promote the recovery of listed species, while section 7(a)(2) prohibits agency actions jeopardizing species or adversely affecting critical habitat. If both mandates apply to all agency actions, as the Solicitor's Opinion in response to the district court

---

53. 741 F.2d at 262.
54. *Id.*
55. *See supra* note 33 for the definition of "conservation."

decision in *Carson-Truckee* points out, the directives to conserve listed species would subsume the section 7(a)(2) jeopardy provisions. Hence, agency actions actually would have to benefit listed species before they would satisfy the ESA. If Congress had intended such a result, it would not have included section 7(a)(2) and the elaborate section 7 exemption process within the statute.[56]

The question thus becomes when to apply the different mandates of the ESA. If federal agencies can decide at their discretion when and under what circumstances to conserve listed species, section 7(a)(1) simply becomes an enabling clause which grants agencies the authority to take all measures necessary to promote species recovery, but it does not obligate agencies to take any action at all. The Solicitor's Opinion adopts this interpretation of section 7(a)(1).

The section 7 regulations take a similar stance. The regulations authorize the Secretary to include "conservation recommendations" in biological opinions.[57] Though these recommendations supposedly are designed to assist Federal agencies in meeting their section 7(a)(1) responsibilities, the regulations make it clear that these conservation recommendations are completely optional and are intended to carry no legal weight.[58]

Alternatively, certain circumstances may trigger mandatory application of the ESA's conservation mandates. In such circumstances, section 7(a)(1), as interpreted by the *Defenders of Wildlife*[59] court and the district court in *Carson-Truckee*, would require agencies to give species recovery priority over all other agency actions. The courts have yet to define what triggers this requirement, however.

The cases which have applied the ESA's conservation mandate at least provide a basis for speculation on future developments in this area. Courts have had no trouble finding that an agency has a duty to conserve a listed species when the agency has already embarked on a program ostensibly aimed at conserving that species. These rulings could be interpreted as establishing a threshold beyond which agencies must give species

---

56. The Solicitor's Opinion, *supra* note 50, emphasizes this point.
57. 50 C.F.R. § 402.14(j).
58. *Id.*
59. 428 F. Supp. at 167.

recovery top priority. For example, in the *Carson-Truckee* case the Secretary may have crossed this threshold when he publicly decided to operate the Stampede Reservoir to benefit the endangered fish downstream. Subsequent to this decision, section 7(a)(1) may require the Secretary to give the endangered fish top priority until they have recovered. If this is the case, the Secretary could not later decide to drop the fish conservation program or relegate conservation measures to a lower priority without violating the ESA.

The threshold theory solves the following problem: suppose that when plaintiffs challenge an agency conservation program as inadequate to achieve species recovery[60] the defendant agency simply drops its entire conservation program, arguing that the ESA merely authorizes but does not obligate agencies to undertake such programs. Currently, there is no clearly articulated judicial decision which precludes this argument. If agency involvement in a plan to conserve a listed species triggers mandatory application of section 7(a)(1), the agency *must* proceed with the species' recovery as its primary aim, as the Ninth Circuit held in *Carson-Truckee*. The problem with this approach is that agencies would no doubt become reluctant to characterize their actions as aimed at promoting species recovery and might even deliberately avoid taking actions which would benefit listed species for fear of triggering section 7(a)(1)'s potentially broad requirements.

Aside from agencies themselves characterizing their action as conservation measures, recovery plans are the only other easily identifiable potential triggers for application of section 7(a)(1). Recovery plans in many ways possess the ideal characteristics to act as triggers for agencies' duty to conserve listed species. They are prepared by experts and contain an outline of steps necessary to promote the conservation of listed species. The plans also often identify which federal agencies are responsible for carrying out specific recovery tasks. Defining agencies' conservation duties by what is set forth in recovery plans would free the courts from sticky problems of attempting to interpret the scope of the ESA's conservation mandate on a case-by-case basis. In addition, binding agency action to the recovery plan goals would remove

---

60. Plaintiff made this type of claim in National Wildlife Federation v. Hodel, 23 Env't Rep. Cas. (BNA) 1089 (E.D. Cal. 1985).

agencies' incentives to avoid characterizing their actions as conservation measures.

Section 4 of the ESA already directs the Secretaries of the Interior and Commerce to implement recovery plans, so interpreting section 7(a)(1) to require recovery plan implementation by all agencies would not impose any additional statutory duties on many federal agencies.

Obviously, reading the ESA's conservation mandate in sections 2(c) and 7(a)(1) to require all federal agencies to carry out the steps outlined in recovery plans would make preparation of the plans an extremely important process. This scheme would raise several important questions about who should participate in recovery plan preparation. Nevertheless, linking the statute's conservation mandate to steps listed in recovery plans may be the best way to define conclusively the scope of sections 2(c) and 7(a)(1).

Once federal agencies decide to take actions to conserve listed species, they must be able factually to justify their efforts as necessary to promote species recovery.[61] In two reported cases, the issue was not whether the ESA obligated federal agencies to take affirmative actions to conserve listed species; rather, plaintiffs argued that federal actions ostensibly aimed at species conservation were themselves unlawful. In *Connor v. Andrus*,[62] the court found that federal agencies need to show a rational basis for affirmative actions aimed at conserving listed species. At issue in the case were FWS regulations banning certain types of hunting in Texas. The agency argued that the ban protected the endangered Mexican duck. The court, noting that "the record is filled to abundance with data to show that hunting presents no threats to the Mexican duck," ruled that plaintiffs had carried their burden of showing the agency's actions were arbitrary and capricious and struck down the challenged regulations.[63]

---

61. Courts review federal actions undertaken pursuant to the ESA's mandate to conserve species using the "arbitrary and capricious" standard. *See infra* Chapter 9, notes 94-97 and accompanying text.

62. 453 F. Supp. 1,037 (W.D. Tex. 1978).

63. *Id.* at 1041. In *State of Louisiana v. Verity*, 853 F.2d 322 (5th Cir. 1988), the Fifth Circuit refused to apply this sort of review to regulations dealing with threatened species promulgated by the Secretary pursuant to section 7(d). Plaintiffs in the case argued that regulations banning takings of sea turtles were arbitrary because the Secretary did not demonstrate that the takings ban would ultimately save turtles from extinction. However, the court held that when exercising his authority under section 7(d) to regulate takings of threatened species, the Secretary need not show any link between the regula-

In a similar case also involving FWS hunting regulations,[64] the agency proposed to close various wildlife refuges to water-fowl hunting starting with the 1986-87 season unless states took action to ban the use of lead shot. FWS found such action necessary to conserve eagles threatened by lead poisoning. Plaintiffs brought suit, however, claiming that the FWS proposal arbitrarily neglected to close the disputed areas prior to the 1985-86 hunting season. Citing significant evidence linking lead shot and eagle lead poisoning, the court found no clearly articulated factors supporting FWS' decision not to close the areas to lead shot immediately. The court enjoined use of lead shot during the 1985-86 season.

Finally, other cases have mentioned agencies' duties under the ESA's conservation mandates, though these duties were not central issues. One court implied that an agency's failure to use the best scientific and commercial data available during consultation constituted a substantive violation of section 7(a)(1), as well as a procedural section 7 violation.[65] A Florida district court, in rejecting a challenge to federal fishing restrictions, noted that the ESA imposed on the Secretary "an affirmative duty . . . not only to protect but also to increase the population of endangered species, such as the American crocodile."[66]

III. THE CONCEPT OF RECOVERY

The ESA and section 7 regulations essentially define a "recovered" species as one that no longer needs special protection to ensure its continued existence.[67] Therefore, the ultimate goal of the ESA is to make itself obsolete—to reach the point at which all listed species are sufficiently numerous to be out of danger of becoming extinct and have adequate habitat in which to thrive. This goal, however, merely begs the ultimate question: Is species recovery possible?

---

tions and the species' chances for survival; the court noted that the Secretary only need demonstrate that regulations adopted pursuant to section 7(d) to prevent takings of threatened species will in fact do so. *Id.* at 333.

64. National Wildlife Federation v. Hodel, 23 Env't Rep. Cas. (BNA) 1089 (E.D. Cal. 1985).

65. Conservation Law Found. v. Watt, 560 F. Supp. 561, 573 (D. Mass. 1983).

66. Organized Fishermen of Florida v. Andrus, 488 F. Supp. 1351, 1356 (S.D. Fla. 1980).

67. *See* definition of "recovery," *supra* note 3. *See also* definition of "conservation," *supra* note 33.

A species will no longer need special protection and will thus be considered recovered only when the factors that initially led to its listing have been redressed so as to no longer imperil the species.[68] When viewed in this manner, recovery of many species becomes much more complex than simply increasing those species' populations. The case of grizzly bears provides a good example. Grizzlies' former range included most of western North America. Today, with the exceptions of Canada and Alaska, grizzlies exist only in isolated pockets of Idaho, Washington, Wyoming and Montana. Even in these areas, resource development and increasing human presence threaten the bears' survival. Intensive interagency efforts between federal and state land management agencies have attempted to ameliorate these threats and increase grizzly populations to recovered levels. Even assuming these efforts prove successful, delisting of grizzlies would eliminate their protected legal status. Without the stringent limitations on activities adversely affecting grizzlies that these protection provide, grizzly numbers would likely decline again. Hence, grizzly recovery becomes a sort of "catch-22"—the ESA defines a recovered species as one no longer in need of the Act's protection, but in order to sustain their populations at such levels, grizzlies need the protection afforded them under the ESA. Many other listed species face similar situations.

The dilemma outlined above clearly illustrates that legal, as well as biological, factors are relevant to species recovery. Therefore, recovery of many species will require concerted efforts on the part of federal and state authorities, as well as private parties, to enact laws and regulations and to reach agreements to protect listed species independent of the ESA. One of the statutory criteria the Secretary considers in listing and delisting species is "the inadequacy of existing regulatory mechanisms."[69] When a species is listed, ESA protections fill this regulatory void. Only when adequate legal mechanisms independent of the ESA are implemented to protect a listed species whose population has rebounded to healthy levels can the species be said to no longer require ESA protection and thus be considered recovered.

In 1988, Congress recognized that even species considered to have recovered and thus removed from the threatened and en-

---

68. 16 U.S.C. § 1533(a)(1)(D).
69. *Id.*

dangered lists may still face threats to their existence.[70] Accordingly, lawmakers amended section 4 by adding a provision which requires the Secretary, acting in cooperation with state governments, to implement a system for monitoring recovered species for at least five years after they are removed from the protected lists.[71] In the event of a "significant risk to the well being" of any such species, the Secretary must use his emergency authority under section 4(b)(7) to re-list the species.[72]

IV. The Recovery Zone Concept

The "recovery zone" concept is becoming increasingly popular among federal agencies.[73] Typically, the recovery zone concept divides the habitat of a listed species into several zones with a different species recovery strategy within each zone. In a three zone system, for example, zone one may be defined as habitat necessary for survival and recovery of the species. Lands in zone one will be protected from impacts adverse to species and managed to the benefit of the listed species. A second zone is defined as marginally important to the species. In these zones, endangered species protection is not paramount; other land uses may prevail when a conflict with species conservation arises. A third zone contains habitat that will not be managed for species conservation. A species' presence in this zone is generally undesirable, and actions may be taken to remove individuals perceived as a threat to ongoing land uses. This recovery zone concept is designed to allow land managers to choose the areas deemed desirable to support a recovered population of the species in question.

This concept suffers serious flaws. Most prominently, it skirts the ESA's critical habitat provisions. Under the recovery zone concept, agencies identify certain geographical areas as necessary for species survival and recovery. This essentially parallels the statutory definition of critical habitat. However, agencies do not designate or recognize areas so identified as critical habitat nor consider the section 7(a)(2) prohibition against destruction or

---

70. S. Rep. No. 240, 100th Cong., 1st Sess. 10 (1987).

71. 16 U.S.C. § 1533(g)(1).

72. *Id.* at § 1533(g)(2).

73. This concept has thus far been applied to large, wide-ranging carnivores, namely wolves and grizzly bears. *See, e.g.*, Interagency Grizzly Bear Guidelines, 51 Fed. Reg. 42,863 (1986). The grizzly guidelines divide grizzly habitat into five "management situations," each of which places a different emphasis on grizzly conservation.

adverse modification of critical habitat in determining whether proposed actions affecting these areas violate section 7.[74] Rather, the agencies themselves define the protection they will accord to areas determined to be necessary to species survival and recovery, as well as the protection applicable to all other "recovery zones."

This system may prove detrimental to listed species in several ways. First, the protection plan agencies decide to implement in each recovery zone may be less stringent than the 7(a)(2) prohibition against destruction or adverse modification of critical habitat. Thus, by calling habitat essential to the conservation of a listed species a "recovery zone," rather than "critical habitat," agencies essentially give themselves discretion to protect that habitat less diligently than required by section 7(a)(2).

Secondly, while the ESA and its implementing regulations outline specific criteria for delineating critical habitat and vest authority to designate critical habitat only in the Secretary, identification of the various zones under the recovery zone concept is left completely to the discretion of the federal agency or agencies administering species' habitat. This creates the possibility that agencies will intentionally manipulate recovery zone boundaries to place the sites of proposed agency actions in a less restrictive recovery zone than is warranted from a biological standpoint.

Another major flaw of the recovery zone concept is that it usurps the section 7 consultation process. Section 7's jeopardy standard prohibits federal actions that reduce the likelihood of a listed species' survival and recovery. One or more of the "recovery zones," however, is usually defined as unnecessary for the survival and recovery of the species in question, or require managers to accommodate species' needs only if feasible.[75] This renders the section 7 consultation process virtually meaningless for these areas. Defining an area as unneeded for species survival and recovery states, in effect, that section 7 does not apply to that

---

74. In a biological opinion rendered on a predecessor to the current Interagency Grizzly Bear Guidelines, which also divided grizzly habitat into zones called "management situations," the Secretary noted that, "[t]he management situations identify areas necessary for species survival and recovery and consequently imply critical habitat. Our biological opinion cannot ratify this implied designation of critical habitat." Interagency Grizzly Bear Committee, *Interagency Grizzly Bear Guidelines* 93 (1986).

75. *See, e.g.*, Interagency Grizzly Bear Guidelines, *supra* note 73 (definitions of Grizzly Bear Management Situations 2 and 3).

area. Similarly, requiring projects to provide for species' needs only if feasible simply ignores the mandates of section 7(a)(2).

The "recovery zone" concept also provides that when species' use of habitat and other land uses are incompatible, other land uses may prevail in management considerations in zones defined as not vital or unnecessary for species survival and recovery. This also undercuts the exacting procedural and substantive requirements of section 7. During interagency consultation, FWS and NMFS must provide those reasonable and prudent alternatives, if any, which would enable a proposed agency action to comply with the mandates of section 7(a)(2). If no such alternatives exist, the federal agency may take the action at the risk of violating section 7, or seek a statutory exemption under section 7(2).[76] For the recovery zone concept to assert that other land uses may prevail over considerations for conservation of listed species simply because those activities occur within a certain zone completely defeats the purpose of these section 7 provisions.

---

76. See *infra* Chapter 7 for a detailed discussion of section 7's substantive requirements.

Chapter 6

Procedural Aspects of Interagency Consultation under Section 7

Among the ESA's most significant provisions are the prohibitions of section 7, which require federal agencies, licensees, and permittees to refrain from taking actions likely to jeopardize the continued existence of listed species or to modify adversely these species' critical habitats. When first enacted, however, the statute gave little guidance to assist agencies in complying with these restrictions, other than a vague directive to consult with expert wildlife agencies for assistance. Subsequently, Congress has greatly expanded section 7, adding several procedural requirements designed to insure that agencies take the necessary steps to comply with section 7's substantive mandates. These procedures play a key role in section 7's protection of listed species since courts equate compliance with section 7's procedural requirements to compliance with the section's substantive provisions.[1] This chapter examines the procedures federal agencies must follow to integrate protection of listed species into their everyday actions.

I. BIOLOGICAL ASSESSMENTS

In 1978, Congress added section 7(c) to the ESA.[2] It requires federal agencies planning an action in a particular region to request information from the Secretary about whether listed species or species proposed for listing may be present in the area.[3] If the Secretary advises, based on the best scientific and commercial data available, that listed or proposed species may occur in the area, the agency taking action must prepare a "biological assessment" which identifies protected species likely to be affected by the proposed action and which outlines the nature and extent

---

1. Thomas v. Peterson, 753 F.2d 764 (9th Cir. 1985).
2. Pub. L. No. 95-632 (1978).
3. 16 U.S.C. § 1536(c); see 50 C.F.R. § 402.12.

of the action's impacts on those species.[4]

Legislative history indicates that lawmakers added section 7(c) "to stimulate the development of additional biological information to assist Federal agencies in complying with section 7."[5] Biological assessments are designed to help agencies determine whether they must formally consult with the Secretary concerning their proposed actions.[6] If a biological assessment indicates that formal consultation is required, the Secretary will use the information contained in the biological assessment, together with other relevant information if necessary, to formulate a biological opinion on the proposed agency action.[7]

In addition to requiring agencies to gather biological information, section 7(c) contains substantive protection for listed and proposed species. Before completion of a biological assessment, the action agency may neither enter contracts for construction, nor begin construction on the proposed project.[8]

It is unclear whether the prohibitions also apply to federal permit applicants whose activities require the permitting agency to prepare a biological assessment. Though legislative history does not specifically discuss why Congress chose to ban contracting and construction during biological assessment preparation, the Congressional policy underlying these restrictions is probably the same as that underlying section 7(d)'s limitation on irreversible and irretrievable commitment of resources while formal section 7 consultation is underway: Congress sought to encourage identification of potential conflicts between projects and protected species before resource commitments create pressure to complete proposed actions.[9] Since section 7(d) expressly applies to both federal agencies and nonfederal applicants, Congress probably intended for section 7(c)'s restrictions against entering into contracts or beginning construction while biological assessments are underway to apply to applicants for federal permits as well as to federal agencies.

---

4. 16 U.S.C. § 1536(c).

5. H.R. REP. No. 1625, 95th Cong., 2d Sess. 20 (1978).

6. For a discussion of what triggers formal consultation, see *infra* notes 36-57 and accompanying text.

7. *See* 50 C.F.R. § 402.12(K)(2).

8. 16 U.S.C. § 1536(c)(1); 50 C.F.R. § 402.12(b)(2). *See also* H.R. REP. No. 1625, 95th Cong., 2d Sess. 20 (1978).

9. *See infra* Chapter 7, notes 4-8 and accompanying text.

A. *Implementing Regulations*

Regulations implementing section 7(c) sharply limit federal agencies' statutory responsibilities to request information on listed and proposed species and prepare biological assessments. Regulations require agencies to follow these procedures only if an agency determines that its action is a "major construction activity,"[10] though agencies may voluntarily prepare biological assessments for actions which do not involve major construction activities.[11] In addition, regulations permit the Secretary to request that an agency prepare a biological assessment; agencies, however, may refuse to comply with such requests.[12]

The above limitations on the scope of section 7(c) seem unjustified. In support of the regulations' interpretation of section 7(c), the Secretary claims that language in the House Conference Report for the 1979 ESA amendments justifies limiting the requirement to request species lists and to perform biological assessments only to major construction activities.[13] The Report provides that "existing law requires Federal agencies to conduct biological assessments *on major Federal actions* initiated after November 10, 1978 and [those which are] designed to result in the building or erection of dams, buildings, pipelines and the like."[14] Although this wording seems to support the regulations' limits on the requirement to prepare biological assessments, the Secretary's reliance on this legislative history to interpret section 7(c) is inappropriate. Congress added the procedures set forth in section 7(c) in 1978; therefore, the conference report accompanying the 1979 ESA amendments is of limited value in interpreting what Congress intended to be the scope of Section 7(c). Moreover, the cited passage from the 1979 Report occurs within a dis-

---

10. The regulations define "major construction activity" to be "a construction project (or other undertaking having similar physical impacts) which is a major Federal action significantly affecting the quality of the human environment as referred to in the National Environmental Policy Act (NEPA), 42 U.S.C. § 4332(2)." 50 C.F.R. § 402.02.

11. *See* 50 C.F.R. § 402.12. For example, even if an agency does not propose a major construction activity, it should voluntarily prepare a biological assessment if the agency anticipates that it will eventually apply for a section 7 exemption. Preparation of a biological assessment is a statutory prerequisite for receiving a permanent exemption from section 7. 16 U.S.C. § 1536(h)(2)(A)(ii).

12. *Id.*

13. *See* 51 Fed. Reg. 19,936-37 (1986) (citing H.R. CONF. REP. No. 697, 96th Cong., 1st Sess. 14 (1979)).

14. H.R. CONF. REP. No. 697, 96th Cong., 1st Sess. 13 (1979).

cussion of an amendment to the section 7 exemption process, rather than accompanying an explanation of section 7(c).

The passage from the 1979 conference report relied on by the Secretary conflicts with the clear language of section 7(c) itself, as well as with the legislative history of the 1978 ESA amendments. Section 7(c) provides that:

> [E]ach Federal agency *shall*, with respect to *any* agency action of such agency for which no contract for construction has been entered into and for which no construction has begun on November 10, 1978, request of the Secretary information whether any species which is listed or proposed to be listed may be present in the area of such proposed action.[15]

If the Secretary informs the agency that such species may be present, section 7(c) goes on to provide that the agency "shall" perform a biological assessment.[16] Far from lending support to limiting the application of section 7(c) only to major construction activities, the language of this provision expressly applies to "any agency action."[17] Legislative history for the 1978 amendments also makes it clear that no special meaning or Congressional intent to limit the ESA's procedural requirements attaches to the word "construction."[18] Rather than referring only to actions designed to erect facilities, dams, buildings and the like, the word "construction" within the context of the ESA is a term of art that refers generally to actions likely to affect listed species. For example, when explaining the limitations of section 7(d), Senator Culver noted that "subsequent to the initiation of consultation, the construction agency [may make] no irreversible or irretrievable commitment of resources. . . ."[19] Since section 7(d) applies to all agency actions involved in section 7 consultation, whether or not the actions include "construction" in a narrow sense of the term, Senator Culver's use of the term "construction agency" includes all agencies whose actions may affect listed species, not merely those agencies engaged in building activities. Thus, the phrase "construction activities" arguably does not limit section 7(c) to *major* construction activities.

Despite claims by the Secretary to the contrary, the regula-

---

15. 16 U.S.C. § 1536(c)(1) (emphasis added).
16. *Id.*
17. *Id.*
18. *See* H.R. REP. No. 1625, 96th Cong., 2d Sess. 19-21 (1978).
19. North Slope v. Andrus, 486 F. Supp. 332, 355 (D. D.C. 1979) (quoting 124 CONG. REC. S10,869 (daily ed. July 7, 1978)).

tions' narrow reading of section 7(c) reduces the protection this section provides to listed and proposed species and their critical habitats. The Secretary argues that even though regulations do not require section 7(c) procedures for all federal actions, this does not decrease ESA protection because all federal agencies still must review their proposed actions to determine whether formal consultation with the Secretary is necessary.[20] However, this view ignores the basic purpose of section 7(c) procedures. Congress added the section 7(c) requirements in order to facilitate "the early discovery of and elucidation of any conflicts between an agency action and a listed species."[21] If an agency decides that its proposed action does not constitute a "major construction activity" within the meaning of section 7,[22] it need not even request advice from the Secretary concerning which listed or proposed species or critical habitats may be present in the project area.[23] It is thus possible for an agency to proceed with an action that harms a protected species or critical habitat simply because the agency is unaware of the species' presence.

Even if an action agency becomes aware that a protected species or critical habitat is indeed present within the area affected by a proposed action, the section 7 regulations' failure to require preparation of biological assessments for all agency actions deprives these species and habitats of significant protection. Preparation of a biological assessment triggers a prohibition against entering into contracts or beginning work on a proposed action until completion of the assessment.[24] The purpose of this restriction is to prevent significant investments in an activity before its effects on protected species are known. Because this rationale applies to major construction activities, as well as to other agency activities, making a distinction between these types of activities for the purpose of section 7(c) seems arbitrary. Finally, a biological assessment determines whether an agency must initiate section 7 consultation with the Secretary over a proposed action. Therefore, biological assessments also serve as the primary bases of agency decisions about whether or not to initiate the section 7 consultation process. Even though an agency must decide

---

20. 51 Fed. Reg. 19,945 (1986) (to be codified at 50 C.F.R. § 402(7)).

21. H.R. REP. No. 1625, 95th Cong., 2d Sess. 20 (1978).

22. *See supra* note 10 for a definition of "major construction activity."

23. 50 C.F.R. § 402.12(b)(1).

24. *See supra* note 8 and accompanying text.

whether consultation is necessary regardless of whether it is required to prepare a biological assessment for a given project, two problems arise when an agency does not prepare a biological assessment. First, without a formal assessment of how a proposed action affects protected species and critical habitats, an agency may decide whether or not to initiate consultation in an ad hoc manner without systematically analyzing all relevant data. Second, lack of biological assessment documenting a proposal's impact on species and on critical habitats could hinder interested parties' evaluations of the federal agency's decision on whether to begin formal section 7 consultation.[25]

It is unclear why the regulations limit section 7(c)'s applicability to major construction activities. Requesting a list of protected species and critical habitat which may be present in project areas does not unduly burden federal agencies. On the contrary, this procedure relieves agencies from the necessity of acquiring the information themselves. Nor does preparation of biological assessments demand much of federal agencies. The contents of a biological assessment are at the discretion of the agencies which prepare them.[26] Far from exhaustive studies, biological assessments need only demonstrate to the agency whether its proposal is likely to adversely affect protected species or critical habitats. The agency must make this determination whether or not it prepares a formal biological assessment.[27] Finally, during formal section 7 consultation, action agencies must provide the Secretary with data on how a proposal affects listed species and their habitats, unless the information is already set forth in a biological assessment.[28] Therefore, by preparing biological assessments agencies may reduce their workload later in the section 7 process.

---

25. This information may be available from other sources, however. For example, the Secretary encourages federal agencies to use NEPA documentation to discuss how a proposal affects species or critical habitats when no biological assessment is prepared. *See* 51 Fed. Reg. 19,945 (1986).

26. 50 C.F.R. § 402.12(f).

27. Whether or not a project is likely to affect a listed species or critical habitat determines whether an agency must initiate formal section 7 consultation. *See infra* notes 36-57 and accompanying text. An agency must determine whether to initiate consultation with the Secretary for all agency actions, including those which are not "major construction activities." *See* 50 C.F.R. § 402.14.

28. *See supra* notes 4-5 and accompanying text.

B. *Judicial Interpretations of Section 7(c)*

Judicial interpretations of the requirements of section 7(c) are few. In *Thomas v. Peterson*,[29] the Ninth Circuit overturned a federal district court ruling and enjoined construction of a road by the Forest Service. The agency had failed to perform a biological assessment, even though it knew that the endangered Rocky Mountain Gray Wolf was present in the area. The appellate court held that "[o]nce an agency is aware that an endangered species may be present in the area of its proposed action, the ESA requires it to prepare a biological assessment," and concluded that failure to conduct an assessment is a substantive violation of the ESA.[30]

In another case addressing the requirement to prepare a biological assessment, the D.C. Circuit Court refused to halt an agency action for an alleged failure to prepare an assessment.[31] In a somewhat unclear opinion, the court apparently held that statements within an EIS prepared for the action were sufficient to constitute a biological assessment. The EIS concluded that listed species either were not present in the area or would not be affected by the proposed action. This approach appears to be valid under the ESA because section 7(c) explicitly links preparation of a biological assessment with NEPA procedures.[32]

Finally, in *No Oilport! v. Carter*,[33] plaintiffs alleged that defendants violated section 7(c) by entering into a contract for construction prior to completion of a biological assessment. The federal district court rejected this argument, finding that defendants' actions prior to completion of the biological assessment did not constitute entry into a contract.[34]

---

29. 589 F. Supp. 1139 (D. Idaho 1984), *aff'd* in part, *rev'd* in part, remanded, 753 F.2d 754 (9th Cir. 1985).

30. *Id.* at 763. A U.S. district court in Vance v. Block, 635 F. Supp. 163, 169 (D. Mont. 1986) held that under the facts of that case the Forest Service's failure to conduct a biological assessment was a *de minimis* ESA violation and thus was not a substantive violation of the statute. However, on appeal the Ninth Circuit dismissed the plaintiffs' ESA claims for lack of jurisdiction. *See* Save the Yaak Committee v. Block, 840 F.2d 714, 721 (9th Cir. 1988).

31. Mobil Oil Corp v. ICC, 685 F.2d 624 (D.C. Cir. 1982).

32. 16 U.S.C. § 1536(c)(1).

33. 520 F. Supp. 334 (W.D. Wash. 1981).

34. 520 F. Supp. at 365. Federal agencies and a private permit applicant, co-defendants in the case, had completed some of the steps necessary to authorize construction of the challenged facility prior to completion of the biological assessment. Noting that the federal defendants had not yet issued a final Notice to Proceed, and further noting that the Notice to Proceed was explicitly contingent upon compliance with the

C.   *Triggering Consultation*

1.   *The statutory scheme.*

Consultation between an agency proposing to take action and the Secretary is the most important of section 7's procedures.[35] The ESA explicitly imposes substantive and procedural duties on agencies while they are involved in formal consultation. The Secretary must study a proposed project's effects on protected species, issue a biological opinion on whether the action violates the substantive mandates of section 7(a)(2), and, if a violation is found, suggest reasonable and prudent alternatives to avoid a violation.[36] In the meantime, the action agency and applicant for a federal permit, if any, must refrain from irreversibly committing resources to the project which would foreclose any reasonable and prudent alternatives to the project under consideration.[37]

The statute is less clear, however, as to when formal consultation becomes mandatory.[38] It remains unclear whether agencies must consult with the Secretary concerning all agency actions, or whether the ESA merely requires that agencies carry out section 7 consultation under limited circumstances. If agencies' duty to

---

ESA, the court construed the permit previously granted by the federal defendants as not being a contract for the purposes of section 7(c). The court cited *Conservation Law Foundation v. Andrus*, 623 F.2d 712 (1st Cir. 1979), as guiding its resolution of the section 7(c) issue.

35. Regulations distinguish between "informal" consultation, an optional process which essentially includes all discussions regarding protected species between an agency and the Secretary prior to consultation, and "formal" consultation, which refers to the statutory process described in 16 U.S.C. sections 1536(a)(2) and 1536(b). *See* 50 C.F.R. § 402.02.

36. 16 U.S.C. § 1536(b).

37. *Id*. at § 1536(d).

38. The ESA clearly sets out at least one set of circumstances in which a federal agency must initiate formal consultation with the Secretary. When a prospective applicant for a federal permit or license reasonably believes that a listed species may be affected by its project, the applicant may request that the permitting or licensing agency initiate consultation with the Secretary. *See* 16 U.S.C. § 1536(a)(3). If the federal agency receives written assurance from the applicant that the applicant has a definite action planned, which it intends to implement if authorized to do so, the federal agency must consult with the Secretary concerning the permit or license. 50 C.F.R. § 402.11(b) - (c).

In addition to the above so-called "early consultation," section 7 regulations permit the Secretary to request that a federal agency enter into consultation on an action to be carried out by that agency. While the regulations do not specify whether such a request creates a duty for the agency to initiate consultation, such a duty exists for all practical purposes since it is unlikely that the Secretary would in such a case concur with a "no adverse affect" finding by the agency. *See infra* notes 44-46 and accompanying text.

consult is limited, a question arises about what circumstances are sufficient to trigger the consultation requirement.

The wording of section 7 supports a broad interpretation of agencies' duty to consult. Section 7 provides that "[e]ach federal agency shall, in consultation with and with the assistance of the Secretary, insure that *any* action authorized, funded, or carried out by such agency" is not likely to jeopardize listed species or adversely modify critical habitat.[39] While this language appears to require that agencies consult with the Secretary on all agency actions, other phrases in section 7(c) suggest that Congress did not intend consultation to be a universal requirement. That section provides that the purpose of a biological assessment is to identify endangered and threatened species "likely to be affected" by agency actions.[40] Since Congress added the biological assessment requirement in 1978 in order to facilitate agency compliance with section 7's substantive requirements,[41] section 7(c) indicates that for purposes of section 7 Congress was concerned only with those agency actions likely to affect listed species.

Nevertheless, section 7 contains nothing suggesting that Congress sought to further limit the reach of this section. Therefore, the statutory language suggests that the ESA requires a federal agency to enter into consultation with the Secretary for *all* actions which the agency determines are likely to affect listed species. The 1978 ESA amendments support the above interpretation. The section 7 regulations in effect in 1978 required federal agencies to initiate section 7 consultation for all actions which an agency determined "may affect" a listed species (these regulations remained in effect until 1986).[42] Congress added the section 7(c) biological assessment requirement in 1978 to facilitate agency compliance with section 7. Therefore, statutory language providing that biological assessments are aimed at determining whether an action is "likely to affect" listed species indicates that Congress implicitly adopted a scheme for triggering section 7 consultation similar to that of the regulations in effect at the time. A provision of section 7 added in 1982 suggests that Congress continued to hold this view. The so-called "early

---

39. 16 U.S.C. § 1536(a)(2) (emphasis added).
40. *Id*. at § 1536(c)(1).
41. *See supra* notes 3-5 and accompanying text.
42. *See* 50 C.F.R. § 402.04 (1985) (superceded).

consultation" provision of section 7(a)(3) also requires consultation for actions which will "likely affect" listed species.[43]

2. *The regulatory framework.*

Current section 7 regulations embody more narrow standards for determining when an agency must formally consult with the Secretary than that suggested by the language of the ESA itself. The regulations require that an agency initiate formal consultation with the Secretary if the agency concludes that its actions "may affect" listed species or critical habitat.[44] The regulations also provide, however, that no formal consultation is necessary when an agency determines, after completing a biological assessment or after informal consultation with the Secretary, that its actions are not likely to affect adversely any listed species or critical habitat.[45] The Secretary must concur in writing with the agency's determination.[46]

The current regulatory scheme implements a controversial modification of the previous section 7 regulations' trigger for consultation. The earlier regulations contained no consultation exception for instances where an agency determines an action would not adversely affect listed species.[47] Despite environmental groups' opposition to this change,[48] the Secretary felt it was justified because "[r]egulatory flexibility is appropriate here to eliminate undue burdens."[49] Responding to fears that the "no adverse effect" exception to consultation weakens section 7 protection, the Secretary asserted that requiring the Secretary's written concurrence with an agency's "no adverse effect" determination would adequately insure the integrity of section 7 procedures.[50]

---

43. 16 U.S.C. § 1536(a)(3).

44. 50 C.F.R. § 402.14(a).

45. 50 C.F.R. § 402.14(b)(1).

46. *Id.*

47. Former section 7 regulations required consultation on *all* agency actions which an agency determined "may affect" listed species. *See* 50 C.F.R. § 402.04(a)(1)(1985) (superceded).

48. *See* 51 Fed. Reg. 19,950 (1986) (discussion of proposed change).

49. *Id.*

50. *Id.* The requirement that the Secretary concur with agencies' "no adverse effect" findings was added when revisions of the section 7 regulations were finalized. As originally proposed, the revised section 7 regulations left the determination of whether an agency action's affects on listed species would be "adverse" to the individual agency's discretion. *See* 48 Fed. Reg. 29,994, 29,998 (1983).

The current section 7 regulations also broaden agencies' discretion while reducing their accountability. The regulations do not define what constitutes an "adverse" effect on listed species, apparently leaving the meaning of this term to the discretion of individual federal agencies. Thus, even when the Secretary concurs with an agency's "no adverse effect" finding, interested outside parties have no means to independently evaluate the finding because there is no standard of what constitutes "adverse" effects.

Despite the Secretary's assurances, the regulations' approach to section 7 may deprive listed species of protection by allowing federal agencies, as well as the Secretary, to make decisions based on incomplete biological information. During formal section 7 consultation, federal agencies and the Secretary must "use the best scientific and commercial data available."[51] When informally consulting about whether an agency proposal will adversely affect listed species, however, the agency and the Secretary are not explicitly subject to a similar requirement.[52] If these entities make a "no adverse effect" finding without the best data available, they run a risk that better information could yield different conclusions on how the proposed action would affect listed species, thus warranting closer scrutiny of the action under formal consultation.

The section 7 regulations may also deny interested parties access to information about a project's effects on listed species. While formal consultation requires the Secretary to issue a biological opinion which details how the activity will affect a listed species,[53] the section 7 regulations allow an agency and the Secretary to agree on a "no adverse effect" determination through

---

51. 16 U.S.C. § 1536(a)(2).

52. One could argue that federal agencies and the Secretary are subject to the ESA's "best scientific and commercial data" requirement even when carrying out informal consultation or preparing biological assessments. Both of these activities are aimed at facilitating ultimate compliance with the substantive mandates of section 7(a)(2), i.e., insuring that agency actions do not jeopardize listed species or modify critical habitat. Section 7(a)(2) mandates that agencies fulfilling these requirements use the best scientific and commercial data available. Therefore, procedures and studies occurring outside the context of formal section 7 consultation, but which help to fulfill these mandates, arguably must also use the best information available. Under this view, the section 7 regulations are deficient in failing to specify that the "no adverse effect" finding must be made using the best scientific and commercial data available.

53. 16 U.S.C. § 1536(c)(1).

"informal" consultation.[54] Informal consultation, simply the regulations' term for communication between the Secretary and an action agency prior to formal consultation,[55] is subject to no statutory or regulatory procedural or disclosure requirements. Consequently, the section 7 regulations apparently permit the Secretary and a federal agency to agree on a "no adverse effect" finding with no formal record of their consultation and no explanation of how the action in question will actually impact listed species. This procedure, which in effect shields the section 7 process from outside scrutiny, may thus weaken the effectiveness of citizen suits as an enforcement mechanism for ESA protection.

It is unclear why the Secretary, through the regulatory process, sought to narrow the scope of section 7's consultation requirement. If an agency action obviously would not adversely affect listed species, formal consultation on that action would likely not be complicated, burdensome, or time-consuming. It would presumably be relatively easy for the Secretary to set out the neutral or beneficial effects of the action in a brief biological opinion, allowing the agency to proceed with its proposed action quickly and with confidence that it had satisfied the mandates of section 7. In addition, the Secretary would provide interested parties with information to support the biological opinion's conclusion. Instead, however, the current regulatory scheme for triggering section 7 consultation seems designed to put project expediency above species conservation, contravening Congressional intent that section 7 be "the institutionalization of caution."[56]

Unfortunately, no courts have examined these issues or directly addressed the statutorily required threshold for initiation of formal consultation.[57]

II.   CONFERENCE ON PROPOSED SPECIES AND CRITICAL HABITATS

In 1979, Congress amended section 7 to require that federal agencies "confer" with the Secretary on any agency action likely

---

54. 50 C.F.R. § 402.14(b)(1).

55. *Id.* at § 402.02.

56. H.R. REP. No. 412, 93d Cong., 1st Sess. 5 (1973) (paraphrased).

57. The court in *Romero Barcel v. Brown* interpreted the section 7 regulations then in effect, and held that the Navy violated section 7 by failing to initiate consultation on an action which crossed the "may affect" consultation threshold. 643 F.2d 835, 857 (1st Cir. 1981). The court was not faced with the question of whether this low threshold for consultation is *required* by the ESA itself.

to jeopardize the continued existence of species proposed for listing or any action likely to destroy or adversely modify proposed critical habitat.[58] It is generally up to federal agencies to determine whether their actions may jeopardize proposed species or adversely modify proposed critical habitat and to initiate the conference.[59] The Secretary, however, may request a conference for an agency action which he or she believes triggers the conference requirement.[60]

Section 7 sets out no procedures which the agency or Secretary must follow during the conference. Regulations term the conference "informal discussions" between the agency and Secretary, during which the Secretary recommends ways for the agency to minimize or avoid adverse impacts to proposed species and proposed critical habitat.[61] The regulations also require the Secretary to document conclusions and recommendations resulting from the conference.[62] This conference requirement provides no substantive protection to proposed species.[63]

A. *Procedures During Consultation*

Perhaps the most difficult section 7 procedural questions arise after a federal agency initiates consultation with the Secretary. This section discusses three related issues: (1) the scope of interagency consultation, specifically the question of what constitutes an "agency action," (2) the requirement that agencies use "the best scientific and commercial data available,"[64] and (3) the consultation process under conditions of uncertainty.

1. *Scope of the term "agency action."*

Both section 7 and its implementing regulations broadly define the term "agency action."[65] The meaning of this term is im-

---

58. 16 U.S.C. § 1536(a)(4). Proposed species or critical habitat include only those species and critical habitat formally proposed for protection under the ESA by the Secretary, and published in the Federal Register. *See* 50 C.F.R. § 402.02.

59. *See* 50 C.F.R. § 402.10(6).

60. *Id.*

61. *Id.* at § 402.10(c).

62. *Id.* at § 402.10(e).

63. *See infra* Chapter 7, notes 155, 158-159 and accompanying text.

64. 16 U.S.C. § 1536(a)(2).

65. Section 7 defines "agency action" as "any action authorized, funded, or carried out by [a Federal] agency." 16 U.S.C. § 1536(a)(2). The regulations define "agency action" to mean:

all activities or programs of any kind authorized, funded, or carried out, in

portant because the scope of an agency action determines the scope of both section 7 consultation and the duties consultation imposes upon the agencies involved.

North Slope Borough v. Andrus[66] involved the question of what constitutes an agency action.[67] There, plaintiffs sought to halt offshore oil leasing in the Beaufort Sea, in part to prevent potential harm to endangered whales in the lease area. The Outer Continental Shelf Lands Act (OCSLA)[68] regulates offshore oil development, dividing the process into three distinct segments: (1) lease sale and pre-exploration activities,[69] (2) exploration,[70] and (3) production.[71] Plaintiffs argued that leasing pursuant to the OCSLA was part of a broad agency action ultimately aimed at offshore oil production, and contended that the Secretary[72] was therefore required to initiate section 7 consultation on all three phases of offshore oil development before leasing took place. Defendants, on the other hand, emphasized the OCSLA's segmented approach to offshore oil development and contended that the initial leasing phase constituted a separate agency action for purposes of section 7 and thus was the only activity subject to scrutiny by the court. Additionally, the defendant Secretary pointed out that a preliminary analysis of the second and third steps of the OCSLA process would be largely speculative because the nature of each successive step depends on the outcome of the previous step.

The district court in *North Slope* rejected the government's po-

---

whole or in part, by Federal agencies in the United States or upon the high seas. Examples include but are not limited to: (a) actions intended to conserve listed species or their habitat; (b) the promulgation of regulations; (c) the granting of licenses, contracts, leases, easements, rights-of-way, permits, or grants-in-aid; or (d) actions directly or indirectly causing modifications to the land, water, or air.

50 C.F.R. § 402.02.

66. 486 F. Supp. 332 (D.D.C. 1980), *aff'd*, 642 F.2d 589 (D.C. Cir. 1980).

67. For further discussion of this aspect of the case, see Erdheim, *Insuring the Effectiveness of ESA Section 7*, 9 ECOLOGY L.Q. 629, 673-78 (1981).

68. 43 U.S.C. § 1331. For a general discussion of several OCSLA cases involving endangered species issues, see Comment, *Circuit Courts Give Go-Ahead to OCS Lease Sales Despite Uncertain Effects on Endangered Whales*, 10 Envtl. L. Rep. (Envtl. L. Inst.) 10,210 (1980).

69. 43 U.S.C. § 1337.

70. *Id.* at § 1340.

71. *Id.* at § 1351.

72. The Secretary of the Interior oversees offshore oil exploitation under OCSLA. The National Marine Fisheries Service serves as the expert wildlife agency for consultations involving listed marine species.

sition, concluding that an agency action under the OCSLA consists of the lease sale and all resulting activities. Otherwise, the court reasoned, "any statute providing an agency with maximum flexibility and planning ability—as the OCSLA does—would also tacitly relieve that agency of much of the scrutiny required by the ESA."[73] The court found that the Secretary had a duty to consult with NMFS until adequate information allowed NMFS to issue a biological opinion for the broadly construed agency action. Though the court agreed with the defendants that inadequate information was then available for such an opinion, the court ordered the Secretary to continue research and consultation until NMFS rendered a comprehensive biological opinion covering the full scope of oil development activities, including leasing, exploration, and production.[74]

In the meantime, however, the decision allowed some leasing-related activities to continue, even though lack of a comprehensive biological opinion meant that the Secretary could not insure that offshore oil development in its entirety would not ultimately jeopardize whales.[75] The court permitted "intermediate" activities, including leasing, so long as the Secretary obtained favorable biological opinions based on adequate information for each activity, made no irreversible commitments of resources in violation of section 7(d), and also obtained a finding from NMFS that there was a "reasonable likelihood" that offshore oil development as a whole would not violate section 7(a)(2).[76]

On appeal, the D.C. Circuit purported to agree with the district court's holdings. The appellate court nevertheless phrased its conclusions in somewhat different language. It expressed "qualified agreement" with the district court on the scope of the agency action involved in the case. The appellate court did not

---

73. 486 F. Supp. at 350.

74. *Id.* at 352.

75. *Id.* To support this finding, the court cited language from the legislative history of the 1979 ESA amendments suggesting that agency actions could proceed even in the face of uncertainty over whether the action would ultimately violate section 7's substantive mandates. For a discussion of this legislative history, as well as its various possible interpretations, see Houck, *The "Institutionalization of Caution" Under Section 7 of the Endangered Species Act: What Do You Do When You Don't Know?*, 12 Envtl. L. Rep. (Envtl. L. Inst.) 15,001 (1982).

76. 486 F. Supp. at 353. For a discussion of the section 7(d) issues involved in this case, *see infra* Chapter 7, notes 28-43 and accompanying text. For a further discussion of incremental consultation, see Erdheim, *The Wake of the Snail Darter: Insuring the Effectiveness of Section 7 of the Endangered Species Act*, 9 ECOLOGY L.Q. 629, 675-78 (1981).

address the Secretary's continuing duty to consult until issuance
of a comprehensive biological opinion on the entire agency action. Instead, it cited a First Circuit OCSLA case for the proposition that the ESA and OCSLA were "melded."[77] In so doing, the
court apparently reasoned that compliance with the ESA would
result from environmental safeguards built into both the OCSLA
and the challenged leases themselves, noting that "satisfaction of
the ESA mandate that no endangered life be jeopardized must be
viewed in light of the full contingent of OCSLA checks and balances and all mitigating measures adopted in pursuance
thereof."[78] The court viewed this as "qualify[ing] somewhat the
broadest practical effect the term ["agency action"] could
have."[79]

The appellate opinion in *North Slope* did not expressly address
the district court's scheme for allowing incremental agency action in the face of overall uncertainty regarding a broadly defined
agency action's ultimate effect on listed species. Nevertheless,
the court implicitly upheld the requirement that the Secretary obtain favorable biological opinions before proceeding with intermediate activities by examining the district court's finding that a
NMFS letter did not constitute such a biological opinion on the
challenged lease sale.[80] Apparently, the appellate court approved the district court's procedural requirements that apply
when the potential effects of an agency's actions on listed species
are unknown.

The Ninth Circuit adopted the procedural scheme created by
the district court in *North Slope* in a case also dealing with the
interaction between the ESA and OCSLA.[81] However, in *Conner
v. Burford*[82] it refused to sanction incremental consultation procedures for on-shore oil and gas leasing pursuant to the Mineral
Leasing Act of 1920 (MLA).[83] *Conner* involved U.S. Forest Ser-

---

77. North Slope Borough v. Andrus, 642 F.2d at 608 (citing Conservation Law
Found. v. Andrus, 623 F.2d 712, 715 (1st Cir. 1979)).

78. 642 F.2d at 609.

79. *Id.*

80. The court of appeals reversed the district court's conclusion. *Id.* However,
had the appellate court disagreed with the district court's holding that an intermediate
biological opinion was required, the D.C. Circuit would not have reached this issue.

81. *See* Village of False Pass v. Watt, 565 F. Supp. 1123 (D. Alaska, 1983), *aff'd*,
Village of False Pass v. Clark, 733 F.2d 605 (9th Cir. 1984).

82. 605 F. Supp. 107 (D. Mont. 1985), *aff'd* in part & *rev'd* in part, 848 F.2d 1441
(9th Cir. 1988).

83. 30 U.S.C. § 181.

vice attempts to lease vast areas of two national forests in Montana for oil and gas development. The Forest Service entered into consultation with the Secretary to assess impacts of oil and gas related activities on threatened and endangered species. The Secretary followed the incremental consultation procedural process created by the district court in *North Slope*, issuing a biological opinion which concluded that leasing itself was not likely to jeopardize listed species, but insufficient data was available to evaluate how subsequent activities authorized by the leases might affect protected species. The Secretary noted that additional consultation would take place prior to further phases of oil and gas development. Plaintiffs challenged the lease sales, arguing that the biological opinion was not based on the best data available, and that the ESA required the Secretary to prepare a comprehensive biological opinion considering all stages of oil and gas related activities. Both the district and appellate courts agreed with this position.

The Ninth Circuit began its analysis by adopting the *North Slope* district court's broad definition of "agency action" in an oil and gas leasing context, holding that this term encompassed the leasing process itself as well as oil and gas development and production.[84] The court then rejected the notion that uncertainty surrounding post-leasing activities excused the Secretary's failure to prepare a comprehensive biological opinion on the entire agency action. It found that the post-leasing and biological information that was available to the Secretary permitted a determination of whether post-leasing activities in certain areas would be incompatible with the continued existence of listed species. The court further noted that Congress had created no exception to the ESA's requirement of a comprehensive biological opinion for situations involving inexact information, and cited a First Circuit ESA case for the proposition that "the Secretary may be required to make projections, based on *potential* locations and levels of oil and gas activity, of the impact of production on protected species."[85] The court held that the Secretary violated the ESA by failing to prepare a comprehensive biological opinion on all oil and gas activities using the best available data.[86]

The defendants in *Conner* maintained that the *North Slope* and

---

84. 848 F.2d at 1453.
85. *Id.* at 1454 (emphasis in original).
86. *Id.*

Village of False Pass cases supported their decision to rely on incremental consultation. The Ninth Circuit, however, refused to sanction use of this procedure for oil and gas leasing pursuant to the MLA. That statute, the court found, lacked the "checks and balances" present within the OCSLA upon which the *North Slope* and *Village of False Pass* decisions relied.[87] The court reasoned:

> We seriously doubt that Congress intended to give federal agencies carte blanche to initiate, *prior* to the completion of a biological opinion, any program subject to continued federal control in the absence of *specific* congressional approval such as that embodied in OCSLA.[88]

The court put particular emphasis on the fact that OCSLA itself divided oil and gas activities into three separate phases whereas the MLA did not.[89] It thus held that permitting incremental consultation on oil and gas development under the MLA would eviscerate Congress' intent to give listed species the benefit of the doubt.[90]

Section 7 regulations, promulgated prior to the *Conner* decision, adopt the *North Slope* district court's procedures for consultation involving agency actions, which consist of distinct incremental steps. Federal agencies may request that the Secretary issue a biological opinion for only a portion of an agency action, so long as "the action is authorized by a statute that allows the agency to take incremental steps toward the completion of the action."[91] When the Secretary issues a biological opinion on the intermediate action, the agency may proceed with the action as long as it satisfies the criteria first set forth by the district court in *North Slope*.[92] If the Secretary concludes that any incre-

---

87. *Id.* at 1456.

88. *Id.* at 1457 n.38.

89. *Id.* at 1456 n.37, 1457 n.39.

90. *Id.* at 1454.

91. 50 C.F.R. § 402.14(K). The regulations provide no guidance, however, as to what types of statutes authorize incremental actions. One could interpret this requirement narrowly, limiting incremental consultation to activities authorized by statutes such as the OCSLA, which expressly breaks actions into distinct stages and requires environmental studies and NEPA documentation at each stage. Alternatively, one could broadly view the regulations as allowing incremental consultation whenever a statute mentions more than one phase of an action it authorizes. In light of the *Conner* decision, where the court refused to extend incremental consultation to a statute without OCSLA's "checks and balances," the narrow interpretation is probably the one a court would adopt.

92. Section 7 regulations permit an agency to proceed with an "intermediate" activity, provided that:

ment of an agency action violates section 7(a)(2), that finding also applies to the agency action as a whole and terminates the incremental consultation process.[93]

Despite its incorporation into section 7 regulations, the incremental consultation process set forth by the *North Slope* district court decision seems internally inconsistent even in an OCSLA context. By permitting an increment of a larger agency action to proceed if any agency obtains an "intermediate" biological opinion, the district court essentially defined the term "agency action" to coincide with the incremental activity. Yet, this is precisely the result the court expressly rejected elsewhere in its opinion.[94]

An example serves to illustrate this conflict: Suppose an offshore oil lease sale and oil exploration plan receive favorable intermediate biological opinions and are allowed to take place despite the unknown impact of oil production on endangered whales. Later, however, the Secretary discovers that oil production jeopardizes the whales and halts all activities. In such a case, the agency action, which the court in *North Slope* broadly defined as all leasing-related activities,[95] must be said to jeopardize the whales. Yet, two-thirds of this action, leasing and exploration, would have already taken place. Hence, by allowing leasing and related activities to proceed with intermediate biological opinions, the court in *North Slope* circumvented its own broad notion of agency action. Though the district court's opinion in *North Slope* and the section 7 regulations note that agencies have a continuing obligation to consult with the Secretary on the consequences of their agency actions as a whole, this requirement is virtually meaningless since agencies may carry out much of their

---

(1) The biological opinion does not conclude that the incremental step would violate section 7(a)(2);

(2) The Federal agency continues consultation with respect to the entire action and obtains biological opinions, as required, for each incremental step;

(3) The Federal agency fulfills its continuing obligation to obtain sufficient data upon which to base the final biological opinion on the entire action;

(4) The incremental step does not violate section 7(d) of the Act concerning irreversible or irretrievable commitment of resources; and

(5) There is a reasonable likelihood that the entire action will not violate section 7(a)(2) of the Act.

50 C.F.R. § 402.14(k).

93. *See* 51 Fed. Reg. 19,955 (1986) ("A 'jeopardy' opinion issued at any stage not only applies to that step but to the entire project as well.").

94. *See supra* note 73 and accompanying text.

95. *See supra* note 73 and accompanying text.

actions in the meantime in smaller increments on the basis of intermediate biological opinions.[96]

The incremental consultation process created by the district court in *North Slope* and adopted by the section 7 regulations also weakens protection section 7 affords to listed species. As an action progresses stage by stage, alternatives to the action become increasingly narrow.[97] Oil and gas leasing provides a good example. Leases grant their holders certain legal rights which depend on the terms of each lease. On the other hand, prior to leasing the agency may have many options to insure that eventual oil production would not adversely affect listed species. These options include not leasing sensitive areas, restrictive stipulations, or ultimately, lease cancellation.[98]

Actions allowed to proceed incrementally also build momentum toward completion, making it difficult as a practical matter to halt a nearly completed activity even if it may harm listed species. Allowing agency actions to proceed in segments despite uncertainty over their ultimate effects on listed species, charac-

---

96. The district court in *North Slope* apparently attempted to avoid this criticism by requiring biological opinions for increments of agency actions to include speculation as to whether there is a "reasonable likelihood" that the agency action as a whole would violate section 7(a)(2)'s substantive mandates. This procedure is of little value for two reasons. First, section 7 requires federal agencies, in consultation with the Secretary, to *insure* that their actions are not likely to violate section 7(a)(2). A finding that an agency action is reasonably likely to comply with section 7(a)(2) falls far short of this statutory standard. More practically, the *North Slope* court created incremental consultation in response to situations where inadequate information hampers preparation of biological opinions for broadly defined agency actions. Hence, any finding on the ultimate effects of such agency actions would necessarily be almost complete conjecture.

97. For a discussion of the potential dangers of incremental consultation applied outside the context of oil and gas leasing, see Luhn, *The Effectiveness of Judicial Review Under the 1979 Amendment to the Endangered Species Act*, 7 J. OF ENERGY L. & POL'Y 145, 159-62 (1986).

98. Courts have recognized that early identification of possible conflicts between agency actions and species protection makes it easier to formulate alternatives. *See, e.g.*, State of California v. Watt, 683 F.2d 1253, 1260 (9th Cir. 1982), *rev'd* in part, 464 U.S. 313 (1984); Village of False Pass v. Watt, 565 F. Supp. 1123 (D. Alaska 1983), *aff'd*, Village of False Pass v. Clark, 733 F.2d 605 (9th Cir. 1984).

On the other hand, the court in *False Pass* also noted that when the ultimate impacts of an action on listed species are uncertain, allowing the action to take place in increments will enable formulation of alternatives based on an expanding base of relevant data, rather than an abstraction and speculation. Village of False Pass v. Watt, 565 F. Supp. at 1157. Yet, this view fails to consider that an alternative suggested by new data may be foreclosed due to the advanced stage of an action. Thus the court's reasoning poses a "Catch-22" situation: concrete data allows agencies to formulate realistic alternatives to their actions, but such data may only be available when it is too late to implement these alternatives.

terized by one commentator as the "full-steam-ahead" approach,[99] creates such momentum.

2. *Best Scientific and Commercial Data Available.*

During section 7 consultation, the ESA requires both federal agencies and the Secretary to use the "best scientific and commercial data available."[100] Though neither the statute itself nor the section 7 regulations define this term, its meaning has been construed by the courts.

In *Roosevelt Campobello International Park Commission v. Environmental Protection Agency*,[101] environmental groups challenged the EPA Administrator's decision to issue a National Pollutant Discharge Elimination System (NPDES) permit to a company proposing to build an oil refinery and deep water supertanker terminal in northern Maine. The First Circuit Court of Appeals held that the EPA had not adequately analyzed risks to endangered marine species using the best scientific data available. The court found that the ESA's requirement to use the best scientific data available applies "not only to such matters as the presence, vulnerability and criticality of the endangered species but also to the likelihood of an occurrence that might jeopardize it. We see no basis for requiring a first class effort on the former and not on the latter."[102] The court set aside the NPDES permit on the ground that a proposed study that would have "contribute[d] a more precise appreciation of risks" posed by the project was not carried out.[103] Although the Coast Guard acknowledged that the proposed study was important in determining whether oil spills would occur, the agency nevertheless refused to conduct the study due to limited funds. The court found this position inconsistent with the Supreme Court's statement in *TVA v. Hill* that the ESA was meant to protect listed species, "regardless of the cost."[104] The court concluded that:

It may very well be that, after conducting real time simulation

---

99. Houck, *supra* note 75, at 15,008.
100. 16 U.S.C. § 1536(a)(2). Though discussed in this chapter, the statutory requirement to use the best scientific and commercial data available is substantive as well as procedural. *See* Conservation Law Found. v. Watt, 560 F. Supp. 561, 573 (1st Cir. 1979).
101. 684 F.2d 1041 (1st Cir. 1982).
102. *Id.* at 1052 n.9.
103. *Id.* at 1055.
104. *Id.* at 1053 (quoting TVA v. Hill, 437 U.S. 153, 188 n.34 (1978)).

studies and any other tests and studies which are suggested by
the best available science and technology, the most informed
judgment of risk of a major oil spill will still have a large component of estimate, its quantitative element being incapable of
precise verification. But at least the EPA will have done all that
was practicable prior to approving a project with such potentially grave environmental costs.[105]

A federal district court relied heavily on *Roosevelt Campobello* in
deciding a case involving OCSLA lease sales.[106] There, plaintiffs
charged that three ongoing studies examining the effects of oil
development on endangered marine species were ignored by the
NMFS in issuing its biological opinion on the lease sale. In halting the sale, the court held that the Secretary of the Interior, by
ignoring the studies, did not do everything practicable to evaluate risks to listed species posed by the sales.[107] The court expressly rejected the defendants' argument that data to be
generated by the studies in the future was not "available" for inclusion in the biological opinion within the meaning of section 7
because the studies were incomplete. The court reasoned that
such an argument misconstrued the Secretary's obligation under
the terms of the ESA. It found the studies to be "demonstrably
feasible" and unquestionably relevant to the proposed lease
sales.[108] Implying that the Secretary must delay his decision on
leases until relevant studies were completed, the court concluded
that the Secretary had erred by not taking the ongoing studies
into account in his decision-making process.[109]

Two additional cases involved challenges to the adequacy of

---

105. *Id.* at 1055.
106. Conservation Law Found. v. Watt, 560 F. Supp. 561 (D. Mass. 1983), *aff'd on other grounds*, 716 F.2d 946, *dismissed as moot*, 586 F. Supp. 1238.
107. *Id.* at 572. The court also held that the Secretary's failure to comply with the ESA's procedural requirement to use the best data available constituted a substantive violation of the Act. *Id.* at 573. The court found that the Secretary had not used "all methods and procedures" at his disposal to insure protection of listed species in violation of his duty to conserve species pursuant to 16 U.S.C. § 1531(c), and further implied that the Secretary had failed to insure against jeopardy to listed species as required by section 7(a)(2). *Id. See also* Thomas v. Peterson, 753 F.2d 754, 764 (9th Cir. 1985) (equating procedural ESA violations with substantive violations of the statute).
108. 560 F. Supp. at 572.
109. The court specifically noted, however, that substantial information then in existence conflicted with the biological opinion and EIS for the lease sales. *Id.* at 572-73. It further observed that the Secretary was aware of the ongoing studies, which had been commissioned prior to issuance of the final EIS. *Id.* The court thus did not decide whether section 7 requires agencies to initiate *new* studies analyzing an action's effects on endangered species if existing data were scarce or inadequate. *See infra* notes 119-124 and accompanying text.

data cited in biological opinions to support findings that the activities in question did not jeopardize the continued existence of listed species. In *Stop H-3 Association v. Dole*,[110] the court conceded that the challenged biological opinion was based on "weak" evidence.[111] Nevertheless, the court noted that although plaintiffs produced testimony which contradicted the biological opinion's conclusions, they did not present any data which FWS had not already evaluated.[112] Applying the "arbitrary and capricious" standard of review, the court upheld the biological opinion's conclusions. *Friends of Endangered Species v. Jantzen* followed a nearly identical pattern.[113]

Though these cases shed light on section 7's requirement to use the "best scientific and commercial data available," they also raise difficult questions. The clearest interpretation of section 7's data requirement, illustrated by the decisions in *Stop H-3* and *Friends of Endangered Species*, is that reviewing courts will presume that agencies engaged in consultation have used the best data available unless parties challenging the consultation can point to data not considered by the agencies. These two cases also demonstrate that courts will defer to an agency's interpretation of data unless the interpretation is arbitrary.[114]

Courts appear to adopt a relevancy test to determine what constitutes the "best scientific and commercial data." To fall within this category for a given section 7 consultation, the data must be relevant to whether the agency action in question jeopardizes listed species or destroys or adversely modifies critical habitat. Though this requirement seems obvious, the difficulty lies in determining whether the data is in fact relevant. Data is clearly relevant when the agencies involved in consultation admit this fact, as was the case in *Roosevelt Campobello*.[115] It is unclear, however, what happens when federal agencies and outside parties dispute the relevancy of particular data. Will courts make independent determinations of relevancy, or will the judiciary defer to agencies' findings as to whether data is relevant? Case law

---

110. 740 F.2d 1442 (9th Cir. 1984), *cert. denied*, Yamasaki v. Stop H-3 Assoc., 471 U.S. 1108 (1985).

111. *Id.* at 1460.

112. *Id.*

113. 760 F.2d 976 (9th Cir. 1985).

114. *See supra* Chapter 9, notes 79-84 and accompanying text.

115. 684 F.2d at 1053. The Coast Guard admitted that data from a proposed study would be important in determining the risk of a large oil spill.

is inconclusive. In *Conservation Law Foundation v. Watt*, the court simply asserted that studies not considered by the federal defendants were relevant to a jeopardy determination.[116] Nothing in the opinion, however, suggests that the defendants argued that the studies were *not* relevant.

Additionally, whether relevant data is "available" within the meaning of section 7 is in itself a complex question. Of course, the feasibility of obtaining certain data plays a key role in determining whether such data is available. The court in *Conservation Law Foundation v. Watt* specifically noted that relevant studies not considered by defendants were "demonstrably feasible."[117] Significantly, the *Roosevelt Campobello* court expressly rejected an argument that a study was not feasible due to cost constraints.[118]

A harder availability question is whether data that may be generated at some point in the future falls within section 7's definition of available data. Under certain circumstances at least, the answer to this question appears to be affirmative. In *Roosevelt Campobello*, the court overturned the EPA's grant of a NPDES permit until the agency initiated and completed studies it acknowledged were important.[119] Similarly, the court in *Conservation Law Foundation v. Watt* expressly rejected defendants' argument that the conclusions of ongoing studies being conducted by entities not involved in the section 7 consultation were not "available" for purposes of section 7.[120] It is unclear, however, whether these courts would have reached the same results if the studies involved would have taken several years or more to complete. The time necessary to complete these studies, however, should be irrelevant because delay is simply one of the costs of the studies, and the court in *Roosevelt Campobello* rejected cost as a viable constraint.[121]

---

116. 560 F. Supp. at 572.

117. *Id.*

118. 684 F.2d at 1052, 1053. On the other hand, if a federal agency argued that a study was not feasible because scientists lacked the knowledge to devise a way to study a certain question, a court likely would defer to the agency's finding. Unlike relevancy, which is basically a legal term, feasibility is usually a scientific question and thus not within a court's competence to decide.

119. 684 F.2d at 1053.

120. 560 F. Supp. at 572, 573.

121. If a court characterized delay as one of the "costs" of relevant studies, the time necessary to complete the studies would be immaterial under the reasoning of the *Roosevelt Campobello* decision, which rejected costs as limiting agencies' duty to use the best information available. *See* 684 F.2d at 1052, 1053.

In both *Roosevelt Campobello* and *Conservation Law Foundation v. Watt*, the defendants essentially admitted that they needed more information to reach a reliable conclusion as to whether the controversial actions would jeopardize listed species.[122] If, on the other hand, the agencies had asserted that they possessed sufficient information to make this determination, it is not clear whether the respective courts would have interpreted section 7 to require the agencies to delay action until other studies were completed, even if the defendants conceded that further studies would be relevant. Indeed, courts may hesitate to take such a position for fear of delaying agency actions indefinitely while opponents pointed to relevant, though not yet completed, studies. Therefore, courts are likely to construe data to be developed in the future as "available" for purposes of section 7 only if, after consultation, an action agency[123] cannot determine with sufficient certainty[124] that its actions will not violate section 7(a)(2)'s substantive mandates.

3. *Uncertainty.*

Related to section 7's requirement to use the best data available is the question of how a lack of available data at the time a federal agency initiates consultation affects the consultation process itself.[125] Uncertainty during section 7 consultation has different implications for expert wildlife agencies, which provide biological opinions, and action agencies, which ultimately decide

---

122. In *Roosevelt Campobello*, the Coast Guard admitted that a real time simulation study was necessary to do a meaningful oil spill risk analysis. 684 F.2d at 1,053. In *Conservation Law Foundation v. Watt*, NMFS concluded in its biological opinion that it was "unable to identify a threshold of [outer continental shelf] activities . . . that would result in significant impacts to listed marine species." 560 F. Supp. at 573.

123. Regardless of the conclusions of the biological opinion for an agency proposal, the federal agency proposing to carry out an activity makes the final decision on whether to proceed.

124. Section 7 sets a high standard of certainty. Agencies must "insure" that their actions are not likely to jeopardize listed species or destroy or adversely modify critical habitat, although addition of the phrase "not likely to" in 1979 may have weakened this standard. *See infra* Chapter 7, notes 97-116 and accompanying text.

125. *See generally* Erdheim, *supra* note 76 at 660-63 (analysis of whether an agency can be said to have complied with section 7(a)(2) when there is not sufficient information to issue a biological opinion); Comment, *Circuit Courts Give Go Ahead to OCS Lease Sales Despite Uncertain Effects on Endangered Whales*, 10 Envtl. L. Rep. (Envtl. L. Inst.) 10,210 (1980) (concerning the effect of lack of information involving challenges to OCSLA lease sales).

whether to carry out their proposed activities in light of section 7's requirements.

When data available during consultation does not permit the Secretary to make a reliable prediction as to whether a project will jeopardize listed species or destroy critical habitat, it is not certain whether the Secretary may issue a "best guess" biological opinion[126] based on whatever information is then available, or whether the Secretary must refrain from issuing a biological opinion until he or she acquires sufficient data for a dependable conclusion.

When confronted with this type of situation, the district court in *North Slope* found that "the duty to consult is not fulfilled until a biological opinion based on adequate information exists."[127] To support this holding, the court cited language from the conference committee report accompanying the 1979 ESA amendments.[128] Citing the same language,[129] however, the Secretary promulgated regulations[130] which require the FWS and the NMFS to issue biological opinions based on whatever information is available at the end of the time period for consultation suggested by section 7,[131] unless an action agency expressly agrees to extend consultation. This, in effect, gives federal agen-

---

126. *See generally* Houck, *supra* note 75.

127. 486 F. Supp. at 352.

128. That report contains the following often cited paragraph discussing the addition of the phrase "not likely to" to section 7(a)(2):

As currently written, however, the law could be interpreted to force the Fish and Wildlife Service and the National Marine Fisheries Service to issue negative biological opinions whenever the action agency cannot guarantee with certainty that the agency action will not jeopardize the continued existence of the listed species or adversely modify its critical habitat. The amendment will permit the wildlife agencies to frame their section 7(b) opinions on the best evidence that is available or can be developed during consultation. If the biological opinion is rendered on the basis of inadequate information then the Federal agency has a continuing obligation to make a reasonable effort to develop that information.

H.R. COMM. REP. NO. 697, 96th Cong., 1st Sess. 12, *reprinted in* 1979 U.S. CODE CONG. & ADMIN. NEWS 4780. For actions taken in incremental steps, however, the court permitted the Secretary to speculate, on the basis of admittedly inadequate data, whether there was a "reasonable likelihood" that the action would not violate Section 7(a)(2). *See supra* text accompanying note 76.

129. 51 Fed. Reg. 19,951 (1986).

130. 50 C.F.R. § 402.14(e) and (f).

131. Section 7 provides that consultation between a federal agency and the Secretary terminates after 90 days unless the agency and the Secretary mutually agree to extend this time period. 16 U.S.C. § 1536(b)(1)(A). When a non-federal applicant is involved, the procedure is somewhat different. *See id.* at § 1536(b)(1)(B).

cies power to force the Secretary to issue a "best guess" biological opinion by refusing to agree to an extension of formal consultation.

The section 7 regulatory scheme thus raises questions about an action agency's responsibilities during consultation when only inadequate information exists. May action agencies refuse to agree to an extension of consultation and still fulfill their duty to insure that their actions do not jeopardize listed species or destroy critical habitat? Does a favorable biological opinion based on admittedly insufficient information mean that an action agency has completely satisfied its section 7 obligations?

Legislative history and case law provide partial answers. Congress noted that action agencies have a "continuing obligation" to develop more data, even after the Secretary issues a "best guess" biological opinion.[132] This ongoing obligation apparently arises from two related section 7 requirements. First, agencies must "insure" that their actions comply with section 7, a standard difficult to satisfy under conditions of uncertainty.[133] Second, the *Roosevelt Campobello* court found that section 7's mandate to use the best data available requires action agencies to do everything "practicable" to obtain determinative information about the projects' impacts on listed species and critical habitats.[134] Unfortunately, however, neither Congress nor the court in *Roosevelt Campobello* mention whether an action agency must continue consultation with the Secretary and obtain a biological opinion based on the additional information it develops.[135]

The district court in *North Slope* settled this issue by holding that an agency has not satisfied its section 7 duties until the Secretary issues a biological opinion based on adequate data.[136] This approach seems most consonant with the purposes which underlie section 7's procedural scheme. Consultation between action agencies and expert wildlife agencies provides the former with an independent, expert interpretation of biological data, as well as presumably unbiased opinions of whether action agencies' projects comply with section 7's substantive commands.

---

132. *See infra* Chapter 7, note 104 and accompanying text.

133. *See supra* notes 122-24 and accompanying text.

134. *See supra* note 105 and accompanying text.

135. It is thus also unclear whether section 7(d)'s limit on the commitment of resources remains in effect, since this limitation terminates when a comprehensive biological opinion is issued.

136. *See supra* note 127 and accompanying text.

These benefits are lost if agencies have no duty to obtain a bio-logical opinion based on information they develop while discharging their "continuing obligation" to collect data in the face of uncertainty.[137]

The foregoing discussion assumes a scenario in which sufficient information—in statutory terms "the best scientific and commercial data available"—does not exist at the end of the ninety days section 7 allots for consultation.[138] This scenario obviously occurs when an action agency acknowledges a lack of needed data or the Secretary issues a biological opinion which admittedly amounts to merely a guess as to whether a proposal complies with section 7.[139] Lacking such admissions, however, it is unclear whether the Secretary or the action agency decides whether sufficient information exists to allow the Secretary to issue a "comprehensive" biological opinion.[140] Phrased differently, who decides whether a biological opinion is based on the "best scientific and commercial data available"?

Section 7 regulations apparently leave this determination to the action agency. The regulations permit the Secretary to request an extension of consultation and further data, but also allow the agency involved to refuse.[141] The regulations expressly note that the Secretary's request should not be construed as expressing an opinion that the action agency has not satisfied section 7's requirement to use the best data available.[142]

This regulatory scheme does not comport with the ESA itself. Section 7 gives the Secretary and action agencies concurrent responsibilities to use the best data available. Action agencies bear the burden of providing the Secretary with biological data to sat-

---

137. Perhaps of utmost importance, a requirement that agencies obtain biological opinions based on further data implies that section 7(d) prohibits action agencies from making any irreversible or irretrievable resource commitments while discharging their continuing obligation to obtain complete data about how projects affect listed species. This restriction thus gives agencies an incentive to vigorously collect more data which may otherwise be lacking.

138. Case law makes it clear that information is not necessarily unavailable for the purposes of Section 7 simply because it will not exist until some point in the future. *See supra* text accompanying notes 119-127.

139. Such was the case in *Roosevelt Campobello*, 684 F.2d 1041 (1st Cir. 1982), and *Conservation Law Foundation v. Watt*, 560 F. Supp. 561 (D. Mass. 1983).

140. *See North Slope*, 486 F. Supp. at 352 ("Consultation must also be continued until a comprehensive biological opinion satisfying the mandate of 7(b) is developed.").

141. 50 C.F.R. § 402.14(f).

142. *Id.*

isfy this requirement.[143] To the extent that data requested by the Secretary is relevant and feasible to obtain, it falls within the meaning of the "best scientific and commercial data available."[144] Therefore, an action agency's failure to provide requested data or agree on extension of consultation to allow time for the Secretary to interpret existing data arguably would violate the agency's section 7 duty to provide the best available data, as well as force the Secretary to issue a biological opinion which is not based on the best available data. Additionally, expert wildlife agencies presumably are more qualified than other federal agencies to determine what data is necessary to evaluate impacts on listed species.

For the reasons discussed above, the Secretary—rather than action agencies—clearly should decide when adequate information exists to formulate a comprehensive biological opinion. If the Secretary determined in a given instance that adequate information did not exist, this finding would presumably trigger the action agency's continuing responsibility to develop more data.[145] After the agency submitted further data, the Secretary would then issue a comprehensive biological opinion.[146]

Involvement of a non-federal applicant in the section 7 process substantially affects the procedures discussed above. Section 7 requires the Secretary to obtain the consent of a permit or license applicant prior to extending consultation to over 150 days after its initiation.[147] Thus, an applicant apparently can force the Secretary to issue a biological opinion based on inadequate data by refusing to consent to a longer consultation period if one is needed to gather more information. Unlike federal agencies, applicants have no responsibilities under section 7, and thus there are apparently no statutory constraints on applicants' ability to withhold such consent.

---

143. *Id.*

144. *See supra* text accompanying notes 115-124.

145. *See supra* note 128.

146. Under this interpretation of section 7, biological opinions based on inadequate data—so-called "best guess" biological opinions—are allowed by section 7 in three situations: (1) when necessary biological data is not scientifically feasible to obtain and thus not "available," (2) when the Secretary speculates whether there is a "reasonable likelihood" of ultimate section 7 compliance during incremental consultation, as created by the *North Slope* decision, and (3) when a non-federal applicant is involved.

147. 16 U.S.C. § 1536(b)(1)(B).

III. REINITIATION OF CONSULTATION

Section 7 regulations require reinitiation of formal consultation between a federal agency and the Secretary if a project that was previously the subject of consultation is modified so that it affects listed species or critical habitats in a way not considered in the previous biological opinion, or if new information reveals effects not previously considered during the consultation.[148] The regulations also require renewed section 7 consultation if a project exceeds the anticipated level of incidental taking, or if a new species is listed, or new critical habitat is designated that may be affected by a project previously subject to consultation.[149]

The Supreme Court in *TVA v. Hill* made it clear that section 7 applies to ongoing, as well as to proposed, federal activities.[150] Therefore, the consultation reinitiation requirements discussed above apply whenever a federal agency retains discretionary involvement with an ongoing action, or when federal intervention in such an action is authorized by law.[151]

In *Pacific Legal Foundation v. Watt*,[152] the plaintiff argued that the defendant federal agency unlawfully failed to reinitiate section 7 consultation with the Secretary after modifying the project in dispute. The federal agency had, however, obtained concurrence from the Secretary that no further consultation was needed. The court dismissed the plaintiff's ESA claim, noting that "[d]eference is due the view of the consulted agency that the prior determinations sufficed."[153]

Sierra Club v. Marsh[154] presented a situation virtually opposite to that in *Pacific Legal Foundation*. There, the U.S. Army Corps of Engineers refused to reinitiate consultation with the Secretary concerning one of its projects, even after the Secretary requested that it do so. In agreeing with the Secretary's conclusion that new information revealed that the project could have effects on listed species not previously considered in the consultation process, the court explained that it was "defer[ing] to the agency

---

148. 50 C.F.R. § 402.16.

149. *Id.*

150. TVA v. Hill, 437 U.S. 153, 180 (1977).

151. *See* 50 C.F.R. § 402.16

152. 539 F. Supp. 841 (C.D. Cal. 1982), *aff'd*, 703 F.2d 576 (9th Cir. 1983), *reh'g denied*, 711 F.2d 1065.

153. *Id.*

154. 816 F.2d 1376 (9th Cir. 1987).

with the more appropriate expertise."[155] The court thus held that the Corps had violated the ESA by failing to reinitiate consultation. This decision means that federal agencies lack discretion to refuse a request from the Secretary to reinitiate consultation.

The *Pacific Legal Foundation* and *Sierra Club v. Marsh* decisions represent the two extremes in disputes over reinitiation of consultation. A situation between these extremes would occur if a plaintiff challenged an agency's decision on whether to reinitiate consultation and the Secretary had neither requested renewed consultation or endorsed the agency's decision not to reinitiate the consultation process. In such an instance, a court would have no expert opinion to which it could defer. Thus, if faced with this type of situation, a court would likely make an independent factual determination of whether new information warranted renewed consultation, considering evidence presented by both the plaintiffs and the agency involved. This is the review standard courts generally apply in ruling on alleged procedural ESA violations.[156]

IV. EXEMPTION PROCEDURES

Section 7's exemption provisions[157] have two particularly noteworthy aspects. First, the section 7 exemption scheme includes the most complex procedures set forth in the ESA. Since its creation in 1978, however, the ESA's exemption mechanism has remained virtually unused.

The exemption scheme's procedural maze is Congress's version of due process for a species essentially on trial for its very existence.[158] Among these procedures, it is particularly noteworthy that Congress made granting a section 7 exemption contingent on a finding that the federal agency or applicant involved did not make irreversible or irretrievable commitments of resources in violation of section 7(d),[159] and made the performance

---

155. *Id.* at 1388.

156. *See generally* Chapter 9 for a discussion of standards of judicial review under the ESA.

157. 16 U.S.C. § 1536(e), (n)-(p).

158. For further discussion and explanation of some of these complex procedures, see Coggins & Russell, *Beyond Shooting Snail Darters in Pork Barrels: The Endangered Species and Land Use in America*, 70 GEO. L. J. 1433, 1485-95 (1982); *The 1978 Amendments to the Endangered Species Act*, 9 Envtl. L. Rep. (Envtl. L. Inst.) 10,031 (1979).

159. 16 U.S.C. § 1536(h)(1)(A)(iv).

of a biological assessment a prerequisite to a permanent exemption.[160] These requirements demonstrate that Congress viewed both strict adherence to section 7(d) and preparation of biological assessments pursuant to section 7(c) as extremely important and provides evidence to contradict narrow interpretations of these requirements adopted by courts or regulations.

Only three applications for section 7 exemptions have been filed to date, all within a year of the 1978 ESA amendments.[161] Non-use of the exemption scheme raises the question of whether this scheme is largely ignored simply because no federal actions or federally authorized actions have faced an unresolvable conflict with the survival of a listed species, or whether resolutions of such conflicts now take place in the context of other ESA procedures. There is evidence that the latter may occur to some degree.[162]

---

160. *Id.* at § 1536(h)(2)(A). A permanent exemption remains in force for a particular federal action regardless of the listing of additional species present in the area, whereas an ordinary exemption only applies to the species involved in the section 7 consultation preceding the exemption application. *See* 51 Fed. Reg. 19,945 (1986).

161. The Endangered Species Committee, in a decision later overturned by Congress, unanimously denied an exemption for the Tellico Dam. The Committee granted an exemption for the Grayrocks Dam, with provisions for mitigating damage to whooping crane habitat. A third application was merely an applicant's implicit challenge to a FWS biological opinion, and EPA refusal to grant a permit. For further discussion of these cases, see *The 1978 Amendments to the Endangered Species Act*, 9 Envtl. L. Rep. (Envtl. L. Inst.) 10,031 (1979).

162. For example, section 4(b)(2) gives the Secretary discretion to take economic impacts into account when designating critical habitats, despite the fact that this procedure seems anomalous in light of the restrictive exemption process. *See supra* Chapter 3, notes 109-115 and accompanying text. Additionally, scientific uncertainty can mask decisions based largely on politics rather than biology. *See* S. YAFFEE, PROHIBITIVE POLICY: IMPLEMENTING THE FEDERAL ENDANGERED SPECIES ACT 86-148 (1982).

Chapter 7

Substantive Protections of Section 7: Avoiding Jeopardy and Habitat Destruction

This chapter examines the substantive constraints section 7 imposes on federal agencies, where Congress and the Secretary have drawn the line between permitted and forbidden activities in order to conserve threatened and endangered species. It considers factors federal agencies, in consultation with the Secretary, must weigh in determining whether their actions comply with section 7's substantive requirements. This chapter also discusses the statutory and regulatory limitations on the conduct of federal agencies, licensees, and permittees during the initial phases of a federally funded or authorized project.

I. LIMITATIONS ON COMMITMENTS OF RESOURCES

A. *The Tellico Dam Controversy*

In the mid 1970's, the Tennessee Valley Authority (TVA) continued to construct Tellico Dam, despite the fact that the Secretary of the Interior had listed snail darters as endangered and had designated the area to be flooded by the dam as the fishes' critical habitat.[1] When TVA's actions were challenged in court, the agency argued that continued congressional commitments of resources to the project, after the threats it posed to the snail darter became known, effectively excepted TVA from the need to comply with the substantive provisions of section 7.[2] The case captured the attention of the media, which pointed out that saving the obscure species of minnow would cost taxpayers over $100 million, the amount of money already invested in the par-

---

1. Tennessee Valley Authority v. Hill, 437 U.S. 153 (1978) [hereinafter TVA v. Hill].
2. *Id.*

tially completed dam.[3]

The uproar surrounding the Tellico Dam case convinced Congress of the importance of resolving or preventing potential conflicts between listed species and federal projects at the earliest possible moment.[4] Congress realized that many federal projects, once begun, were extremely difficult to halt, especially when agencies committed public resources to such endeavors and created expectations on the part of people or entities who stood to benefit from federal projects, permits, or licenses. As a direct result of the Tellico Dam controversy, lawmakers enacted section 7(d)[5] in 1978[6] to prevent federal agencies and advocates of specific federal actions from "steamrolling"[7] those actions to completion, regardless of their impacts on listed species. Congress also made section 7 exemptions contingent upon compliance with section 7(d)'s limits on commitment of economic resources to prevent project advocates from citing "sunk costs" as reasons for granting exemptions.[8]

B.   *Section 7(d)*

   1.   *Irreversible or irretrievable commitment of resources.*

Section 7(d) prohibits federal agencies as well as federal permittees and licensees from making "any irreversible or irretrievable commitment of resources . . . which has the effect of foreclosing the formulation or implementation of any reasonable and prudent alternatives which would not violate subsection (a)(2)."[9] Subsection (a)(2) prohibits actions that jeopardize the

---

3. One magazine article satirically predicted the opening of the "Tellico Dam All-Weather Outdoor Drive-In Movie Theatre" as a constructive use of the 400-foot high concrete slab, if impoundment of the Little Tennessee River was enjoined to protect snail darters. *See* S. YAFFEE, PROHIBITIVE POLICY: IMPLEMENTING THE FEDERAL ENDANGERED SPECIES ACT 143 (1982).

4. *See* 124 CONG. REC. S21,131-S21,135 (July 17, 1978) (statement of Senator Culver) [hereinafter Culver Statement].

5. 16 U.S.C. § 1536(d).

6. Section 7(d) codified FWS regulations enacted earlier in 1978, which prohibited irreversible and irretrievable commitments of resources and which precluded adoption of alternatives inconsistent with the mandates of section 7. *See* 43 Fed. Reg. 875 (1978), 50 C.F.R. § 402.04(a)(3) (superseded).

7. *See* North Slope Borough v. Andrus, 486 F. Supp. 332, 356 (D.D.C. 1980), *aff'd*, 642 F.2d 589 (D.C. Cir. 1980).

8. *Id.* at 355 n.80 (quoting a House of Representatives report on the 1978 ESA amendments).

9. 16 U.S.C. § 1536(d). *See also id.* at § 1536(a)(2). Even though the phrase "irreversible or irretrievable" within this provision is cast in the disjunctive tense, courts

continued existence of listed species or that destroy or adversely modify critical habitat. It is important to note that this mandate does not absolutely prohibit agencies from making resource commitments even in the face of uncertainty over the proposed actions' effects on listed species—section 7(d) outlaws only "irreversible" or "irretrievable" resource commitments. Neither the ESA itself nor section 7 regulations define these terms. Therefore, a key question is what sort of resource commitments are reversible or retrievable.

The question of whether a resource commitment is reversible within the meaning of section 7(d) appears to be relatively straightfoward. A resource commitment is clearly reversible if the status quo could be restored at no cost. For example, awarding a contract is a resource commitment, but that commitment is reversible if the contract is subject to cancellation without compensation.[10] Conversely, Congressional concern over avoiding situations like the Tellico Dam controversy, where the federal agency faced having to abandon a project after already spending a great deal of money, suggests that a commitment of resources is not reversible if returning to the status quo entails costs to a federal agency or applicant. Thus, a contract subject to cancellation only upon some type of compensation would be irreversible; similarly, beginning construction of a project would be an irreversible resource commitment even if subsequent work could restore the site to its original condition. The district court's opinion in *North Slope Borough v. Andrus*,[11] applying section 7(d), implicitly equated a retrievable resource commitment with one that was "salvageable." The court then created a two-part test to determine whether a given resource commitment is salvageable. This test considered (1) whether the resources expended could be used in a manner different from the one proposed in the original plan, or (2) whether the resources could be devoted to another project altogether—provided that neither of these alternate resource uses violated section 7(a)(2).[12] For example, section

---

apparently have interpreted it as if phrased conjunctively. Thus, courts have found no violation of section 7(d) where agency resource commitments, though irreversible, were found to be retrievable or "salvageable." *See infra* notes 23-45 and accompanying text.

10. This assumes one does not consider the transaction costs involved in drafting and evaluating the contract.

11. 486 F. Supp. 332 (D.D.C. 1980), *aff'd*, 642 F.2d 589 (D.C. Cir. 1980).

12. *Id.* at 356. Remarks by Senator Culver in 1978 support the court's notion that the independent utility of the resource expenditure need not be related to the original

7(d) may not prohibit acquisition of land for a damsite because the government could designate the land as a wildlife refuge if the ESA ultimately prevents construction of the dam itself.

One could push this notion of salvageability to the extreme by arguing that section 7(d) does not prohibit construction of a dam, even if it may later have to be abandoned due to its adverse impact on listed species, because the structure itself has independent utility as art or perhaps as a giant drive-in movie screen.[13] This seemingly absurd notion raises an important point. An otherwise useless dam may indeed have utility as a movie screen, though that utility would obviously not be commensurate with the millions of dollars it cost to build the structure. Therefore, the salvageability notion inherent in section 7(d) must implicitly embody a "relative value test." Under such a test, a commitment of resources is retrievable only if the value of those resources in their potential alternatives uses is reasonably similar to the value of the resources in their intended use.[14]

2. *The "Effect of Foreclosing" standard.*

Despite limits on what is considered salvageable, allowing resource commitments as long as they are somehow reversible or retrievable seems somewhat at odds with Congress' purpose in enacting section 7(d)—namely to prevent completion of projects through steamrolling. For instance, even though land acquired for a dam and reservoir could theoretically serve as a wildlife refuge if a conflict with a listed species later develops, the acquisition of land to begin the project would undoubtedly raise the expectations of members of local communities who stood to benefit from the dam. These people would probably apply political pressure against attempts to curtail the project. In addition, bureaucratic inertia tends to resist radical changes in plans. These forces could conceivably prompt a reevaluation of the project's effects on protected species and could potentially succeed in pushing the project to completion despite threats to listed species.[15]

---

purpose: "It may be feasible to utilize resources already expended or lands acquired for a proposed action to carry out alternatives, such as the development of parks or wildlife refuges, which are unrelated to the initial project." Culver Statement, *supra* note 4.

13. *See* S. YAFFEE, *supra* note 3, at 143.

14. *See* Erdheim, *The Wake of the Snail Darter: Insuring the Effectiveness of Section 7 of the Endangered Species Act*, 9 ECOLOGY L.Q. 629, 648 (1981).

15. Yaffee contends that politics inevitably plays an important role in seemingly

Section 7(d) arguably attempts to prevent the scenario described above by prohibiting resource commitments that merely have "the effect of foreclosing" project alternatives.[16] This language seems to temper Congress' sanction of reversible and retrievable resource commitments by forbidding those commitments that, while theoretically reversible or retrievable, may effectively allow a project to steamroll to completion.

The "effect of foreclosing" standard may prove difficult to apply, however. Courts are often reluctant to examine the role politics play in interpreting and administering legal mandates, assuming instead that administrators will carry out the intent of the law. Thus, it may be difficult for plaintiffs to challenge a resource commitment by arguing prospectively that momentum created by the commitment will foreclose alternatives to the project underway.[17]

Courts have examined the "effect of foreclosing" standard only indirectly. In *Nebraska v. Rural Electrification Administration*,[18] the court determined that defendants had made an unlawful commitment of resources by allowing construction of a dam to begin prior to analysis of the dam's effect on whooping cranes. The court observed that: "A different site, split sites, less impoundment, less use of water for the power plant, conservation techniques, or other such alternatives, are not built into the Project's plans. Further considerations of them is not impossible, to be sure, but, *as a practical matter . . .* it is foreclosed."[19] The First Circuit took an opposite approach in *Conservation Law Foundation v. Andrus*.[20] The court simply assumed that the Secretary of the Interior would cancel offshore oil and gas leases or restrict lessees' actions if proposed activities were found to harm endan-

---

technical questions involving the status of listed species and their habitat. *See generally* S. YAFFEE, *supra* note 3.

16. 16 U.S.C. § 1536(d).

17. One commentator suggests that "courts would do well to examine the commitments and their 'effect of foreclosing' as realistically as they would the effects of similar commitments affecting their own habits, their courthouses, residences, and personal lives; this is no more than we request routinely of juries." Houck, *The "Institutionalization of Caution" Under Section 7 of the Endangered Species Act: What Do You Do When You Don't Know?*, 12 Envtl. L. Rep. (Envtl. L. Inst.) 15,001, 15,010 (1982). *Compare with* Erdheim, *supra* note 14, at 651 n.172-73 and accompanying text. Erdheim suggests that section 7(d) is not violated unless it is "quite likely" that a federal agency would succumb to political pressure.

18. 12 Env't Rep. Cas. (BNA) 1156, 1172 (D. Neb. 1978).

19. *Id.* (emphasis added).

20. 623 F.2d 712 (1st Cir. 1979).

gered whales.[21] The court did not discuss, nor, apparently, did it consider whether granting oil and gas leases would make later cancellation or restriction of the leases practically or politically impossible.[22]

3. *Judicial construction of section 7(d).*

Conservation Law Foundation v. Andrus[23] was one of the first cases to discuss section 7(d). Plaintiffs filed suit in an attempt to halt oil and gas leasing on the Georges Bank. Adopting a somewhat awkward interpretation of section 7(d), plaintiffs argued that listed species received fewer protections under the Outer Continental Shelf Leasing Act (OCSLA) as compared to protections afforded by the ESA, and thus the Secretary's act of leasing violated section 7(d) by irreversibly giving up the opportunity to apply the ESA's strict protections.[24] The court disposed of this claim by observing that compliance with the ESA was an implied condition of an OCSLA lease.[25] The plaintiffs did not allege, and the court did not decide, whether the act of leasing itself was an unlawful commitment of resources. Nevertheless, subsequent decisions have erroneously cited this case as standing for the proposition that leasing pursuant to the OCSLA does not violate section 7(d).[26]

North Slope Borough v. Andrus[27] dealt with a question left open in the Georges Bank case: whether oil and gas leasing itself constitutes an unlawful commitment of resources if leases are granted prior to analyzing the effects of related activities on listed species. The district court discussed this question in detail. The court began its analysis by noting that the project or agency action involved in the case included not only the lease transactions themselves, which alone would not affect endangered whales, but also all subsequent related physical activities on the leaseholds, even though such actions may eventually require sep-

---

21. *Id.* at 715.
22. The court may not have reached this question because plaintiffs in the case did not contend that granting the leases was itself an unlawful commitment of resources.
23. 623 F.2d 712 (1st Cir. 1979).
24. *Id.* at 715.
25. *Id.*
26. *See* Village of False Pass v. Watt, 565 F. Supp. 1123, 1163 (D. Alaska 1983), *aff'd*, 733 F.2d 605 (9th Cir. 1984); State of California v. Watt, 520 F. Supp. 1359, 1387 (C.D. Cal. 1981), *aff'd*, 683 F.2d 1253 (9th Cir. 1982), *rev'd*, 464 U.S. 312 (1984); No Oilport! v. Carter, 520 F. Supp. 334, 365 (W.D. Wash. 1981).
27. 486 F. Supp. 332, 356 (D.D.C. 1979), *aff'd*, 642 F.2d 589 (D.C. Cir. 1980).

arate government approval.[28] The decision then set forth a two-part test governing interpretation of the statute. A section 7(d) violation occurs, according to the court, if: (1) at the time an agency commits resources to a project there is a reasonable likelihood that the project, at any stage of development, will violate section 7(a)(2), and (2) the resource expenditure is not salvageable, i.e., useful for another approach to the project or for an entirely different project.[29]

Applying this test to the challenged lease sales, the court determined that there was no indication of ultimate non-compliance with section 7(a)(2).[30] The court also found that resources expended on oil and gas exploration and development were salvageable, even if the ESA ultimately prohibited any oil and gas production.[31] The court supported this conclusion by noting that money spent on exploration activities produces information valuable in its own right, even apart from its utility for oil and gas production. It further asserted that Congress had accepted the inherently risky nature of oil and gas investment and therefore Congress did not contemplate that the assumption of those risks would constitute a section 7(d) violation.[32] As a result, the court denied plaintiffs' section 7(d) claims. The appellate court affirmed this holding with a brief discussion that simply summarized the lower court's findings.[33]

The district court's analysis of the section 7(d) issues presented by offshore oil and gas leasing is flawed in several respects. The first part of the court's two-part test, a project's likelihood of ultimately complying with section 7(a)(2), demonstrates a fundamental misunderstanding of section 7(d). If courts or federal agencies could reliably predict whether a project would ultimately comply with section 7(a)(2) when the project is in its initial stages, there would be little need for *any* limitation on commitment of resources and little need for the section 7 consultation process.[34] Moreover, if an initial guess that a project will

28. *Id.* at 351.
29. *Id.* at 356.
30. *Id.* at 358.
31. *Id.* at 357.
32. *Id.*
33. 642 F.2d 589, 611 (D.C. Cir. 1980).
34. The *North Slope* district court based its conclusion that there was a reasonable likelihood of ultimate compliance with section 7(a)(2) largely on the lack of evidence of ultimate non-compliance, even though the court recognized that little information on the impacts of oil and gas related activities existed. *See* 486 F. Supp. at 357-58. The lack

ultimately comply with section 7(a)(2) later turns out to be in error after significant resources are committed, the project may have gathered enough momentum to steamroll to completion regardless of its effects on listed species. This is precisely the result Congress intended to prevent by enacting section 7(d). Congress recognized that the initial phases of virtually *all* projects proceed under conditions of uncertainty over how the project will affect protected species and enacted section 7(d) in an attempt to maintain the status quo, or at least to prevent foreclosure of project alternatives until consultation with an expert agency discloses information on the project's effects on listed species. Uninformed speculation about a project's ultimate compliance with the ESA on the part of a court or federal agency without biological expertise does not further these purposes.[35]

The second element of the *North Slope* court's section 7(d) test, whether a resource commitment is unsalvageable, correctly interpreted the statute. Unfortunately, however, the court incorrectly applied its own test. The court argued that resources spent looking for oil and gas are not wasted and thus are salvageable even if the ESA ultimately prohibits oil and gas production because information gleaned from these activities would be valuable in its own right.[36] While this assertion may be nominally correct, there is likely to be a huge disparity between the value of this information in the abstract and the value of the information if used to produce oil and gas. The opinion noted that pre-exploration activities alone would cost $157 million.[37] It is improbable that an oil company would spend such vast resources simply to gain information in the abstract. Therefore, such a resource commitment is not truly salvageable from the perspective

---

of reliability inherent in basing a conclusion that an event will occur solely upon the absence of any indication that the event will not occur is readily apparent. More fundamentally, the notion that a judge or federal agency could draw any meaningful conclusions on how a project will ultimately affect listed species with virtually no biological information or expertise is ludicrous.

35. The *North Slope* court may have included the likelihood of ultimate compliance with section 7(a)(2) as a factor in its test for section 7(d) violations because ultimate compliance with section 7(a)(2), as well as compliance with section 7(d), are elements of the court's test for applying its incremental consultation scheme. *See supra* Chapter 6, note 76 and accompanying text. Incremental consultation procedures are not relevant for determining whether a resource commitment violates section 7(d). In fact, the *North Slope* court made compliance with section 7(d) a prerequisite for incremental consultation. *See id.*

36. 486 F. Supp. at 357.

37. *Id.*

of the oil company, if it is not valuable in the potential production of oil and gas.[38]

Though unrelated to either part of its test for determining compliance with section 7(d), the *North Slope* district court also cited industrial willingness to accept the risk that the ESA may not permit oil and gas production under the challenged leases as a reason why leasing does not violate section 7(d).[39] However, acceptance of risk in this case should have been irrelevant for purposes of the ESA's limitation on commitment of resources. The opinion correctly noted that oil and gas production is a highly risky business because oil companies traditionally expend significant resources despite high chances that exploration will reveal that no hydrocarbons exist on a particular leasehold. This gamble, however, must be distinguished from the risk present in *North Slope* that oil and gas may exist in great quantities on the leaseholds, but danger to protected whale or other species may preclude production of those resources.[40] Oil companies traditionally do not assume this type of risk, nor is it likely they would quietly acquiesce to foregone production in order to protect whales after making substantial investments in leasing and exploration. One would expect oil companies to do everything in their power to circumvent restrictions on production, including section 7(d) restrictions on commitment of resources, despite their avowed acceptance of the risk that the ESA would preclude production. Moreover, allowing commitments of resources under section 7(d), even when an actor expressed a willingness to forego those resources if a conflict with listed species eventually occurs, destroys the fundamental aim of section 7(d): to permit only salvageable resource expenditures.

The lease sales at issue in *North Slope*, contrary to the court's decision, were arguably an unlawful commitment of resources within the meaning of section 7(d). The sales precluded an alternative to leasing which would not violate section 7(a)(2), namely no sale of leases at all. The lease sales also constituted an irreversible and irretrievable commitment of resources because the government would have to compensate the oil companies if dan-

---

38. *See supra* text accompanying note 14 (arguing that a resource commitment is salvageable only if the value of those resources in their potential alternative uses is reasonably similar to their value in their intended use).

39. 486 F. Supp. at 357.

40. *See* Erdheim, *supra* note 14, at 649.

ger to whales later required it to cancel the leases.[41] Leasing and exploration expenses incurred by the oil companies are also unsalvageable.[42] Finally, the lease sales and investment in preliminary exploration activities, particularly if the activities discover oil and gas, undoubtedly create political and bureaucratic pressure to produce oil and gas regardless of the danger this activity poses to endangered species, and may ultimately have the effect of precluding alternatives to production.

Unfortunately, other courts have followed the *North Slope* court's reasoning in dismissing similar section 7(d) claims. The court in *No Oilport! v. Carter*[43] applied a *North Slope*-type section 7(d) analysis to a challenge to a Federal permit granting right of way for an oil pipeline through Puget Sound.[44] Noting that use of the right of way required the permittee to obtain a Notice to Proceed, which was expressly contingent upon compliance with the ESA, the court held that granting the right of way did not constitute an unlawful commitment of resources.[45]

It is difficult to evaluate this decision because the opinion does not indicate whether the government was entitled to withhold the Notice to Proceed, thus rendering the right of way useless, without compensating the permittee for the value of the right of way. If compensation were required, this decision would suffer from the same defects present in *North Slope*. In addition, the *No Oilport!* court made no attempt to analyze whether granting the right of way as a practical matter made granting the Notice to Proceed inevitable, in which case the government's grant of the right of way would constitute an unlawful commitment of resources because this action would preclude alternatives to the oil pipeline.

4.   *Resource commitments and consultation.*

Section 7(d)'s limits on resource commitments begin "[a]fter initiation of consultation required under [section 7(a)(2)]."[46]

---

41. With respect to cancellation of any lease or permit, Congress requires that lessees receive compensation. *See* 43 U.S.C. § 1334(a)(2)(C).

42. *See supra* text accompanying note 38.

43. 520 F. Supp. 334 (W.D. Wash. 1981).

44. The court erroneously cites *Conservation Law Foundation v. Andrus*, rather than *North Slope*, for the proposition that oil and gas leasing itself is not an unlawful commitment of resources. *Id.* at 365. *See supra* note 26 and accompanying text.

45. 520 F. Supp. at 365.

46. 16 U.S.C. § 1536(d).

This raises the question whether federal agencies or applicants may make irreversible and irretrievable commitments of resources that foreclose alternatives prior to initiation of formal consultation.[47]

Section 7(c) and its implementing regulations prohibit beginning construction on projects or even entering into contracts for construction while an agency or applicant is preparing a biological assessment,[48] an ESA procedural step preceding consultation.[49] This requirement is obviously aimed at preventing the same sort of commitment of resources that section 7(d) attempts to prevent. Therefore, though no cases have addressed this issue, section 7(c) arguably embodies the same sort of prohibitions as does section 7(d), but section 7(c) applies the prohibitions immediately after listed species are discovered in a project area, rather than upon initiation of "formal" consultation.[50]

Section 7 regulations narrowly construe the circumstances requiring preparation of a biological assessment.[51] However, even if regulations do not require preparation of a biological assessment for a certain project, the action agency still must determine whether its project will "adversely affect" listed species or critical habitat through an informal consultation process.[52] The limitations of section 7(d) arguably begin when this informal consultation process is initiated. Otherwise, actions which do not require preparation of a biological assessment would escape any limits on resource commitments.

Even though the language of the statute is ambiguous, the

47. *See* 50 C.F.R. § 402.14 (formal consultation).

48. 16 U.S.C. § 1536(c)(1); 50 C.F.R. § 402.12(b)(2). In *No Oilport! v. Carter* the court refused to find a violation of this provision. It determined that a permit granted by a federal agency was not a "contract" because the permittees needed to obtain additional government approval prior to acting on the permit. 520 F. Supp. at 365. For further discussion of biological assessments, see *supra* Chapter 6.

49. 50 C.F.R. § 402.14(b) (formal consultation not necessary where biological assessment indicates that the proposed action is unlikely to adversely affect listed species or critical habitats).

50. The prohibitions of section 7(c) may even be stricter than those of section 7(d). The latter provision does not prohibit entering into contracts as long as the contracts are not irreversible or do not result in irretrievable resource commitments. Section 7(c), however, prohibits all contracts for construction, and therefore all activities which move projects toward completion.

51. 50 C.F.R. § 402.12(b).

52. *See* 50 C.F.R. § 402.13 (optional informal consultation); 50 C.F.R. § 402.14(b) (formal consultation required except when biological assessment or informal consultation indicate the proposed action is not likely to have adverse effects on endangered species).

North Slope district court opinion spells out when section 7(d) no longer applies to an agency action. The court observed that section 7(d) is linked with the provisions of section 7(a)(2). As a result, the court held that section 7(d) remains viable until consultation between the Secretary and action agency to determine whether an action complies with section 7(a)(2) has terminated, i.e., until the Secretary issues a comprehensive biological opinion on the entire agency action.[53]

II.   PROHIBITIONS ON JEOPARDIZING ENDANGERED SPECIES

Section 7(a)(2)'s requirement that federal agencies refrain from actions likely to jeopardize the continued existence of listed species,[54] often referred to as the jeopardy standard, is section 7's most commonly applied substantive protection. The ESA, however, does not define the meaning of the phrase "jeopardize the continued existence of." Therefore, one of the ESA's most important provisions for protection of threatened and endangered species hinges on how the Secretary and courts interpret this phrase.

A.   *Regulatory Interpretations of the Jeopardy Standard*

Regulations promulgated in 1978 read as follows:

> "Jeopardize the continued existence of" means to engage in an activity or program which reasonably would be expected to reduce the reproduction, numbers or distribution of a listed species to such an extent as to appreciably reduce the likelihood of the survival and recovery of that species in the wild. The level of reduction necessary to constitute "jeopardy" would be expected to vary among listed species.[55]

A key ambiguity in this definition was whether a project which appreciably reduced the likelihood of a listed species' recovery, but which did not threaten the species' bare survival, jeopardized that species.[56]

Revision of the jeopardy definition in 1986 resolved this ambiguity. Current regulations provide that:

> "Jeopardize the continued existence of" means to engage in an

---

53.   486 F. Supp. at 354-55.

54.   16 U.S.C. § 1536(a)(2).

55.   50 C.F.R. § 402.02 (1985) (superceded).

56.   This assumes that it is possible for a project to adversely affect a species' chances for recovery without also imperiling its very survival. For a discussion on the interrelationship of survival and recovery, see *infra* notes 58-60 and accompanying text.

action which would be expected, directly or indirectly, to reduce appreciably the likelihood of *both the survival and recovery* of a listed species in the wild by reducing the reproduction, numbers, or distribution of that species.[57]

Under this definition, therefore, a project which harms a species' chances of recovery but which does not pose a likelihood of entirely wiping out the species does not violate the jeopardy standard of section 7(a)(2). An agency action must imperil the survival as well as recovery of a species to run afoul of the ESA's jeopardy prohibition. Obviously, any action which appreciably reduces the likelihood that a species will survive necessarily reduces that species' chances of recovery.[58] Thus the word "recovery" within the regulatory definition of jeopardy is superfluous; the extent to which a project affects listed species' recovery is irrelevant for purposes of determining whether the project jeopardizes those species. Only a project's effects on species' survival are meaningful under the jeopardy standard.[59]

This regulatory interpretation of the jeopardy standard has two extremely important ramifications on the scope of protection which section 7(a)(2) extends to listed species. First, because the section 7 regulations also afford no protection for the recovery of listed species in section 7(a)(2)'s prohibition against destroying critical habitat, the Secretary interprets section 7(a)(2) as merely requiring federal agencies to refrain from threatening the bare survival of listed species. Moreover, since the ESA gives no indication of what constitutes "survival" or "continued existence" of a species from a biological perspective, the Secretary and federal agencies have complete discretion over how to interpret these terms.[60]

---

57. 50 C.F.R. § 402.02 (1987) (emphasis added). It is important to read this definition in conjunction with the statutory definition of the term "species." *See* 16 U.S.C. § 1532(16). Since "species" may refer to a distinct population segment of vertebrate fish or wildlife, a project could jeopardize a species even though the project affects only a portion of that species' total population. See Chapter 3 for further discussion of this point.

58. The Secretary explicitly noted this fact in the explanation accompanying the section 7 regulations. *See* 51 Fed. Reg. 19,934 (1986) ("If survival is jeopardized, recovery is also jeopardized.").

59. However, the effects of a federal agency action on a species' recovery may be relevant in determining whether the action agency has fulfilled its duties under section 7(a)(1) to conserve listed species. *See supra* Chapter 5, notes 32-36 and accompanying text.

60. This distinction between survival and recovery is absurd from a biological point of view. Biologically, the survival of a species cannot be equated with its mere "continued existence." The critical factor from a scientific perspective is not whether a

III. Protection of Critical Habitat

In addition to forbidding agency actions which jeopardize species' continued existence, section 7(a)(2) prohibits federal agencies from destroying or adversely modifying habitat of listed species that the Secretary determines to be critical.[61] This statutory protection of critical habitat,[62] however, is often misinterpreted by both the general public and federal agencies charged with administering the ESA. Moreover, the Secretary commonly ignores the critical habitat portion of section 7.[63]

A. *Public Perception of the Critical Habitat Problem*

Many people view critical habitat as akin to a wildlife preserve, equating section 7's protection of critical habitat with virtually complete restrictions on uses of land identified as critical to a listed species. This view overstates the case. Like the jeopardy standard, section 7(a)(2)'s critical habitat provisions apply only to federal or federally authorized activities. Moreover, these protections do not preclude all uses of critical habitat unrelated to species conservation. Only uses which destroy or adversely modify physical or biological features essential to conservation of

---

few or even many individuals of a species continue to exist, but whether a viable population of that species exists. A viable population describes the number of individuals of a species necessary to have a given chance of maintaining that species for a given time period. It is a variable definition, for example, if one defines a viable population as having a ninety percent chance of existing for 100 years, a certain species' population containing 100 individuals might be viable. If one defines a viable population as having a ninety percent chance of surviving for a thousand years, however, that species' population would probably have to be much larger to be considered viable. Section 7 contains a legal standard of species viability: federal agencies must *insure* that their actions are not likely to jeopardize a species' continued existence. However, neither the statute nor its implementing regulations translates this legal definition into a biological definition of a viable population. Thus, for each listed species, the ESA sets no minimum viable population. This fundamental omission thus allows the Secretary almost unfettered discretion in determining what impacts threaten the viability of a species and therefore constitute jeopardy in violation of section 7(a)(2).

For further discussion of the concept of a viable population and related concepts in conservation biology, see Shaffer, *Minimum Population Sizes for Species Conservation*, 31 BIOSCIENCE 131 (1981). *See generally* M. SOULE & B. WILCOX, CONSERVATION BIOLOGY (1980); M. SOULE, CONSERVATION BIOLOGY (1984).

   61. 16 U.S.C. § 1536(a)(2).
   62. For a discussion of the definition of critical habitat and when the Secretary must designate critical habitat, see *supra* Chapter 3. For a discussion of section 7's critical habitat protection of land not officially designated as critical habitat, see *infra* notes 85-95 and accompanying text.
   63. *See infra* notes 77-78 and accompanying text.

listed species violate section 7(a)(2).[64] Despite these limitations, statutory protection for critical habitat remains controversial principally because it affects discrete parcels of land. In contrast, the jeopardy standard applies to mobile populations of listed species.[65]

B.   *Regulatory Interpretations of the Critical Habitat Provision*

The significance of section 7's protection for critical habitat depends on its scope, specifically whether the prohibition against destruction or adverse modification of critical habitat affords listed species and their habitats legal protection in addition to the protection all species enjoy under the jeopardy standard. In other words, does the critical habitat portion of section 7(a)(2) grant listed species substantive protection not found elsewhere in the ESA or are critical habitat provisions simply redundant?

As interpreted by current section 7 regulations, the statutory language in section 7(a)(2) forbidding destruction or adverse modification of critical habitat gives species *no* substantive protection beyond that to which species are entitled under the jeopardy standard. The phrase "destruction or adverse modification," not defined by the ESA itself, is interpreted by the section 7 regulations as follows:

> "Destruction or adverse modification" means a direct or indirect alteration that appreciably diminishes the value of critical habitat for both the survival and recovery of a listed species. Such alterations include, but are not limited to, alterations adversely modifying any of those physical or biological features that were the basis for determining the habitat to be critical.[66]

As in the regulatory definition of "jeopardize the continued existence of,"[67] the key phrase in this definition is "both the survival

---

64. *See* 16 U.S.C. § 1532(5)(a).

65. Advocates of federal projects often argue that a project does not jeopardize listed species because the species can simply go elsewhere. Frantic attempts to transplant snail darters from the doomed Little Tennessee River in order to allow completion of the Tellico Dam provide a particularly notorious example of this type of thinking. Even expert wildlife agencies occasionally rely on the mobility of listed species in order to avoid a jeopardy finding. For instance, FWS issued a "no jeopardy" biological opinion for the massive Grant Village development in Yellowstone National Park, rationalizing that habitat improvements miles away would compensate for the development's adverse impacts on grizzlies. Had the Secretary determined the Grant Village area to be critical habitat, this rationale would not have worked because critical habitat protection focuses on specific land areas, rather than net impacts on an entire species.

66. 50 C.F.R. § 402.02.

67. *See supra* note 57 and accompanying text.

and recovery of a listed species." Conjunctive use of the terms survival and recovery means that an activity must threaten the bare survival of a listed species in order to constitute destruction or adverse modification of critical habitat; an action reducing a species' chances of recovery without also threatening to wipe out the species itself does not meet the regulatory definition.[68]

This definition of destruction or adverse modification of critical habitat is virtually identical to the regulatory definition of the jeopardy standard. The regulations set forth the same test for jeopardy as for destruction or adverse modification of critical habitat—threat to the very survival of a listed species. Since a jeopardy finding alone is sufficient to constitute a section 7 violation, the ESA's critical habitat mandate, as interpreted by the regulations, adds nothing to section 7's substantive protection and is therefore simply redundant.[69]

This interpretation, however, is greatly in error. By essentially reading the prohibition of destruction or adverse modification of critical habitat out of section 7(a)(2), the section 7 regulations clearly conflict with the intent of the ESA, as well as with express statutory language. The statute seeks to "provide a means whereby the ecosystems upon which endangered species and threatened species depend may be conserved, [and] to provide a program for the conservation of such endangered species and threatened species. . . ."[70] The term conservation means to bring about the recovery of listed species.[71] Therefore, the ESA aims to foster the recovery of protected species. Congress designed section 7's critical habitat mandate to carry out this pur-

---

68. *See supra* notes 56-59 and accompanying text.

69. Since a jeopardy determination is by itself sufficient to trigger section 7(a)(2)'s prohibition of agency actions adversely affecting listed species, once a jeopardy determination is made it becomes meaningless to determine whether a proposed action also destroys or adversely modifies critical habitat. If the consultation process determines that a proposed action does not jeopardize a listed species, the proposed action by definition does not destroy or adversely modify critical habitat. Note that in addition to being interpreted as superfluous, the critical habitat portion of section 7(a)(2) is commonly ignored. *See infra* notes 77-78 and accompanying text.

70. 16 U.S.C. § 1531(b).

71. The ESA defines conservation as ". . . the use of all methods and procedures which are necessary to bring any endangered species or threatened species to the point at which the measures provided pursuant to this chapter are no longer necessary." 16 U.S.C. § 1532(3). Regulations define recovery as ". . . improvement in the status of listed species to the point at which listing is no longer appropriate. . . ." 50 C.F.R. § 402.02. Thus, conservation consists of procedures necessary to bring about the recovery of listed species.

pose. The ESA defines critical habitat as containing physical or biological features "essential to the conservation of "[listed] species,"[72] in other words features essential to the recovery of listed species. Thus, section 7(a)(2)'s prohibition against "destruction or adverse modification" of critical habitat necessarily proscribes actions which affect critical habitat so as to impair the recovery of listed species.

The section 7 regulations err by providing that an agency action within critical habitat which adversely affects a listed species' recovery without also imperiling that species' very survival does not violate section 7(a)(2). By erroneously equating the substantive protections of the critical habitat mandate with those of the jeopardy standard, thereby rendering section 7's critical habitat provisions redundant,[73] the current regulations deprive listed species of legal protection for their recovery[74] and thus thwart the ESA's fundamental purpose.[75]

The regulations' approach to section 7(a)(2)'s critical habitat mandate is also at odds with Congressional intent. In 1978, Congress amended the ESA to require the Secretary to designate critical habitat for a species at the same time the Secretary adds that

---

72. 16 U.S.C. § 1532(5)(A).

73. Note that by interpreting the critical habitat provision of section 7(a)(2) as inconsequential, the section 7 regulations violate a basic principle of statutory construction. A statute should be construed to give effect to all of its provisions, so that no part is superfluous or insignificant. *See* J. SUTHERLAND, STATUTORY CONSTRUCTION § 46.06 (4th ed. 1984).

74. Sections 2(c) and 7(a)(1) also are designed to protect listed species' recovery. The Secretary apparently interprets these provisions, however, as merely authorizing rather than mandating federal agencies to take steps to promote recovery of listed species. *See* Chapter 5. Therefore, the critical habitat mandate in section 7(a)(2) becomes crucial to protect recovery.

75. The current regulations' requirement that an action threaten both the survival and recovery of a listed species in order to constitute destruction or adverse modification of critical habitat represents a complete reversal from the way the Secretary previously (and correctly) interpreted the critical habitat portion of the section 7(a)(2) mandate. In a 1975 Federal Register notice, FWS noted that:

> Actions by a Federal agency which result in the destruction or modification of habitat considered "critical habitat" for a given Endangered or Threatened species would not conform with section 7 of the Endangered Species Act of 1973, if such an action might be expected to result in a reduction in the numbers or distribution of that species of sufficient magnitude to place that species in further jeopardy, *or* restrict the potential and reasonable expansion or recovery of that species.

40 Fed. Reg. 17,765 (1975) (emphasis added).

species to the endangered or threatened list.[76] This requirement is virtually meaningless unless having adequate critical habitat provides species with increased statutory protection. Congress clearly views critical habitat protection as an important element of section 7, rather than as superfluous.

C.   *Other Benefits of Critical Habitat*

Critical habitat primarily protects species' recovery. In addition, the critical habitat portion of the section 7(a)(2) mandate indirectly benefits listed species. Official designation of critical habitat notifies all Federal agencies, permittees and licensees that any proposed activity within that area may be restricted. This notice serves dual purposes. First, a proposed activity in critical habitat is less likely to be "steamrolled" to completion. Steamrolling occurs when an agency proposal creates expectations in certain groups or individuals who stand to benefit from the project. If subsequent conflicts with a listed species affect these expectations, both the action agency and the Secretary may come under pressure from those interested in project completion to follow through with the action with weakened protection for the species. Critical habitat designation notifies agencies and interested parties from the beginning that projects must accommodate a species' needs, thus preventing creation of unreasonable expectations. Second, it is usually easier and less expensive to plan a project with a species' requirements in mind, rather than to attempt to incorporate mitigation measures into existing plans.

D.   *When to Apply Critical Habitat Protection*

1.   *Ignoring the provision.*

The regulatory interpretation of section 7 holds that critical habitat protection applies only when the Secretary formally designates an area as critical habitat.[77] Under this interpretation, if a species has no designated critical habitat, section 7 consultations and subsequent agency decisions need only consider whether a proposed action would jeopardize the continued existence of the species in question. The Secretary, as well as action

---

76. 16 U.S.C. § 1533(a)(3); *see supra* Chapter 3 for a discussion of critical habitat designation.

77. Regulations promulgated under section 7 define critical habitat as an area which the Secretary has designated as critical habitat. *See* 50 C.F.R. § 402.02.

agencies, ignores the section 7(a)(2) prohibition against destroying or adversely modifying critical habitat when no such area is officially recognized.

If critical habitat protection provisions are interpreted as redundant, this scheme becomes largely inconsequential. Though formal critical habitat designation would still serve to notify federal agencies that projects within the area must accommodate a particular species, official critical habitat designation would create no further legal protection benefiting that species. Therefore, when the action and wildlife agencies ignore the critical habitat portion of the section 7(a)(2) mandate, listed species lose nothing. Clearly, however, the critical habitat provision of section 7 affords listed species protection beyond merely prohibiting agency action which jeopardize species' continued existence.[78] Therefore, a key question becomes when to apply this protection.

2. *The problem of official notice of critical habitat.*

The ESA defines critical habitat as a physical rather than legal entity.[79] The physical nature of the term "critical habitat" contrasts with the legal nature of, for example, the term "wilderness." Under the Wilderness Act,[80] when an area is designated as wilderness, that designation represents how that land will be managed. "Wilderness" describes the land's legal status. Areas classified as wilderness must meet certain physical criteria,[81] but all lands meeting these criteria are not necessarily classified and managed as wilderness.[82]

Conversely, critical habitat represents the term for physical and biological features necessary for a depleted species to recover to the extent that ESA protection is no longer necessary. The only qualification of this definition is that these physical features "may require special management considerations or protection."[83] It therefore follows that critical habitat must exist for every threatened and endangered species whose precarious sta-

---

78. *See supra* notes 70-76 and accompanying text.
79. *See* 16 U.S.C. § 1532(5)(a) (definition of critical habitat).
80. 16 U.S.C. § 1131(a).
81. *Id.*
82. Only Congress has the power to designate Wilderness Areas pursuant to the Wilderness Act. 16 U.S.C. § 1131(a). Land meeting the Wilderness Act's description of wilderness but not formally accorded wilderness status by Congress is not protected under the Wilderness Act.
83. 16 U.S.C. § 1532(5)(A)(i)(II).

tus can be traced in whole or in part to negative impacts on habitat.[84]

When the Secretary officially designates critical habitat, he or she identifies the physical area containing features believed necessary for a species' recovery.[85] It is important to note, however, that critical habitat, as the ESA defines this term, may exist for a species even if none has been formally identified. Because the term critical habitat describes a physical rather than legal entity, the Secretary does not "create" critical habitat by designating certain land as such. Critical habitat exists when protection of certain land or a certain biological feature is necessary for recovery of a certain species, regardless of whether the Secretary has officially designated critical habitat for that species.

This line of reasoning suggests that agencies may not justifiably ignore the critical habitat portion of the 7(a)(2) mandate when considering a proposal that may affect a listed species for which the Secretary has not designated critical habitat. Because the critical habitat portion of section 7(a)(2) provides additional protection to listed species beyond merely prohibiting "jeopardy," the conclusion that federal agencies must consider critical habitat in all section 7 consultations, *whether critical habitat is officially designated or not*, becomes inescapable.

Consider the following scenario: A proposed agency action may adversely affect a listed species. The Secretary has not officially designated critical habitat for the species, but human encroachment on the species' habitat has contributed to its endangered or threatened status. During consultation, the Secretary determines that the project's impacts on habitat will adversely affect species recovery, but will not threaten the survival of the species' population as a whole. Under the regulatory definition of "jeopardize the continued existence of," the wildlife agency could issue a "no jeopardy" biological opinion, allowing the action agency to proceed with its plans.[86] Under standard procedure, the agencies would ignore the critical habitat provi-

---

84. For example, if a species was listed as endangered or threatened only because excessive hunting or disease reduced its numbers, habitat protection presumably would not be essential to its recovery. Therefore, no critical habitat would exist for the species because its habitat would not require special management considerations or protection.

85. For further discussion of critical habitat designation, see *supra* Chapter 3, notes 76-120 and accompanying text.

86. *See supra* notes 57-60 and accompanying text.

sion of 7(a)(2) because no officially designated critical habitat exists for the species in question.

The above procedure deprives the species of the additional protection accorded them under the critical habitat provision of section 7(a)(2) and thus violates the ESA. The goal of the ESA is species recovery.[87] Critical habitat by statutory definition consists of physical and biological features essential to recovery.[88] In the hypothetical example above, the Secretary and action agency may take actions adverse to the species' recovery simply because they do not officially recognize the affected area as critical habitat and therefore do not apply 7(a)(2) critical habitat protection. Yet, lack of official habitat designation does not change the biological fact that the agency action adversely affects features important to the species and hurts species recovery. Thus, even though the action receives a "no jeopardy" opinion, it nevertheless may violate the ESA. If the section 7(a)(2) prohibition against destroying or adversely modifying critical habitat were applied, the action would likely be precluded and the species' recovery would not be threatened.

3. *A biological critical habitat standard.*

It seems ludicrous to allow agencies to apply habitat protection of section 7 depending on whether or not the Secretary takes official notice of biological facts. An alternative interpretation of section 7 more consistent with the intent of the ESA would require the Secretary to consider the critical habitat portion of 7(a)(2) in all consultations, even if critical habitat was not officially designated.[89] This procedure would work as follows: For species with designated critical habitat, the Secretary and action agency would apply section 7(a)(2) critical habitat protection within the designated area. For agency actions affecting the species but occurring outside its designated critical habitat, the wildlife agency could assume the habitat was not critical and ignore the portion of 7(a)(2) dealing with critical habitat.[90] For agency proposals affecting species with no officially designated critical habitat, however, the Secretary, within the context of section 7

---

87. 16 U.S.C. § 1531(b); *see also supra* notes 70-71 and accompanying text.

88. 16 U.S.C. §§ 1532(3), 1532(5)(A)(ii).

89. *See* Mallory, *Obligations of Federal Agencies under Section 7 of the Endangered Species Act of 1973*, 28 STAN. L. REV. 1247, 1261-62 (1976).

90. Such an assumption would be valid provided that all features essential to a full recovery of the species were included within the designated critical habitat.

consultation, would be required to make a finding as to whether the physical area or biological features to be affected by the proposed action were critical habitat within that term's statutory definition. If the area was found to be critical habitat, section 7(a)(2)'s substantive critical habitat protection would apply. Only if the wildlife agency determined the area was not critical habitat could the agencies ignore the critical habitat portion of section 7(a)(2).

This approach is consistent with the wording of section 7(a)(2) itself. Section 7 prohibits "destruction or adverse modification of habitat . . . which is determined . . . to be critical." This provision does not imply that only officially recognized critical habitat cannot be destroyed or adversely modified.[91] An analogous provision of the Department of Transportation Act of 1966 proscribes highway construction on public lands "of national, State or local significance as determined by the Federal, State or local officials having jurisdiction thereof."[92] Interpreting this clause, a federal district court found that "Congressional use of the word 'determined' *requires* a finding of significance, either affirmative or negative, by the officials having jurisdiction of the [land] involved."[93] Similarly, rather than ignoring critical habitat protection if not officially designated, federal agencies, in consultation with the Secretary, should determine on a case-by-case basis whether or not proposed agency actions affect critical habitat as the ESA defines this term.

Such a scheme could substantially complicate section 7 consultations.[94] Nevertheless, it would provide wildlife agencies with incentives to designate critical habitats for all listed species in order to avoid making costly and time-consuming piecemeal

---

91. Section 7 regulations erroneously conclude that Section 7(a)(2)'s critical habitat protection applies only to designated critical habitat because the regulations define the term critical habitat in a *legal* sense, i.e., land the Secretary formally designates as such. *See* 50 C.F.R. § 402.02. This view conflicts with the *physical* definition of critical habitat embodied in the ESA, i.e., land containing features essential to the conservation of listed species. *See* 16 U.S.C. § 1532 (5)(A).

92. 49 U.S.C. § 1653(f).

93. Harrisburg Coalition Against Ruining the Environment v. Volpe, 330 F. Supp. 918, 929 (M.D. Pa. 1971) (emphasis added); *see also* Arlington Coalition on Transportation v. Volpe, 458 F.2d 1323, 1335-36 (4th Cir.), *cert. denied*, 409 U.S. 1000 (1972) ("land 'presumed' significant unless explicitly determined otherwise").

94. It is unclear whether the ESA would require the Secretary to take economic and other impacts into account when making critical habitat determinations on a case-by-case basis. *See supra* Chapter 3, notes 109-113 and accompanying text.

determinations in the context of individual consultations. Most importantly, this procedure would insure that all listed species receive the full protection of section 7(a)(2), specifically protection of species' recovery.[95]

IV. A STANDARD OF CERTAINTY

A. *The 1979 Amendments*

Section 7 requires federal agencies to "insure" that their actions are "not likely to jeopardize" listed species or to destroy or adversely modify critical habitat.[96] Congress added the phrase "not likely to" in 1979, amending what up to that time had been an absolute statutory directive to insure against jeopardy or critical habitat modification.[97] Precisely how this amendment modified the standard of certainty agencies must meet to satisfy the ESA remains unclear, though legislative history and subsequent case law suggest that the 1979 change weakened this standard.

Congress' explanation for adding the words "not likely to" to section 7's basic mandate is somewhat confusing. On the one hand, lawmakers attempted to soft-pedal the amendment as simply "bring[ing] the language of the statute into conformity with existing agency practice" while still giving listed species "the benefit of the doubt."[98] On the other hand, Congress apparently intended to prevent section 7 from being interpreted to require federal agencies to "guarantee with certainty" that their actions would not violate section 7(a)(2).[99]

---

95. On the other hand, a portion of the ESA's legislative history could be read to support the current practice of applying Section 7(a)(2)'s critical habitat mandate only to designated critical habitats. A House Report which accompanied the House version of 1978 ESA amendments contains the following passage: "The mandate of section 7 applies once a species is listed or once 'critical habitat' is designated for any listed species." H.R. REP. No. 1625, 95th Cong., 2d Sess. 7, *reprinted in* 1978 U.S. CODE CONG. & ADMIN. NEWS 9453, 9458. This sentence, however, is far from conclusive in resolving the question of when to apply critical habitat protection. Even if one interprets the House Report to mean that section 7 applies only to designated critical habitats, the ESA arguably imposes a duty on the Secretary formally to designate critical habitat within the context of individual consultations if the habitat which is the subject of consultation is necessary for the recovery of a listed species. The basic point is that critical habitat is a biological entity, not a legal concept that the Secretary may apply at his or her discretion.

96. 16 U.S.C. § 1536(a)(2).

97. Pub. L. No. 96-159, § 4, 93 Stat. 1225, 1226 (1979) (amending 16 U.S.C. § 1536(a)(2)).

98. H.R. CONF. REP. No. 697, 96th Cong., 1st Sess. 12, *reprinted in* 1979 U.S. CODE CONG. & ADMIN. NEWS 2572, 2576.

99. *Id.*

The 1979 ESA amendments were influenced by the Supreme Court decision in *TVA v. Hill*[100] and subsequent perception of the ESA as a very powerful yet highly inflexible statute.[101] Congress was obviously concerned that federal projects would be delayed indefinitely while action agencies, in consultation with the Secretary, attempted to gather enough evidence to insure with certainty that federal actions would not violate section 7(a)(2).[102] The conference committee report accompanying the 1979 amendments suggests that Congress modified section 7(a)(2) to allow agency actions to proceed even if existing information after consultation was complete did not allow the Secretary or the action agency to insure against jeopardy or critical habitat destruction.[103] Nevertheless, the conference report also indicates that Congress hedged what would have been a drastic change in section 7 by noting that federal agencies which proceed without adequate information on how projects affect listed species do so at the risk of violating section 7(a)(2), and in addition have a "continuing obligation" to develop more information.[104] This flip-flop nature of Congress' approach to section 7(a)(2) raises difficult procedural questions concerning when consultation ends and the extent of agencies' obligation to gather information in the face of uncertainty.[105] The 1979 addition of "not likely to" to section 7(a)(2) also raises substantive issues, namely when federal agencies may act without "guaranteeing with certainty" that their actions will not violate section 7(a)(2), and exactly what standard of certainty short of a guarantee agencies must satisfy.

B. *Judicial Interpretations of the Section 7 Standard of Certainty*

In *Sierra Club v. March*,[106] the Ninth Circuit court examined whether the Army Corps of Engineers had insured that a disputed project was not likely to jeopardize two endangered bird species or was not likely to adversely modify their critical habitat.

---

100. 437 U.S. 153 (1978).

101. *See* Luhn, *The Effectiveness of Judicial Review under the 1979 Amendment to the Endangered Species Act*, 7 J. ENERGY L. & POL'Y 145, 149-52 (1986).

102. H.R. CONF. REP. No. 697, 96th Cong., 1st Sess. 12, *reprinted in* 1979 U.S. CODE CONG. & ADMIN. NEWS 2572, 2576.

103. *Id.*

104. *Id.*

105. *See supra* Chapter 6, notes 125-147 and accompanying text. *See also* Houck, *supra* note 17, at 15,006-09.

106. 816 F.2d 1376 (9th Cir. 1987).

In order to avoid jeopardizing the birds, FWS concluded that
public acquisition of 188 acres of nearby wetlands was necessary.[107] When the Corps' rights in wetlands that it was attempting to acquire became clouded, environmental groups filed suit
to halt the project. The court rejected the Corps' argument that
it should not have to halt construction because the plaintiffs' had
allegedly failed to prove that the Corps would not prevail in its
attempt to acquire the necessary wetlands.[108] Instead, the court
held that the Corps' "insurance" against jeopardy to the endangered birds lapsed when the Corps discovered that its expectations under its wetlands acquisition agreement were not being
fulfilled.[109]

Further case law suggests that the 1979 amendment lowered
section 7(a)(2)'s standard of certainty only for those instances
where adequate information on how a project affects listed species is not available.[110] In *Roosevelt Campobello International Park
Commission v. U.S. Environmental Protection Agency*,[111] plaintiffs challenged an administrative law judge's order to the EPA to issue a
permit necessary for construction of an oil refinery, which the
agency had previously denied to protect listed species present in
the area. Despite lack of a study that the EPA considered important for assessing the risk of a major oil spill,[112] the administrative law judge (ALJ) found that the risk of such a spill was
minuscule and that therefore the project did not threaten any
listed species.[113] In reviewing the ALJ's findings and order, the
First Circuit court noted that Congress in 1979 had "softened the
obligation" of agencies to insure that their actions did not violate
section 7(a)(2).[114] The court nevertheless found that such a violation had occurred. In overturning the ALJ's decision, the court
held that without using the best scientific data available, including the study asked for by EPA, the agency could not insure that
the project was unlikely to violate section 7(a)(2).[115]

---

107. *Id.* at 1385.

108. *Id.*

109. *Id.* at 1386.

110. For discussion of when information should be considered "available," see
supra Chapter 6, notes 117-124 and accompanying text.

111. 684 F.2d 1041 (1st Cir. 1982).

112. *Id.* at 1053.

113. *Id.* at 1050.

114. *Id.* at 1048.

115. *Id.* at 1052-53, 1055. For discussion of section 7's requirements to use the
best scientific and commercial data available, see *supra* Chapter 6.

This decision is significant because the court refused to adopt a lower section 7(a)(2) standard of certainty, despite the 1979 amendment and despite some evidence in the record supporting the ALJ's findings. The appellate court could have excused performance of the study requested by EPA by finding that the weight of the existing evidence considered by the ALJ showed that jeopardy was not likely. Instead, the court linked section 7's requirement to insure against the likelihood of jeopardy or critical habitat modification with section 7's requirement to use the best scientific and commercial data available, holding in effect that any violation of the latter requirement automatically means that an agency has failed to insure that its actions are not likely to violate section 7(a)(2).[116]

When complete information on how a proposed federal action may affect listed species is not available, however, courts have been willing to allow the action to proceed even though neither the action agency nor the Secretary could guarantee that no section 7(a)(2) violation would take place. In two cases involving disputed offshore oil and gas lease issuance pursuant to the OCSLA, courts cited the conference report accompanying the 1979 ESA amendments to support holdings that section 7(a)(2) does not absolutely bar federal actions when the action agency cannot insure ultimate compliance with section 7(a)(2).[117] In both cases the ultimate impact on listed species of the agency actions in question could not be determined at the time of leasing due to uncertainty over where, if anywhere at all, exploration and production would take place on the leased tracts.[118]

Even though courts have clearly applied a lower standard of certainty in the context of section 7(a)(2) when crucial biological information is unavailable, only one decision has attempted to articulate that standard. The district court in *North Slope Borough v. Andrus* noted that a section 7 violation would occur when an agency proceeds with a project despite a "reasonable likelihood"

---

116. A federal district court reached virtually the same conclusion when federal defendants failed to wait for conclusion of ongoing studies relevant to defendants' decision on compliance with Section 7(a)(2). *See* Conservation Law Found. v. Watt, 560 F. Supp. 561, 572 (D. Mass. 1983).

117. North Slope Borough v. Andrus, 486 F. Supp. 332, 352 (D.D.C.), *aff'd in part and rev'd in part*, 642 F.2d 589 (D.C. Cir. 1980); Village of False Pass v. Watt, 565 F. Supp. 1123, 1154-55 (D. Alaska 1983).

118. For further discussion of OCSLA leasing cases, see *supra* Chapter 6, notes 66-79 and accompanying text.

that the project would ultimately violate section 7(a)(2).[119] The legislative history of the 1979 amendments, on the other hand, does not clearly set forth a standard of certainty to use in the face of skimpy biological data; it instead simply refers to a vague "continuing obligation" to develop more information.[120]

V. IMPACTS AGENCIES MUST CONSIDER IN COMPLYING WITH SECTION 7

Federal agencies, in consultation with the Secretary, must evaluate how proposed projects or permits might affect listed species, as well as determine the magnitude of those effects. These dual considerations form the basis of decisions about whether federal actions jeopardize the continued existence of listed species or destroy or adversely modify critical habitat.

Human activities may affect listed species in many ways. Actions may result in direct species mortality, or activities may directly modify habitat upon which species depend. Projects also indirectly affect protected species by setting other events or projects in motion. Finally, an action by itself may not jeopardize species or destroy critical habitat, but could nevertheless prove to be fatal when considered together with a host of other activities.

During consultation on a proposed agency action, section 7 regulations require the Secretary to evaluate the effects of the action on listed species or critical habitat.[121] The regulations also define the term "effects of the action."[122]

---

119. *North Slope*, 486 F. Supp. at 356. Although the court articulated this standard in discussing the requirements of section 7(d), it clearly linked the standard to section 7(a)(2).

120. *See supra* notes 98-104 and accompanying text. *See also supra* Chapter 6, notes 125-146 and accompanying text for a discussion of agencies' "continuing obligation" to develop more information.

121. 50 C.F.R. § 402.14(g)(3).

122. Regulations define "effects of the action" as follows:

"*Effects of the action*" refers to the direct and indirect effects on the species or critical habitat, together with the effects of other activities that are interrelated or interdependent with that action, that will be added to the environmental baseline. The environmental baseline includes the past and present impacts of all Federal, State, or private actions and other human activities in the action area, the anticipated impacts of all proposed Federal projects in the action area that have already undergone formal or early section 7 consultation, and the impact of State or private actions which are contemporaneous with the consultation in process. Indirect effects are those that are caused by the proposed action and are later in time, but are still reasonably certain to occur. Interre-

"Effects of the action" include a project's direct as well as indirect effects on listed species and critical habitat. Inclusion of indirect effects as a factor the Secretary must consider follows from *National Wildlife Federation v. Coleman*.[123] In *Coleman*, the court enjoined construction of a highway because the federal agency involved failed to consider how private development resulting from building the road would affect endangered cranes. Even though the court recognized that the federal government had no formal control over private development near the highway, the court noted that the government exercised substantial de facto control simply through placement of the highway and interchanges.[124] The court therefore ordered defendants to take private development near the highway into account in the section 7 review process as an indirect effect of highway construction.[125]

While the section 7 regulations require analysis of indirect effects, they apparently attempt to narrow the scope of activities considered indirect effects of a federal action. Indirect effects include only activities "reasonably certain" to occur.[126] A Solicitor's Opinion explaining this "reasonably certain" standard provides that:

> [a] non-federal action is "reasonably certain" to occur if the action requires the approval of a state or local land use control agency and such agencies have approved the action, and the project is ready to proceed. Other indicators which also may support such a determination include whether the project sponsors provide assurance that the action will proceed, whether contracting has been initiated, whether there is obligated venture capital, or whether state or local planning agencies indicate that grant of authority for the action is imminent. These indicators must show more than the *possibility* that the non-federal project will occur; they must demonstrate with reasonable certainty that it *will occur*.[127]

The "reasonably certain" standard of the section 7 regulations

---

lated actions are those that are part of a larger action and depend on the larger action for their justification. Interdependent actions are those that have no independent utility apart from the action under consideration.
Id. at § 402.02 (emphasis in original). For further discussion of this definition, see 51 Fed. Reg. 19,932 (1986).

123. 529 F.2d 359 (5th Cir. 1976).

124. *Id.* at 374.

125. *See also* Riverside Irrigation District v. Andrews, 568 F. Supp. 583, 588 (D. Colo. 1983) (agency required to consider indirect effects of dam on whooping cranes downstream from damsite).

126. 50 C.F.R. § 402.02.

127. 88 Interior Dec. 903, 908 (1981) (emphasis in original).

goes too far. It sets a higher standard of certainty than the one applied by the court in *Coleman*. That case neither contained discussion of local government approvals or economic viability, nor mentioned any specific development proposals. It merely referred in the abstract to the likelihood of private development near the disputed highway. This approach appears more in line with other regulatory definitions of indirect effects. For example, NEPA regulations recognize indirect effects as those which are "reasonably foreseeable" as a result of the action in question.[128]

Section 7 regulations also require the Secretary to consider cumulative effects on listed species during consultation.[129] At this point, it is helpful to emphasize the distinction between indirect effects and cumulative effects. Indirect effects of an action are actually *caused by* and subsequent to that action, as in private development spawned by construction of a highway. Cumulative effects refer to the additive impacts of past, present and future actions on listed species, where the actions are not necessarily related.

A 1978 Solicitor's Opinion initially applied cumulative effects analysis to section 7 consultation under the ESA.[130] The Opinion essentially tracked the NEPA regulatory definition of cumulative effects. It directed the Secretary to consider, within the context of individual consultations, the potential impacts on listed species of pending projects that could reasonably be anticipated to occur either before or after the completion of the federal project in question. The pending projects could include private, state, or other federal projects.

A 1981 Solicitor's Opinion superseded this interpretation.[131] The more recent Opinion takes the position that cumulative effects analysis as developed under NEPA regulations and cases should not be applied without modification to section 7 consultations. It therefore adopts a complex definition of cumulative effects unique to the ESA. The Opinion defines the scope of a federal project to include the project itself and connected activi-

---

128. *See* 40 C.F.R. § 1508.8.
129. 50 C.F.R. § 402.14(g)(3). Regulations define cumulative effects as follows: " '*Cumulative effects*' are those effects of future State or private activities, not involving Federal activities, that are reasonably certain to occur within the action area of the Federal action subject to consultation." *Id.* at § 402.02. For further discussion of this definition, see 51 Fed. Reg. 19,932 (1986).
130. *See* 85 Interior Dec. 275 (1978).
131. 88 Interior Dec. 903 (1981).

ties interrelated or interdependent on the proposed project. "Interdependent" actions are defined as having no independent utility apart from the proposed project; "interrelated" actions are defined as actually a part of the proposed project that cannot proceed unless other actions are taken previously or simultaneously.[132]

The Secretary begins an ESA cumulative effects analysis by figuring the total impacts of the project and its connected activities on a hypothetical resource "cushion." The Solicitor defines this resource cushion as "that amount of a particular natural resource like water, air, vegetation or habitat (upon which a given listed species is dependent), that could be utilized or consumed, without jeopardy to the continued existence of the species."[133]

Next, other *proposed* federal actions previously the subject of section 7 consultation which have received a "no jeopardy" biological opinion are also considered under the cumulative effects analysis. The anticipated effects of such projects are subtracted from the resource "cushion" available to the proposal under consideration. The effects of other proposed federal projects which have *not* been the subject of section 7 consultation are *not* considered in the cumulative effects analysis, since such projects must themselves later comply with the mandates of section 7 before they are approved. The Opinion thus envisions a "first-in-time, first-in-right" scheme for federal projects.[134] In other words, whether a proposed federal project is authorized depends on how much of the resource "cushion" is left for consumption at the time it undergoes section 7 consultation.

The cumulative effects analysis for a given federal project must also consider impacts of contemporaneous state or private actions.[135] Additionally, future state or private actions "reasonably certain" to occur are also classified as cumulative effects to be considered under section 7.[136] The Solicitor's Opinion classifies reasonably certain events as including those for which required state or local approval is obtained, financial backing is assured, and other similar indicators suggest the activity will

---

132. *Id.* at 906.
133. Memorandum to Regional Solicitor, Rocky Mountain Region from Associate Solicitor, Conservation and Wildlife, U.S. Department of the Interior, 1 (July 6, 1982) (on file with the author) [hereinafter cited as *Memorandum*].
134. 88 Interior Dec. 903, 907 (1981).
135. *Id.* at 908.
136. *Id.*

occur.[137]

In sum, the cumulative effects analysis scheme essentially links all section 7 consultations dealing with the same species in a given ecosystem. Once consultation identifies constituent resources of the "cushion" upon which a listed species depends, as well as the status quo of that cushion, subsequent section 7 consultations merely determine how much additional effect a proposed federal action will have on the ecosystem. This amount, together with the effects of state and private actions "reasonably certain" to occur, is subtracted from the cushion's status quo as determined by the previous consultation. If this calculation indicates that the proposed federal action will affect the cushion to the extent that species are jeopardized or critical habitat is modified, then section 7 would prohibit the action. All future federal activities requiring "consumption" of the resource cushion in that ecosystem would likewise be forbidden. Thus, once the Secretary issues a jeopardy opinion for a given species in a given ecosystem, federal agencies are put on notice that section 7 precludes further activities in that ecosystem adversely affecting that species.[138]

The rationale set forth by the 1981 Solicitor's Opinion to justify creating a specialized ESA cumulative effects analysis procedure in place of the NEPA-style procedure used in section 7 consultations prior to 1981 is unconvincing. Under NEPA-style cumulative effects analysis, federal agencies must consider the likely impacts of all "reasonably foreseeable" federal and nonfederal actions.[139] Current ESA cumulative effects analysis, on the other hand, requires the Secretary to consider only the impacts of "reasonably certain" nonfederal actions.[140] The 1981 Solicitor's Opinion justifies the higher "reasonably certain" standard by noting that the ESA imposes substantive limitations on federal activities, whereas NEPA merely imposes procedural obligations.[141] Therefore, the argument continues, "prerequisite authority for a proposed action subject to [section 7] consultation

---

137. *Id. See supra* text accompanying note 127.
138. A clarification of this procedure provides that "[o]nce this 'cushion' is allocated, additional utilization of the particular resource can be authorized if further effects are offset by other means, so that the net result is no further adverse impact on the species." *Memorandum, supra* note 133.
139. 40 C.F.R. § 1508.7.
140. 50 C.F.R. § 402.02.
141. 88 Interior Dec. 903, 905 (1981).

could be denied because of the effects of other speculative and unrelated future actions which might be likely to jeopardize a listed species."[142]

This line of reasoning has two important flaws. First, it is irrelevant whether future impacts on listed species are caused by actions unrelated to the proposed federal activity in question. The purpose of cumulative effects analysis is to look at the additive impacts of *all* actions on listed species, regardless of whether the actions are related. Second, actions which are reasonably foreseeable are not "speculative" and therefore should be considered within a cumulative effects analysis. This is not unreasonable because many legal questions turn on the question of what is reasonably foreseeable. Significantly, section 7's legislative history makes it clear that listed species are to be accorded the benefit of the doubt and, thus, greater protection.[143] Therefore, as in the definition of indirect effects,[144] the "reasonably certain" standard within the meaning of cumulative effects is too high.

The 1981 Solicitor's Opinion also reasons that an ESA cumulative effects analysis should not consider the impacts of other proposed federal actions that are not yet the subject of section 7 consultation because such actions must eventually undergo consultation and would be proscribed at that time if the hypothetical resource cushion had already been used up.[145] This type of "first-come, first-served" scheme for federal projects presents substantial practical dangers. The first project to undergo section 7 consultation will not necessarily be the most valuable use of certain resources nor the most politically popular project. Thus, there is a danger that more desirable projects may be approved even after the available species resource "cushion" has been used up by less socially valuable projects, if project proponents can "steamroll" the project to completion. It would make much more sense to consider the cumulative effects of all proposed federal projects in a given area at the earliest possible moment, allowing decisionmakers themselves to set priorities among the various projects, rather than simply determining pri-

---

142. *Id.*

143. *See* H.R. CONF. REP. No. 697, 96th Cong., 1st Sess. 159, *reprinted in* 1979 U.S. CODE CONG. & ADMIN. NEWS 2572, 2576.

144. *See supra* notes 126-127 and accompanying text.

145. 88 Interior Dec. 903, 907 (1981).

ority based upon which projects undergo section 7 consultation first.

For the above reasons, NEPA cumulative effects procedures should apply in an ESA context, as they did prior to 1981.

VI. EXPERIMENTAL POPULATIONS

In 1982, Congress added a subsection to the ESA dealing with so-called experimental populations. These provisions are significant primarily because they contain a limited exception to the substantive protection of section 7.

The ESA defines an experimental population as a population of a listed species established by the Secretary outside the current range of that species and which remains geographically separate from other populations.[146] The Secretary may establish experimental populations to conserve listed species.[147] All experimental populations are classified as threatened species, regardless of whether non-experimental populations of the same species are listed as endangered or threatened.[148] When establishing an experimental population, the Secretary must determine, on the basis of the best available information, whether that population is "essential to the continued existence" of the particular species as a whole.[149] This finding is very important because "non-essential" experimental populations which occur outside national parks or national wildlife refuges are treated as species proposed for listing *for purposes of section 7 only*.[150] This means that non-essential experimental populations outside national parks and national wildlife refuges are entitled to no substantive section 7 protection.[151] Experimental populations determined to be essential to the continued existence of a listed species, or non-

---

146. 16 U.S.C. § 1539(j)(l).

147. *Id.* at § 1539(j)(2)(A).

148. *Id.* at § 1539(j)(2)(C).

149. *Id.* at § 1539(j)(2)(B). Regulations implementing the ESA's experimental population provisions define an experimental population as essential to the continued existence of a listed species if loss of the experimental population "would be likely to appreciably reduce the likelihood of the survival of the species in the wild." 50 C.F.R. § 17.80(b) (1986). The regulations classify all other experimental populations as non-essential. *Id.*

150. 16 U.S.C. § 1539(j)(2)(C)(i).

151. Species proposed for listing receive no substantive section 7 protection and are subject only to the procedural conference requirements. In addition, the Secretary may not designate critical habitat for non-essential experimental populations. *See* 16 U.S.C. § 1539(j)(2)(C)(ii).

essential populations occurring in national parks and national wildlife refuges, receive the full protection of section 7.[152] The existence of experimental populations of a certain species in no way affects the application of section 7 to non-experimental populations of that species.

Since all experimental populations are treated as threatened species, the prohibitions listed in ESA section 9 do not automatically apply to experimental populations. Instead, as for other threatened species, the Secretary must promulgate regulations which further the conservation of experimental populations.[153]

VII.   UNLISTED SPECIES, PROPOSED SPECIES, AND PROPOSED CRITICAL HABITAT

With one minor exception,[154] species not on the endangered or threatened lists or proposed for listing receive no substantive protection under section 7.[155] Federal agencies must "confer" with the Secretary whenever an agency action is likely to jeopardize the continued existence of a species proposed for listing.[156] This requirement, however, is merely procedural.[157] The ESA expressly provides that the restrictions of section 7(d) do not apply to proposed species.[158] Additionally, the legislative history indicates that no other substantive section 7 protection attaches until a species is formally added to the endangered or threatened lists.[159] Congress warned, however, that actions affecting a proposed species that are lawful when taken may constitute section 7 violations if the species is subsequently listed.[160]

Agencies also must confer with the Secretary on actions likely to destroy or adversely modify proposed critical habitat.[161]

---

152. Such experimental populations are considered threatened species for purposes of section 7. Hence, like other threatened species, they enjoy the full protection of section 7.

153. *See supra* Chapter 4 for a discussion of threatened species.

154. The Secretary may promulgate regulations protecting unlisted species which are similar in appearance to listed species. *See* 16 U.S.C. § 1533(e).

155. *See* Wilson v. Block, 708 F.2d 735, 747-51 (D.C. Cir. 1983); Enos v. Marsh, 769 F.2d 1363, 1369 (9th Cir. 1985).

156. 16 U.S.C. § 1536(a)(4). *See also* 50 C.F.R. § 402.10.

157. For a summary of conference procedural requirements, see *supra* Chapter 6, notes 58-63 and accompanying text.

158. 16 U.S.C. § 1536(a)(4).

159. H.R. CONF. REP. No. 697, 96th Cong., 1st Sess. 159, *reprinted in* 1979 U.S. CODE CONG. & ADMIN. NEWS 2572, 2577.

160. *Id.*

161. 16 U.S.C. § 1536(a)(4).

Whether the substantive section 7 mandate to refrain from destroying or adversely modifying critical habitat applies to proposed critical habitat is similar to the question of whether this mandate applies to land necessary to the recovery of a listed species but not formally designated as critical habitat.[162]

---

162. *See supra* notes 79-95 and accompanying text.

Chapter 8

International Aspects

The problem of human-caused species extinctions crosses international boundaries. Congress cited the plight of rare species in other countries as one reason for the United States to enact strong protective legislation and saw the ESA in part as setting an important precedent for other nations to follow.[1] Accordingly, the ESA implements two major international species conservation agreements and contains several other provisions designed to further protection of listed species around the globe.

I. Convention Implementation

ESA section 8[2] implements the Convention on Nature Protection and Wildlife Preservation in the Western Hemisphere.[3] This relatively little known Convention, signed in 1940, has potentially broad ramifications but has had little concrete effect.[4] In 1982, however, Congress amended the ESA to direct the Secretary of the Interior, acting in cooperation with the Secretary of State, to take steps to put the Convention into effect.[5] This provision specifically directs the Secretary to cooperate with other parties to the Convention to identify measures necessary to protect migratory birds and plants.[6]

The ESA also implements[7] the Convention on International Trade in Endangered Species of Wild Fauna and Flora[8] (CITES), probably the most significant international regulation of trade in

---

1. *See, e.g.*, H. R. REP. No. 412, 93d Cong., 1st Sess. 4-6 (1973).
2. 16 U.S.C. § 1537a(e).
3. Oct. 12, 1940, 56 Stat. 1354, T.S. No. 981.
4. For a brief discussion of the provisions of the Convention, see M. BEAN, THE EVOLUTION OF NATIONAL WILDLIFE LAW 313-18 (1977). *See also* Guilbert, *Wilderness Preservation I: A Recent Case and a Not-So-Recent Treaty*, 3 Envtl. L. Rep. (Envtl. L. Inst.) 50,023 (1973); Guilbert, *Wilderness Preservation II: Bringing the Convention into Court*, 3 Envtl. L. Rep. (Envtl. L. Inst.) 50,044 (1973).
5. 16 U.S.C. § 1537a(e)(2).
6. 16 U.S.C. §§ 1537a(e)(2)(B)-(C).
7. *Id.* at §§ 1538(c), 1537(a)-(d).
8. Mar. 3, 1973, 27 U.S.T. 1087, T.I.A.S. No. 8249.

rare species.[9] In 1982, Congress amended the ESA explicitly to forbid the Secretary from requiring that states estimate population sizes of species covered by CITES,[10] reversing a decision by the D.C. Court of Appeals.[11]

II. INTERNATIONAL COOPERATION AND ENFORCEMENT

Section 8 contains a number of provisions designed to encourage international efforts to protect rare species, especially species listed as threatened or endangered pursuant to the ESA. It gives the President power to provide financial assistance to foreign nations for species conservation programs.[12] Section 8 also directs the Secretary of the Interior, acting through the Secretary of State, to encourage foreign governments or individuals to protect rare species and to encourage the development and signing of agreements between the United States and other countries on species conservation.[13] After consulting the Secretary of State, the Secretary of the Interior may also offer the services of federal personnel to foreign nations or to international organizations attempting to conserve fish, wildlife, or plants. The United States may also provide or finance training of foreign wildlife experts.[14] Finally, section 8 authorizes law enforcement and research operations abroad.[15]

III. LISTING, CRITICAL HABITAT DESIGNATION, AND RECOVERY PLANS

The ESA permits the Secretary to list species even if they are not found in the United States. Accordingly, only about 425 species of the 925 species listed as threatened or endangered at

---

9. For a brief outline of how CITES works, see *supra* Chapter 2, notes 77-79 and accompanying text; *see also* Kosloff & Trexler, *The Convention on International Trade in Endangered Species: No Carrot, but Where's the Stick?* 17 Envtl. L. Rep. (Envtl. L. Inst.) 10,222 (1987); Schonfeld, *International Trade in Wildlife: How Effective is the Endangered Species Treaty?*, 15 CAL. W. INT'L L. J. 111 (1985); Melick, *Regulation of International Trade in Endangered Wildlife*, 1 B. U. INT'L L. J. 249 (1982).

10. 16 U.S.C. § 1537a(c)(2).

11. Defenders of Wildlife v. Endangered Species Scientific Authority, 659 F.2d 168 (D.C. Cir.), *cert. denied*, 454 U.S. 963 (1981).

12. 16 U.S.C. § 1537(a).

13. *Id.* at § 1537(b).

14. *Id.* at § 1537(c).

15. *Id.* at § 1537(d).

the end of 1986 are native to the United States.[16] Section 4 directs the Secretary to consider listing species identified by foreign governments as in danger of extinction, as well as species which foreign nations or international agreements protect from unrestricted commerce.[17] When listing foreign species, the Secretary must consider efforts by other countries to conserve the species.[18]

As a matter of policy, the Secretary does not designate critical habitats for species found outside the United States or on the high seas. A 1976 Solicitor's Opinion concluded that the ESA does not require designation of critical habitats outside the United States.[19] The Opinion based its conclusion on the fact that the ESA's critical habitat provisions do not require or even mention involvement of the Secretary of State or consultation with foreign governments, unlike other ESA provisions dealing with foreign species. The Opinion also noted that due to obvious constraints on U.S. government personnel working abroad it would often be very difficult to define precisely the critical habitat of foreign species. Though the Secretary's policy of not designating critical habitats in foreign countries generated considerable controversy,[20] Congress apparently resolved this issue in 1982. The House Report accompanying the 1982 amendments expressed agreement with the conclusion of the Solicitor's Opinion.[21]

The Secretary also generally does not prepare recovery plans for foreign species listed pursuant to the ESA. This is apparently a result of the Secretary's recovery priority scheme, however, rather than a matter of policy. The Secretary's recovery priority guidelines note that priority for preparing and implementing recovery plans goes to species with the greatest potential for recov-

---

16. DEFENDERS OF WILDLIFE, SAVING ENDANGERED SPECIES: IMPLEMENTATION OF THE ENDANGERED SPECIES ACT, 6 (1987) (pamphlet in author's files).

17. 16 U.S.C. § 1533(b)(1)(B).

18. *Id.* at § 1533(b)(1)(A).

19. Memorandum to the Associate Director, U.S. Fish and Wildlife Service, from the Assistant Solicitor for Fish and Wildlife, U.S. Department of the Interior (Feb. 13, 1976) (copy in author's files).

20. This policy was challenged in court in Colorado River Water Conservation District v. Andrus, 476 F. Supp. 966 (D. Colo. 1979). The court ordered the Secretary to designate critical habitat for a listed fish species found in Mexico. Congress, however, implicitly reversed this holding in 1982. *See infra* text accompanying note 21.

21. H.R. REP. No. 567, 97th Cong., 2d Sess., pt. 1, at 20, *reprinted in* 1982 U.S. CODE CONG. & ADMIN. NEWS 2820.

ery success.[22] Since the Secretary's ability to promote recovery of foreign species is obviously more limited than for domestic species, the Secretary views preparation of recovery plans for domestic species as a higher priority than recovery plan preparation for foreign species.[23] Recovery plans *are* prepared for migratory species, such as whooping cranes, which spend only part of their life cycle in the United States.

IV. PROHIBITIONS

Section 9 prohibits import into the United States of all species listed as endangered, including exclusively foreign species.[24] This section also forbids anyone subject to United States jurisdiction from transporting, receiving, delivering, carrying, shipping, selling, or offering endangered species for sale in foreign commerce.[25] The ESA broadly defines foreign commerce to include transactions between persons in foreign countries, transactions between a person in the United States and a person in a foreign country, and even transactions between persons in the United States when endangered species move in commerce within foreign countries.[26]

Finally, section 9 prohibits those subject to United States jurisdiction from taking endangered species in the United States, its territorial seas, and on the high seas.[27] Last-minute opposition by hunter groups in 1973 prevented passage of a provision which would have extended the takings ban to foreign

---

22. 48 Fed. Reg. 43,098, 43,104 (1983).

23. Telephone interview with Larry Thomas, U.S. Fish and Wildlife Service, Office of Endangered Species, Washington, D.C. (Oct. 8, 1987). The wisdom of this approach, however, is questionable. The United States may be able to significantly affect the conservation of foreign species on the protected lists by strictly enforcing section 9's prohibitions on imports of listed species and commerce in listed species or by refraining from taking actions within other countries which imperil listed species. The Secretary's recovery guidelines themselves also suggest that the Secretary should give recovery plan preparation for at least some foreign species higher priority than for some domestic species. The recovery guidelines accord species facing a high degree of threat relatively high priority, even if those species have low "recovery potential" ratings under the Secretary's recovery priority guidelines. *See* 48 Fed. Reg. 43,098, 43,104 (1983).

24. 16 U.S.C. § 1538(a)(1)(A). The Secretary has discretion to prohibit by regulation imports of all threatened species into the United States but has not done so.

25. *Id.* at § 1538(a)(1)(E)-(F).

26. *Id.* at § 1532(9).

27. *Id.* at § 1538(a)(1)(B)-(C).

countries.[28]

V.   SECTION 7'S JEOPARDY STANDARD

In 1986, the Secretary issued new section 7 regulations which interpret section 7(a)(2)'s directive to federal agencies to refrain from taking actions likely to jeopardize listed species as applying only to federal actions carried out within the United States or on the high seas.[29] This interpretation reversed the position adopted in previous section 7 regulations, which explicitly provided that federal activities within foreign countries were subject to section 7(a)(2)'s jeopardy standard.[30]

To justify eliminating the requirement that federal actions overseas comply with the jeopardy standard and section 7's consultation procedures, the explanation accompanying the 1986 section 7 regulations cited the "apparent domestic orientation" of section 7's consultation and exemption processes, as well as potential interference with sovereignty of foreign nations should the jeopardy standard apply to American actions in other countries.[31] These justifications appear to track the reasoning of a 1981 Solicitor's Opinion which also concluded that section 7 does not apply to federal actions in foreign countries.[32] The Solicitor argued that the ESA's section 7 exemption process "fails to expressly reflect the possibility that an exemption may be necessary for a federal action in a foreign country"[33] and thus supports an interpretation giving section 7 no extraterritorial applicability. To bolster this argument, the Solicitor noted that the exemption process makes provisions to include governors of affected states but is silent about including consultation with foreign governments. Finally, the Solicitor asserted that section 7 consultation on federal actions abroad would interfere with foreign sovereignty with respect to foreign nations' development priorities and species conservation programs.

The arguments against applying section 7 to federal actions

---

28. *See* S. YAFFEE, PROHIBITIVE POLICY: IMPLEMENTATION OF THE FEDERAL ENDANGERED SPECIES ACT 56 (1982).

29. *See* 50 C.F.R. § 402.01(a).

30. 50 C.F.R. § 402.01 (1985) (superseded).

31. 51 Fed. Reg. 19,926, 19,929 (1986).

32. Memorandum to the Assistant Secretary of the Interior, Fish, Wildlife and Parks, from the Associate Solicitor for Conservation and Wildlife, U.S. Department of the Interior (Aug. 31, 1981) (copy in author's files).

33. *Id.* at 4.

overseas have little merit. Contrary to the position taken by the
Solicitor's Opinion and the explanation accompanying the 1986
section 7 regulations, the statutory section 7 exemption process
does in fact appear to recognize that federal actions overseas
could be the subject of an exemption application. For example,
section 7 provides that "[a] Federal agency, the Governor of the
State in which an agency action will occur, *if any*, or a permit or
license applicant may apply to the Secretary for an exemption
. . . ."[34] Additionally, section 7 provides that the D.C. Circuit has
jurisdiction to review exemption decisions concerning agency actions to take place outside the United States.[35] Furthermore,
since section 7 applies exclusively to United States federal agencies, there is also little likelihood that consultation on federal actions overseas to conserve threatened and endangered species
would interfere with foreign sovereignty. The United States
commonly attaches strings to its foreign aid without consulting
affected countries. If these countries are uncomfortable with certain United States activities on their soil, they may simply refuse
to permit the offensive actions. Finally, it is almost inconceivable
that Congress, while terming the value of endangered species
"incalculable"[36] and citing the importance of global efforts to
conserve species,[37] could simultaneously condone federal actions
abroad which may jeopardize the continued existence of listed
species.[38]

After the section 7 regulations were published in 1986, Defenders of Wildlife and two other organizations filed suit challenging the Secretary's decision to limit section 7's reach to
domestic species. After a dispute over standing was resolved in

---

34. 16 U.S.C. § 1536(g)(1) (emphasis added).

35. *Id.* at § 1536(n).

36. H.R. REP. No. 412, 93d Cong., 1st Sess. 4 (1973).

37. *Id.* at 1-6.

38. In the Senate report accompanying the 1988 ESA amendments, lawmakers left
little doubt as to how Congress viewed regulations restricting the scope of section 7's
mandates. The report provides:

To the extent [section 7] regulations attempt to restrict the Act's requirements
that each federal agency consult with the Secretary to ensure that its actions are
not likely to jeopardize the continued existence and recovery of any listed species, the regulations have no statutory basis, are contrary to congressional intent, and are contrary to the law.

S. REP. No. 240, 100th Cong., 1st Sess. 6-7 (1987).

One commentator also builds a compelling case that section 7 applies to federal
actions in foreign countries. *See* Erdheim, *Insuring the Effectiveness of Endangered Species Act
Section 7*, 9 ECOLOGY L.Q. 629, 668-73 (1981).

favor of the plaintiffs,[39] a federal district court ordered the Secretary to promulgate revised regulations applying section 7 procedures to federal actions abroad.[40]

---

39. *See* Defenders of Wildlife v. Hodel, 658 F. Supp. 43 (D. Minn. 1987), *rev'd*, 851 F.2d 1035 (8th Cir. 1988).

40. Defenders of Wildlife v. Hodel, No. 3-86 Civ. 757 (D. Minn. Feb. 15, 1989).

Chapter 9

Species Conservation and the Courts: Judicial Review under the Endangered Species Act

The ESA contains strong measures to enforce its protection of endangered and threatened species. Many of these statutory enforcement mechanisms are available not only to federal officials charged with administering the ESA, but to interested individuals as well. The latter commonly seek to further the protection of listed species through the federal courts. Accordingly, a large body of law has developed which deals with the procedural requirements of judicial review under the ESA, as well as the substantive review standards courts apply to disputes involving listed species.

I. PUBLIC ENFORCEMENT

ESA section 11 grants the Secretary broad enforcement powers. The Secretary may impose civil penalties up to $10,000 for each violation of the statute after giving alleged violators notice and an opportunity for a hearing.[1] The Secretary also has authority to conduct searches[2] and may confiscate listed species or their products which have been taken, sold, shipped, or exported in a manner contrary to the ESA.[3]

Section 11 also subjects persons who knowingly violate any provision of the ESA to criminal penalties of up to one year in jail and to up to $20,000 in fines.[4] Those convicted of criminal ESA violations face suspension, or in some cases even revocation, of federal licenses and permits relating to wildlife trade or livestock

---

1. 16 U.S.C. § 1540(a)(1). For specific procedures governing how the Secretary conducts hearings on the assessment of civil penalties pursuant to the ESA, see 16 U.S.C. § 1540(a)(2).
2. *Id.* at § 1540(e)(3).
3. *Id.* at § 1540(e)(4)(A).
4. *Id.* at § 1540(b)(1).

grazing.[5] Additionally, the federal government may permanently confiscate equipment from persons convicted under the ESA, ranging from guns to airplanes used to commit specified violations of the statute.[6]

Finally, in 1982 Congress amended section 11 to empower the U.S. Attorney General to seek injunctions against any persons[7] alleged to be in violation of an ESA provision or regulation issued under authority of the statute.[8]

A. *Jurisdiction and Venue*

Federal district courts have jurisdiction over disputes arising under the ESA without regard to the citizenship of the parties or the amount in controversy.[9] Section 11 also provides that citizen suits *may* be brought in the judicial district in which the violation occurs.[10] This has been construed to be a venue provision only.[11]

B. *Citizen Suits and Standing*

Section 11 contains a liberal citizen suit provision. It allows any person[12] to maintain an action against another person, including governmental entities to the extent permitted by the Eleventh Amendment, alleged to be in violation of any provision of the statute or its implementing regulations.[13] In addition, section 11 specifically authorizes any person to sue the Secretary to

---

5. *Id.* at § 1540(b)(2).

6. *Id.* at § 1540(e)(4)(B).

7. The ESA broadly defines the word "person" as any "individual, corporation, partnership, trust, association, or any other private entity, or any officer, employee, agent, department, or instrumentality of the Federal Government, of any state or political subdivision thereof, or of any foreign government." *Id.* at § 1532(13) (1982). The 1988 Amendments to the ESA expanded the definition of "person" to include states, municipalities, other political subdivisions of a state, "or any other entity subject to the jurisdiction of the United States. H.R. Conf. Rep. No. 928, 100th Cong., 2d Sess. 1 (1988).

8. 16 U.S.C. § 1540(e)(6).

9. *Id.* at § 1540(g)(1).

10. *Id.* at § 1540(g)(3)(A).

11. *See* Colorado River Water Conservation District v. Andrus, 476 F. Supp. 966 (D. Colo. 1979).

12. The ESA contains a broad definition of "person." *See supra* note 7. Courts have apparently expanded this definition. In at least two cases, the listed species involved was itself named as the plaintiff, with various environmental organizations as co-plaintiffs.

13. 16 U.S.C. § 1540(g)(1)(A).

compel enforcement of ESA taking prohibitions in emergency situations,[14] or compel the Secretary to perform a non-discretionary duty arising under section 4.[15]

The ESA also indirectly provides private persons with judicially enforceable rights under the Convention on International Trade in Endangered Species (CITES) by implementing the Convention.[16] Therefore, section 11's citizen suit provisions presumably apply to facilitate private enforcement of CITES, as well as to the ESA itself.

Section 11 contains two express limitations on private enforcement. It bars citizen suits when the Secretary is pursuing civil penalties against an alleged violator or when the United States is pressing criminal charges.[17] Citizen suits are also barred when the Secretary has commenced action to determine whether an emergency situation justifies action under section 6.[18]

Despite the fact that the ESA's liberal citizen suit provision implies a low threshold for standing,[19] a small number of courts have found that plaintiffs lacked standing to assert an ESA claim. The Tenth Circuit in *Glover River Organization v. U.S. Department of the Interior*[20] held that plaintiffs challenging a listing action lacked standing because no facts supported existence of a substantial nexus between the relief plaintiffs requested and elimination of plaintiffs' alleged injuries. Two other courts faced with claims similar to those advanced in *Glover* also reached the same conclusions on standing.[21] Each of these cases involved attempts by plaintiffs to block addition of a species to the protected lists. The plaintiff in *Glover*, for example, opposed listing of a small fish because it feared the listing would preclude construction of dams

---

14. *Id.* at § 1540(g)(1)(B).

15. *Id.* at § 1540(g)(1)(C).

16. *See* Defenders of Wildlife v. Endangered Species Scientific Authority, 659 F.2d 168, 175 (D.C. Cir. 1981), *cert. denied*, International Association of Fish & Wildlife Agencies v. Defenders of Wildlife, 454 U.S. 963 (1981). *See also supra* Chapter 8 for a discussion of CITES.

17. 16 U.S.C. § 1540(g)(2)(A).

18. *Id.* at § 1540(g)(2)(B)(ii).

19. *See, e.g.*, Pacific Legal Foundation v. Watt, 703 F.2d 576 (9th Cir. 1983) ("We impose a relatively low threshold with respect to environmental litigation in general and the Endangered Species Act in particular.").

20. 675 F.2d 251 (10th Cir. 1982).

21. *See* Colorado River Water Conservation District v. Andrus, 476 F. Supp. 966 (D. Colo. 1979); Pacific Legal Foundation v. Andrus, 13 Env't Rep. Cas. (BNA) 1266 (1979), *aff'd on other grounds*, 657 F.2d 829 (6th Cir. 1981).

desired by the plaintiff.[22] The courts' refusals to reach the merits
in these cases suggests that plaintiffs whose aims are not consistent with conserving rare species face substantial standing hur-
dles to asserting an ESA claim even under the citizen suit
provision of section 11.

Defenders of Wildlife v. Hodel[23] dealt extensively with standing
issues under the ESA. There, plaintiffs sought to challenge regulations which eliminated the applicability of section 7 to U.S. federal actions in foreign countries.[24] In dismissing plaintiffs'
claims, the district court noted that the plaintiffs' complaint alleged an interest in proper enforcement of the ESA to insure full
protection of listed species but that it did not cite any specific
instances in foreign countries where listed species suffered as a
result of the Secretary's reinterpretation of section 7. Citing *Sierra Club v. Morton*,[25] the court held that this mere allegation of
interest was an insufficient injury for standing purposes.[26] In a
later brief, however, plaintiffs listed several U.S. activities in foreign countries which allegedly harmed or threatened to harm
listed species. The court found these further allegations still insufficient to show injury. It found no indication that the listed
projects would harm listed species. The court also put particular
emphasis on the fact that plaintiffs did not seek to enjoin the enu-
merated activities. The court observed that limited judicial resources counselled against deciding cases when plaintiffs failed
to request a remedy to redress an alleged injury relied upon to
show standing.[27]

The Eighth Circuit court reversed on appeal, holding that the
plaintiffs had shown an actual or threatened injury in fact traceable to the Secretary's promulgation of the challenged regulation.[28] While agreeing with the district court that a mere interest

---

22. Although the court in *Glover* refused to grant plaintiff the relief it requested,
the court determined that plaintiff's allegation of threatened future flood damage if
dams were not built was sufficient to constitute a concrete injury for standing purposes.
675 F.2d at 254.

23. 658 F. Supp. 43 (D. Minn. 1987), *rev'd sub nom.*, Defenders of Wildlife, Friends
of Animals v. Hodel, 851 F.2d 1035 (8th Cir. 1988).

24. *See supra* Chapter 8, note 29 and accompanying text.

25. 405 U.S. 727 (1972) (mere interest in environmental protection insufficient to
confer standing).

26. 658 F. Supp. at 46.

27. *Id.* at 48.

28. Defenders of Wildlife, Friends of Animals v. Hodel, 851 F.2d 1035, 1040-41
(8th Cir. 1988).

in enforcing the ESA would be insufficient to confer standing, the court of appeals found plaintiffs' allegation—that specific foreign projects increased the rate of extinction of endangered species in countries plaintiffs' members visited—sufficient to constitute injury in fact.[29] The court further determined that the plaintiffs had pleaded a judicially cognizable procedural injury under the ESA by alleging that the Secretary had refused to carry out a statutorily mandated procedure: the Secretary failed to promulgate regulations requiring federal agencies to consult on agency actions abroad which may affect listed species.[30]

The appellate court also rejected the Secretary's arguments that the plaintiffs' alleged injuries were not traceable to the Secretary's actions and that injunctive relief sought by the plaintiffs would not redress their alleged injuries. The court of appeals disagreed with the district court's observation that there was no indication that specific projects cited by the plaintiffs would affect listed species. The appellate court noted that requiring such evidence as a prerequisite to standing would require environmental plaintiffs to conduct their own independent investigation before commencing an action. The court quoted from an opinion in which the Ninth Circuit court held that one's standing under NEPA did not depend on the plaintiffs' ability to prove that certain environmental effects would occur.[31] The court also held that relief sought by the plaintiffs—an order compelling the Secretary to require consultation on agency actions abroad—would redress plaintiffs' alleged injuries. To support this conclusion, the court reasoned that "Congress has determined that the remedy for the harm to [plaintiffs'] personal, professional, and aesthetic interest in endangered species is consultation between the Secretary and the action agency."[32] By characterizing the remedy for plaintiffs' alleged injuries as procedural rather than substantive, the Eighth Circuit court rejected the district court's conclusion, based on plaintiffs' failure to ask for injunctions against specific U.S. agency activities affecting listed species abroad, that the plaintiff environmental organizations had neglected to request relief for their alleged injuries.

---

29. *Id.* at 1040.

30. *Id.* at 1040-41.

31. *Id.* at 1042 (citing City of Davis v. Coleman, 521 F.2d 661, 670-71 (9th Cir. 1975)).

32. 851 F.2d at 1043.

In addition to demonstrating that standing requirements under the ESA are minimal, the *Defenders* decision is significant because it affords plaintiffs standing to seek broad changes in the way the Secretary implements the ESA without tying their claims to any specific actions. The existence of a judicially recognizable procedural injury under the ESA may prove to be especially significant with regard to litigation involving section 7, which contains a number of procedural requirements designed to buttress substantive prohibitions against jeopardizing listed species or adversely modifying critical habitats.

II.   The ESA and Federalism

When it passed the ESA, Congress gave the federal government power over wildlife that was previously exercised by the states.[33] Hence, the ESA occasionally gives rise to difficult issues of federalism.[34]

Section 11 permits any person to sue state governments or political subdivisions thereof to the extent permitted by the Eleventh Amendment to the U.S. Constitution.[35] In *Palila v. Hawaii Department of Land and Natural Resources*[36] (*Palila I*), the district court examined whether the Eleventh Amendment barred a suit against State alleged to be in violation of the ESA. The court found that the statutory reference to the Eleventh Amendment in section 11(g) does not constitute a blanket sovereign immunity exception to private enforcement of the ESA. The court reasoned that a contrary conclusion would seriously impair achievement of a congressional purpose to conserve listed species and lead to a right without an effective remedy. The court concluded that State of Hawaii implicitly consented to be sued by participating in species conservation activities covered by federal legislation. Hawaii's participation in a cooperative agreement under ESA section 6 and passage of a state endangered species law to further this agreement were cited by the court as evidence of Ha-

---

33. For example, prior to passage of the ESA, only the states regulated the taking of wildlife within their borders. (Migratory birds represent an exception to this rule. The federal government has long had a input into the harvest of these species.) ESA section 9 now regulates taking of listed species with the states.

34. For additional discussion of these issues, see M. Bean, The Evolution of National Wildlife Law 375-78 (1983).

35. 16 U.S.C. § 1540(g)(1)(A). *See also* 16 U.S.C. § 1532(13) (definition of "person").

36. 471 F. Supp. 985, 995-98, *aff'd*, 639 F.2d 495 (9th Cir. 1981).

waii's participation in activities regulated by the Federal government.

Also in the *Palila I* case, the defendant state agency argued that the Tenth Amendment prohibited the United States from enforcing the ESA against the State of Hawaii, particularly since no federal funds or federal land was involved in the dispute. Citing *Douglas v. Seacoast Products, Inc.*[37] and *Missouri v. Holland*,[38] the court observed that Congress has power under the Commerce Clause to preempt state control over wildlife. After also discussing various international treaties relating to wildlife, including those specifically noted by the ESA, the court concluded that the Tenth Amendment does not restrict enforcement of the ESA against states because of Congressional power to enact legislation implementing treaties and regulating commerce.

Whether the ESA preempts state regulation of trade in endangered species has been the subject of considerable controversy.[39] Courts are split on this issue. In *Man Hing Ivory and Imports v. Deukmejian*[40] and *Fouke Co. v. Brown*,[41] courts held that the ESA preempted state law. On the other hand, the court in *H.J. Justin & Sons, Inc. v. Brown*[42] upheld state law.

Finally, ESA section 6 provides for cooperative agreements between the states and the federal government to conserve listed species.[43]

III. NOTICE REQUIREMENTS PRIOR TO FILING SUIT

In limited instances, the ESA allows for immediate judicial review of disputes arising under the statute. In the event of "an emergency posing a significant risk to the well-being" of any listed species, any person may bring an action seeking to compel the Secretary to carry out a non-discretionary duty under section

---

37. 431 U.S. 265 (1977).

38. 252 U.S. 416 (1920).

39. *See generally* Phillips, *Federal Preemption of State Commerce Bans Under the Endangered Species Act*, 34 STAN. L. REV. 1323 (1982) (arguing that the ESA preempts state law only under narrow circumstances); Nelson, *State Governments Fall Prey to the Endangered Species Act of 1973*, 10 ECOLOGY L.Q. 281 (1982).

40. 702 F.2d 760, 764 (9th Cir. 1982).

41. 463 F. Supp. 1142 (E.D. Cal. 1979).

42. 519 F. Supp. 1383 (E.D. Cal. 1981). For an extensive analysis of this case and the *Fouke* case, see M. BEAN, *supra* note 34, at 377-80.

43. 16 U.S.C. § 1535. For further discussion of the mechanics of these agreements, see M. BEAN, *supra* note 34, at 376-77.

4.[44] In such a case, the plaintiff must first provide the Secretary with written notice of intent to sue. Immediately upon the Secretary's receipt of this notification, the plaintiff may bring suit.[45] Plaintiffs may also obtain immediate judicial review if the Secretary denies action on a petition to add or remove a species from the lists of threatened and endangered species.[46] Finally, no advance notice is necessary to obtain judicial review of exemptions to section 7 granted by the Endangered Species Committee.[47]

In other circumstances, persons wishing to exercise their right to file suit under section 11 must provide the Secretary and any alleged violator with written notice of the violation sixty days prior to commencing court action.[48] Of course, filing a sixty day notice does not obligate a potential plaintiff actually to file suit.

The ESA does not specify requirements for the content of a sixty day notice. Nevertheless, the notice should inform prospective defendants of the nature of a plaintiff's allegations in order to allow defendants to evaluate and possibly to alter their conduct.[49] Failure to outline all violations in the notice likely will not bar prospective plaintiffs from making related claims in their lawsuit, so long as alleged violators had general notice of plaintiffs' claims. Though this issue has not arisen in context of the ESA, judicial interpretation of a similar sixty day notice requirement of the Federal Water Pollution Control Act[50] suggests that courts may take a lenient position regarding related claims. In *Rivers Unlimited v. Costle*[51] the court held that "[t]he plaintiff's notice fairly informs the defendant of the nature of its complaints even though the plaintiff has now expanded the scope of the relief which it seeks."[52]

Courts have split on the importance of technical and formal aspects of a sixty day notice. In *National Wildlife Federation v. Coleman*,[53] the federal defendants challenged jurisdiction on the basis

44. 16 U.S.C. § 1540(g)(2)(C).
45. *Id.*
46. *Id.* at § 1533(b)(3)(C)(ii).
47. *Id.* at § 1536(m).
48. *Id.* at § 1540(g)(2)(A)(i).
49. *See, e.g.*, Rivers Unlimited v. Costle, 11 Env't Rep. Cas. (BNA) 1681, 1683 (S.D. Ohio 1978) (construing a similar sixty day notice provision in the Clean Water Act).
50. 33 U.S.C. § 1365(b).
51. 11 Env't Rep. Cas. (BNA) at 1683.
52. *Id.*
53. 400 F. Supp. 705 (S.D. Miss. 1975), *rev'd on other grounds*, 529 F.2d 359 (5th Cir. 1976).

that the plaintiff had failed to provide adequate notice. Noting that the ESA does not require sixty day notices to take any particular form, the district court found a letter from the plaintiff to defendants alleging that violations of the ESA constituted adequate notice, even though the letter did not purport to be the notice required by section 11.[54] On the other hand, in *Save the Yaak Committee v. Block*[55] the Ninth Circuit cited several deficiencies in finding the plaintiffs' notice inadequate to satisfy the ESA's notice requirement. The court noted that a letter relied on by the plaintiffs failed specifically to give notice of an ESA violation and failed specifically to mention an intention to file suit.[56] Even if these weaknesses were not enough to render the plaintiffs' written notice inadequate, the court continued, the notice was faulty because it was not sent to the Secretary of the Interior, as required by the statute.[57] The court implicitly construed "Secretary of the Interior" to mean the actual cabinet official, rather than merely one of his or her subordinates: the plaintiffs had sent a letter to a U.S. Fish and Wildlife Service Regional Director, a subordinate of the Secretary of the Interior.

In general, courts have liberally construed the timing of sixty day notices under the ESA. In several instances, courts have asserted jurisdiction over ESA claims even though plaintiffs filed suit prior to expiration of sixty days.[58] In rejecting arguments for strict observance of the sixty day notice requirement, courts have generally cited defendants' knowledge of their alleged violations as an indication that the purpose of the statutory notice requirement had been fulfilled and that further delay of judicial review of plaintiffs' claims to force technical compliance with the sixty day requirement would serve no useful purpose. In *Sierra Club v. Block*,[59] the court suggested in dicta that if defendants could show

---

54. 400 F. Supp. at 709-10.
55. 840 F.2d 714 (9th Cir. 1988).
56. *Id.* at 721.
57. *Id.*
58. *See, e.g.*, Jackson Hole Alliance for Responsible Planning v. Watt, 13 Envtl. L. Rep. (Envtl. L. Inst.) 20,994, 20,998 (D. Wyo. Sept. 8, 1983); Village of Kaktovik v. Corps of Engineers, 12 Env't Rep. Cas. (BNA) 1740, 1744 (D. Alaska 1978); Sierra Club v. Froehlke, 534 F.2d 1289, 1302 (8th Cir. 1976) (the number of experts on the endangered species was so small that allowing defendant's additional time to prepare for trial would produce no helpful new evidence); Sierra Club v. Block, 614 F. Supp. 488, 492 (D.D.C. 1985); Fund For Animals v. Andrus, 11 Env't Rep. Cas. (BNA) 2,189 (D. Minn. 1978).
59. 614 F. Supp. 488 (D.D.C. 1985).

any prejudice as a result of less than sixty days' notice, or that if defendants could show that they were reconsidering their allegedly illegal position, plaintiffs may be barred from filing suit prior to sixty days after notifying defendants of their intentions.[60]

Despite lenient interpretations by previous decisions, the Ninth Circuit's opinion in *Save the Yaak Committee v. Block*[61] may signal a dramatic change in the importance of timing of sixty day notices. In *Save the Yaak*, plaintiffs filed suit thirty-eight days after sending a formal notice of their intention to do so.[62] Citing a decision construing the notice provision of the Resources Conservation and Recovery Act as jurisdictional rather than procedural, the court similarly interpreted the ESA's notice requirement.[63] The court thus held that it lacked jurisdiction to consider an ESA claim because the plaintiffs had failed to provide timely notice before filing suit.[64] This decision, if followed by other courts, would make strict compliance with the sixty day notice requirement imperative since a court could not otherwise assume jurisdiction over an ESA claim. In addition to the *Save the Yaak* opinion, there is at least one instance of a court dismissing an ESA claim for lack of jurisdiction due to lack of sixty days notice.[65]

IV. STANDARD OF JUDICIAL REVIEW

The ESA does not explicitly provide a standard for judicial review of discretionary federal actions[66] made under the statute.

---

60. *Id.* at 492.

61. 840 F.2d 714 (9th Cir. 1988).

62. An earlier notice upon which plaintiffs relied to satisfy the ESA's notice requirement was found by the court to be inadequate. *See supra* note 57 and accompanying text.

63. 840 F.2d at 721 (citing Hallstrom v. Tillamook County, 831 F.2d 889 (9th Cir. 1987)).

64. *Id.*

65. Del-Aware v. Baldwin, Civ. No. 82-5115 (E.D. Penn. 1982). Additionally, the district court in *Romero-Barcelo v. Brown*, 478 F. Supp. 646 (D.P.R. 1979), declined to take jurisdiction over ESA claims due to the plaintiff's lack of compliance with the statute's sixty-day notice provision. *Id.* at 691. The Court of Appeals implicitly overruled this judgment, however, by considering ESA claims and remanding them to the district court. Romero-Barcelo v. Brown, 643 F.2d 835 (1st Cir. 1981), *rev'd sub nom.* Weinberger v. Romero-Barcelo, 456 U.S. 305 (1982).

66. It is important to distinguish between discretionary and non-discretionary federal actions in an ESA context. Discretionary actions and decisions involve determinations of fact made by an expert federal agency. For example, the Secretary's assessment in a biological opinion of whether an agency action jeopardizes listed species is discretionary. Courts give this type of agency determination deference unless it is completely

In *Cabinet Mountains Wilderness/Scotchmans' Peak Grizzly Bears v. Peterson*,[67] plaintiffs attempted to exploit this ambiguity by arguing that Congress mandated *de novo* review. The court held that since the ESA does not specify a standard of review, judicial review of agency actions allegedly violating the statute is governed by the "arbitrary and capricious" standard of section 706 of the Administrative Procedure Act.[68] No subsequent ESA cases have adopted a substantially different review standard.

While the "arbitrary and capricious" standard accords agency decisions substantial deference, it nevertheless requires agencies to demonstrate that their actions are rational. In deciding whether an agency has met this burden in a specific instance, a court will inquire into whether the agency has "considered the relevant factors and articulated a rational connection between the facts found and the choice made."[69] This test has been explicitly employed to strike down an agency action challenged on ESA grounds.[70]

A. *Judicial Review Under Section 4*

Section 4 explicitly provides for the availability of judicial review whenever (1) the Secretary finds that a petition to add or remove a species from the protected lists does not present substantial information indicating that the action may be warranted, (2) when the Secretary rejects such a petition as not warranted, and (3) when the Secretary declines to act on a petition found to be warranted because of other pending listing proposals.[71] The ESA's legislative history indicates that the arbitrary and capricious standard applies to court review of these determinations.[72]

Congress directed courts to take an especially close look at instances where the Secretary declines to list a species simply be-

---

arbitrary. On the other hand, non-discretionary matters involve determinations of law. For example, the decision whether to carry out a procedural ESA obligation, such as preparing a biological assessment, is non-discretionary. Courts make their own independent determinations in disputes over non-discretionary ESA obligations.

67. 685 F.2d 678 (D.C. Cir. 1982).

68. *Id.* at 685.

69. Baltimore Gas & Electric Co. v. Natural Resources Defense Council, 462 U.S. 87, 105 (1983).

70. National Wildlife Federation v. Hodel, 23 Env't Rep. Cas. (BNA) 1089, 1091-92 (E.D. Cal. 1985).

71. 16 U.S.C. § 1533(b)(3)(C)(ii).

72. H.R. Conf. Rep. No. 835, 97th Cong., 2d Sess. 21-22 (1982), *reprinted in* 1982 U.S. Code Cong. & Admin. News 2362-63.

cause of listing work already in progress, even though this review is carried out under the arbitrary and capricious standard. In an explanation of the 1982 amendments, lawmakers noted:

> First, the Secretary must be actively working on other listings and delistings and must determine and publish a finding that such other work has resulted in pending proposals which actually preclude his proposing the petitioned action at that time. Second, the Secretary must determine and present evidence that he is, in fact, making expeditious progress in the process of listing and delisting other species. In cases challenging the Secretary's claim on inability to propose an otherwise warranted petitioned action, the court will, in essence, be called on to separate justifications grounded in the purposes of the Act from the foot-dragging efforts of a delinquent agency.[73]

A consideration undoubtedly relevant to whether challenged inaction by the Secretary on a listing petition is "grounded in the purposes of the Act" is the priority number of the species under petition relative to the priorities of species whose listings have precluded action on the species under petition.[74]

Section 4 also directs the Secretary to promulgate regulations to conserve threatened species.[75] While promulgation of such regulations is mandatory, the Secretary has discretion to determine the content of the regulations, provided they are designed to further the conservation of threatened species.[76] Therefore, courts will review these regulations under the arbitrary and capricious standard.[77]

Finally, section 4 directs the Secretary to implement recovery plans.[78] This duty is apparently mandatory. Thus, whether the Secretary has implemented a recovery plan in a given instance simply presents a factual question for the reviewing court to resolve.

---

73. *Id.*
74. For discussion of the ESA's priority system requirement, as well as the Secretary's priority system, see *supra* Chapter 3, notes 45-53 and accompanying text.
75. 16 U.S.C. § 1533(d). For extensive discussion of this requirement, see Chapter 4.
76. If regulations promulgated under Section 4(d) are not designed to conserve threatened species within the statutory definition of conservation, the Secretary has exceeded his authority. This reasoning proved successful to plaintiffs challenging Section 4(d) regulations which permitted takings of threatened timber wolves. *See supra* Chapter 4, notes 65-68 and accompanying text. *See also* State of Louisiana v. Verity, 853 F.2d 322, 333 (5th Cir. 1988) (regulations aimed at preventing the taking of a protected species are presumed to be designed to preserve the species).
77. *See State of Louisiana* 853 F.2d at 326-27.
78. 16 U.S.C. § 1533(f).

B. *Judicial Review Under Section 7*

Section 7 contains a somewhat confusing mix of discretionary and non-discretionary provisions; therefore, one must carefully classify the type of ESA claim involved in a specific case before the applicable standard of review becomes clear. ESA claims generally fall into four categories: (1) allegations that a federal action is likely to jeopardize listed species or adversely affect critical habitat in violation of section 7(a)(2); (2) allegations that a federal agency has made an irreversible and irretrievable commitment of resources during consultation in violation of section 7(d); (3) claims involving section 7(a)(1)'s mandate to conserve listed species; and (4) allegations of violations of procedural requirements set forth in section 7. The standard of judicial review relevant to each type of claim is discussed below.

1. *Allegations of substantive Section 7(a)(2) violations.*

Section 7(a)(2) flatly prohibits agency actions likely to jeopardize listed species or destroy or adversely modify critical habitat. To assist agencies in complying with this provision, section 7 contains elaborate requirements for consultation between the Secretary and federal agencies proposing to carry out actions which may affect listed species. Due to section 7's consultation mechanism, courts do not make independent determinations of whether challenged agency actions violate section 7(a)(2) as a matter of law. Instead, courts evaluate the consultation process. If a court determines that consultation was properly conducted, it will not disturb the finding made as a result of consultation as to whether an agency action complies with section 7(a)(2). On the other hand, if a reviewing court determines that the Secretary or federal agency reached an arbitrary conclusion, or if the court finds procedural violations,[79] it will conclude that the challenged agency action has not satisfied the substantive mandates of section 7(a)(2).

Federal agencies carry out two basic types of discretionary action relevant to agencies' substantive compliance with the mandates of section 7(a)(2). The Secretary, in the context of consultation with agencies proposing to carry out or to authorize activities, determines whether federal actions are likely to jeop-

---

79. For a discussion of judicial review of procedural section 7 violations, see *infra* notes 98-102 and accompanying text.

ardize listed species or destroy or adversely modify critical habitat. The Secretary relays these determinations, together with reasonable and prudent alternatives to projects in danger of violating section 7(a)(2), to action agencies in the form of a biological opinion. Taking into account the biological opinion and other relevant factors, other federal agencies decide whether proceeding with their proposed actions will jeopardize listed species or adversely affect critical habitat. The conclusions of biological opinions and decisions of whether or not to proceed with proposed activities are therefore discretionary because they require determinations of fact (e.g., determinations of how agency actions affect listed species). Thus, courts will review them only under the deferential arbitrary and capricious standard.

Substantive challenges to the conclusions of biological opinions seldom succeed because courts will not substitute their judgments of fact for those of expert wildlife agencies. For instance, in *Friends of Endangered Species, Inc. v. Jantzen*,[80] the plaintiff argued that the Secretary did not use the best scientific evidence available in rendering a biological opinion. The plaintiff organization based its claim on the allegation that uncontroverted evidence from plaintiff's experts revealed major mistakes in the field studies upon which the biological opinion relied. Though couched in procedural terms of section 7's best scientific evidence requirement, this claim was in fact a substantive challenge to the biological opinion's conclusions. The key factor which distinguishes the plaintiff's arguments in *Jantzen* from true procedural challenges to a biological opinion[81] is that the plaintiff in the *Jantzen* litigation failed to direct the Secretary or the reviewing court to any relevant evidence which the Secretary did not consider in rendering the disputed biological opinion. Rather, the plaintiff in *Jantzen* simply presented expert testimony to the court which refuted the Secretary's conclusions. Citing this fact, the court upheld the Secretary's findings after concluding that the findings were not arbitrary and capricious.

Had the court adopted the plaintiff's position in *Jantzen*, it would have been forced to weigh the testimony of the plaintiff's experts attacking the biological opinion against the Secretary's

---

80. 760 F.2d 976 (9th Cir. 1985).

81. For a discussion of procedural challenges based on section 7's best scientific data requirement, see *infra* notes 101-102 and accompanying text. *See also supra* Chapter 6, notes 100-124 and accompanying text.

experts and reach its own determination on the validity of factual conclusions in the biological opinion. Under the arbitrary and capricious review standard, courts will not attempt to perform such balancing since such a procedure would put the court in the position of substituting its own judgment for the determinations of an expert federal agency.[82] Therefore, when reviewing the conclusions of a biological opinion under the arbitrary and capricious standard, courts will consider plaintiffs' evidence and expert testimony only to the extent such information sheds light on relevant information which the Secretary did not consider in rendering the biological opinion.

Courts likewise accord deference to the decision of a federal agency whether or not to proceed with a proposed project when the decision is made after consideration of the Secretary's biological opinion. For example, in *Stop H-3 Association v. Dole*[83] plaintiff alleged that the defendant agency's proposed action jeopardized a listed species, even though a U.S. Fish and Wildlife Service (FWS) biological opinion reached the opposite conclusion. Plaintiff argued that since action agencies make the final decision on whether to proceed with a proposal, the defendant could not rely solely on the favorable biological opinion to establish that its planned action complied with the directives of section 7(a)(2). In response, the court conceded that the defendant agency bore the ultimate responsibility under section 7 for insuring that its actions did not jeopardize listed species. It also recognized that section 7 required the agency to use the best scientific data available in making this finding. The court noted, however, that plaintiff failed to point out any relevant information not already considered by the Secretary in the biological opinion.[84] Therefore, the court concluded that the defendant had not acted un-

---

82. *See, e.g.*, Cabinet Mountain Wilderness/Scotchman's Peak Grizzly Bears v. Peterson, 685 F.2d 678, 685 (D.C. Cir. 1982).

83. 740 F.2d 1442 (9th Cir. 1984).

84. Plaintiffs also presented evidence that the proposed action would in fact jeopardize the species in question, contrary to the biological opinion. The court rejected this implicit challenge to the conclusion of the biological opinion, observing that the plaintiffs did not establish that the biological opinion findings were arbitrary and capricious merely by presenting information which conflicted with the opinion. Even though the biological opinion itself conceded that its conclusions were based on weak evidence and plaintiffs presented testimony that the opinion was incorrect, the court noted that it was obliged to defer to the agency's judgment of the factual issues. *Id.* at 1460. This reasoning is virtually identical to that of the court in *Friends of Endangered Species v. Jantzen. See* 760 F.2d 976, 985 (9th Cir. 1985). The *Jantzen* court, in fact, cited *Stop H-3* for the above proposition.

reasonably when it relied on the biological opinion in deciding to act.

The decision in *Stop H-3* is consistent with prior cases, as well as with the ESA's legislative history, which indicate that courts give great weight to biological opinions in determining whether agencies have complied with the substantive mandates of section 7(a)(2).[85] A corollary to the rule that courts give biological opinions great weight is that courts will be hesitant to uphold challenged agency actions which are inconsistent with biological opinions. In *Village of False Pass v. Watt*,[86] the court determined that the defendant agency had not adopted reasonable and prudent alternatives which would avoid jeopardizing endangered whales and which were suggested by the Secretary's biological opinion. Finding no justification in the administrative record for the agency's failure to adopt the biological opinion's suggestions, the court found the defendant's actions arbitrary and thus unlawful under section 7(a)(2).[87] It is likely that other courts will reach similar conclusions (1) if an agency proceeds with a project despite a biological opinion concluding that the action will violate section 7, (2) if an agency fails to adopt reasonable and prudent alternatives contained in a biological opinion, or (3) if an agency's actions are otherwise inconsistent with a biological opinion. On the other hand, the court in *False Pass* also held that *substantial* compliance with a biological opinion is adequate under section 7.[88]

Occasionally, however, no biological opinion may exist for a challenged agency action. Regulations permit an agency to avoid the section 7 consultation process if it determines, with concurrence from the Secretary, that its action will not adversely affect listed species.[89] Since this determination involves fact-finding rather than a question of law,[90] courts will likely review it under

---

85. *See, e.g.*, Roosevelt Campobello International Park Comm'n v. U.S. Environmental Protection Agency, 684 F.2d 1041, 1049 (1st Cir. 1982). *See also* H.R. Rep. No. 1625, 95th Cong., 2d Sess. 11 (1978).

86. Village of False Pass v. Watt, 565 F. Supp. 1123 (D. Alaska 1983), *aff'd*, Village of False Pass v. Clark, 733 F.2d 605 (9th Cir. 1984).

87. *Id.* at 1163.

88. *Id.* at 1162.

89. 50 C.F.R. § 402.14(b). For extensive discussion of this regulatory scheme, see *supra* Chapter 6, notes 44-57 and accompanying text.

90. It is at least arguable, however, that as a matter of law section 7 requires consultation on *all* agency actions that affect listed species. *See supra* Chapter 6, notes 39-43 and accompanying text.

the arbitrary and capricious standard. Though this standard gives deference to determinations by the Secretary and the action agency as to whether a project adversely affects listed species, it requires the Secretary and agency at least to set forth the basis of their decision in order for the court to evaluate whether the decision was rational or simply arbitrary.[91]

2. *Allegations of Section 7(d) violations.*

Section 7(d) affords agencies no discretion; it flatly prohibits irreversible and irretrievable commitments of resources during consultation which have the effect of foreclosing alternatives to agencies' proposed actions.[92] Therefore, courts independently determine whether agency actions challenged on section 4(d) grounds are valid or not as a matter of law.[93]

3. *Allegations of Section 7(a)(1) violations.*

Unlike disputes arising under section 7(a)(2), the standard of review applicable to alleged violations of section 7(a)(1)'s mandate to conserve listed species is unclear simply because the scope of this mandate remains ambiguous. Both agencies and courts have yet to define precisely federal agencies' duties under section 7(a)(1).[94] Whether these duties are mandatory or merely discretionary also is uncertain. As a result, it is unclear whether courts should defer to agencies' interpretations of their duties under section 7(a)(1) or simply order agencies to implement conservation measures as a matter of law.

Cases construing section 7(a)(1)'s conservation mandate have split on which review standard to apply, though no decision has carefully considered the question: In *Defenders of Wildlife v. Andrus*,[95] the court held that section 7(a)(1) imposes a duty on federal agencies to increase the populations of listed species. The court struck down as arbitrary hunting regulations that it found

---

91. *See supra* notes 68-69 and accompanying text. Curiously, however, the section 7 regulations do not require the agency or the Secretary to set forth their reasons for concluding that a project will not adversely affect listed species. *See* 50 C.F.R. § 402.14(b).

92. 16 U.S.C. § 1536(d). *See supra* Chapter 7 for discussion of this provision.

93. *See, e.g.,* North Slope Borough v. Andrus, 486 F. Supp. 332 (D.D.C. 1980), *aff'd in part, rev'd in part,* 642 F.2d 589 (D.C. Cir. 1980).

94. For extensive discussion of the ESA's mandate to conserve listed species and uncertainties over its scope, see *supra* Chapter 5.

95. 428 F. Supp. 167 (D. D.C. 1977).

conflicted with this duty. On the other hand, the court in *Carson-Truckee Water Conservancy District v. Watt* [96] found as a matter of law that section 7(a)(1) obligated the Bureau of Reclamation to operate a dam for the conservation of listed species.

In two other cases involving section 7(a)(1), whether the ESA's conservation mandate affirmatively requires agencies to carry out conservation measures was not at issue. Instead, plaintiffs in both cases challenged the purported conservation programs themselves. Both courts reviewed the disputed programs under the arbitrary and capricious standard.[97]

4. *Allegations of procedural Section 7 violations.*

Under circumstances specified by the ESA and its implementing regulations, section 7 obligates the Secretary and other federal agencies to carry out several non-discretionary procedural duties. Such duties include preparing biological assessments and using the best scientific and commercial data available. Significantly, courts equate failure to comply with section 7's procedural requirements with a violation of its substantive mandates as well.[98]

Courts make their own independent determinations of whether the Secretary and federal agencies have complied with section 7's procedural requirements. Plaintiffs bear the burden of establishing a procedural violation by showing that the circumstances triggering a procedural requirement exist and that the required procedures have not been followed.[99] How an agency action actually affects listed species is irrelevant to a procedural section 7 claim.[100]

One of the most common section 7 procedural claims is that the Secretary or a federal agency did not use the best scientific

---

96. Carson-Truckee Water Conservancy v. Watt, 537 F. Supp. 106 (D. Nev. 1982), *aff'd in part, rev'd in part*, Carson-Truckee Water Conservancy v. Clark, 741 F.2d 257 (9th Cir. 1984).

97. *See* Conner v. Andrus, 453 F. Supp. 1037 (W.D. Tex. 1978); National Wildlife Federation v. Hodel, 23 Env't Rep. Cas. (BNA) 1089 (E.D. Cal. 1985).

98. *See, e.g.*, Conservation Law Found. v. Watt, 560 F. Supp. 561, 573 (D. Mass. 1983); Thomas v. Peterson, 753 F.2d 754, 764 (9th Cir. 1985). *But see supra* Chapter 6, note 30.

99. Thomas v. Peterson, 753 F.2d at 765.

100. *Id.* ("It is not the responsibility of the plaintiffs to prove, nor the function of the courts to judge, the effect of a proposed action on an endangered species when proper procedures have not been followed.").

and commercial data available[101] when deciding whether an agency action met the requirements of section 7(a)(2). These challenges succeed only when plaintiffs can point out relevant data that was *not considered* by the Secretary or agency.[102]

C. *Judicial Review under Section 9*

Section 9 contains a list of several prohibited acts, most notably a ban on taking endangered species.[103] Courts determine whether a disputed activity violates this section by weighing the evidence presented by plaintiffs and defendants.[104] Plaintiffs bear the burden of establishing a section 9 violation.[105] When a person alleged to have violated a section 9 prohibitions claims the benefit of any statutory exemption, however, that person bears the burden of showing that the exemption applies.[106]

In 1982, Congress amended the ESA to authorize the Secretary to permit limited takings "incidental to, and not the purpose of" otherwise lawful activities.[107] Before issuing an incidental take permit to private persons, however, the Secretary must find that a conservation plan submitted by an applicant satisfies several statutory requirements, including a requirement that the taking will not reduce the likelihood of survival and recovery of the species to be taken. In *Friends of Endangered Species v. Jantzen*,[108] plaintiff challenged issuance of a permit to incidentally take endangered butterflies. The court evaluated the Secretary's biological findings in connection with the permit application, as well as the Secretary's decision to issue the permit, under the arbitrary and capricious standard. Courts will undoubtedly also apply this standard to the Secretary's decisions to allow federal agencies in-

---

101. For discussion of this requirement, see *supra* Chapter 6, notes 100-124 and accompanying text.

102. *See, e.g.*, Roosevelt Campobello International Park Comm'n v. U.S. Environmental Protection Agency, 684 F.2d 1041 (1st Cir. 1981); Conservation Law Found. v. Watt, 560 F. Supp. 561 (D. Mass. 1983). Contrast these decisions with *Friends of Endangered Species v. Jantzen*, 760 F.2d 976 (9th Cir. 1985) and *Stop H-3 Association v. Dole*, 740 F.2d 1442 (9th Cir. 1984).

103. *See generally* Chapter 4.

104. *See, e.g.*, Palila v. Hawaii Department of Land and Natural Resources, 649 F. Supp. 1070 (D. Hawaii 1981) (Palila II), *aff'd*, 852 F.2d 1106 (9th Cir. 1988); Sierra Club v. Lyng, 694 F. Supp. 1260 (E.D. Tex. 1988); Sierra Club v. Block, 614 F. Supp. 488 (D. D.C. 1985).

105. *See, e.g.*, Sierra Club v. Block, 614 F. Supp. at 492.

106. 16 U.S.C. § 1539(g).

107. *Id.* at § 1539(a)(1)(B).

108. 760 F.2d 976.

cidental taking of listed species.[109]

V. RELIEF GRANTED FOR ESA VIOLATIONS

A. *Injunctions*

Courts usually grant injunctive relief when they determine that an ESA violation has occurred. In *Thomas v. Peterson*,[110] the court held that an injunction is the proper remedy for ESA procedural violations absent "unusual circumstances."[111] Though the court did not speculate what unusual circumstances may make an injunction inappropriate, it noted that unusual circumstances in a NEPA context refer to instances where irreparable harm would flow from issuance of an injunction.[112] *National Wildlife Federation v. Hodel*[113] followed the *Thomas v. Peterson* rationale to enjoin a federal action which violated substantive ESA requirements. The court in *National Wildlife Federation* also considered two types of unusual circumstances which it acknowledged could conceivably harm the species involved in the case as a result of issuance of an injunction.[114] The court found, however, that this potential harm was outweighed by the harm likely to result without an injunction. Therefore, the court enjoined the challenged federal activity.

In *Vance v. Block*,[115] a federal district court conceded that "a technical violation of the ESA may have occurred," but nevertheless refused to grant injunctive relief.[116] Distinguishing its factual findings from the situation in *Thomas v. Peterson*, the court held that the ESA violation in the case at bar was *de minimis*; therefore, the court did not even consider granting an injunction.[117] Plaintiffs' ESA claim was dismissed on appeal for lack of

---

109. *See* 16 U.S.C. § 1536(b)(4).

110. 753 F.2d 754.

111. *Id.* at 764.

112. *Id.* at n.8.

113. 23 Env't Rep. Cas. (BNA) 1089 (E.D. Cal. 1985).

114. The plaintiff in the case attempted to halt use of lead shotgun pellets in order to protect bald eagles from lead poisoning. The defendants, however, argued that an injunction against use of lead shot would decrease hunting, decrease revenue from hunting licenses, and thereby force a cutback on programs to benefit waterfowl, a major food source of eagles. The defendants also argued that an injunction would create animosity toward federal wildlife agencies and would disrupt waterfowl conservation efforts.

115. 635 F. Supp. 163 (N.D. Ill. 1986).

116. *Id.* at 169.

117. *Id.*

jurisdiction.[118]

In *Village of False Pass v. Watt*,[119] the court carefully examined the question of what remedies are appropriate for ESA violations. It concluded that an injunction need not always issue for violations of the statute, but did not elaborate on what sort of violations would not call for injunctive relief.[120] The court also found that an injunction was necessary in the case at bar. The district court dissolved its injunction prior to appeal, however, so the appellate court did not examine the question of appropriate remedies for ESA violations.[121]

In *Sierra Club v. Marsh*,[122] the Ninth Circuit noted that "the balance of hardships and the public interest tip heavily in favor of endangered species."[123] Accordingly, the court held that plaintiffs were entitled to an injunction if defendants violated a substantive or procedural provision of the ESA.[124]

B. *Attorneys' Fees*

The ESA authorizes courts to award costs of litigation, including reasonable attorney and expert witness fees, to any party to a suit brought under the statute's citizen suit provision.[125] Such an award is made whenever the court determines it is "appropriate."

In *Ruckelshaus v. Sierra Club*,[126] the United States Supreme Court construed the citizen suit provision of the Clean Air Act, which is substantially similar to that of the ESA. The court rejected a claim that an award of fees could be appropriate even if the party seeking reimbursement lost its suit. To qualify for fees, the court held that a party must be at least "partially prevailing" or achieve "some success, even if not major success."[127] The court emphasized, however, that "trivial success on the merits, or purely procedural victories" would be insufficient to render an award of fees appropriate.[128]

---

118. Save the Yaak Committee v. Block, 840 F.2d 714, 721 (9th Cir. 1988).
119. 565 F. Supp. 1123 (D. Alaska 1983), *aff'd*, Village of False Pass v. Clark, 733 F.2d 605 (9th Cir. 1984).
120. *Id.* at 1164.
121. Village of False Pass v. Clark, 733 F.2d 605, 609 (9th Cir. 1984).
122. 816 F.2d 1376 (9th Cir. 1987).
123. *Id.* at 1383 (citing TVA v. Hill, 437 U.S. at 187-88).
124. *Id.* at 1384.
125. 16 U.S.C. § 1540(g)(4).
126. 463 U.S. 680 (1983).
127. *Id.* at 688.
128. *Id.* at n.9.

Appellate courts have applied the logic of *Ruckelshaus* to the fee award provision of the ESA. In *Conservation Law Foundation v. Secretary of the Interior*,[129] the First Circuit interpreted *Ruckelshaus* to allow fee awards to parties who achieve "notable progress, short of full achievement, on any issue of substance."[130] The court went on to hold that plaintiffs' success in obtaining a preliminary injunction could support an award of fees even though the case was later dismissed as moot. The court noted that obtaining a preliminary injunction will not always entitle the prevailing party to fees, but it may make a fee award appropriate when the court's findings and rulings on a motion for preliminary injunction come close to the relief ultimately sought. Nevertheless, the *Conservation Law Foundation* court reversed the district court's award of fees for ESA claims. The First Circuit determined that plaintiffs' ESA claims involved differing proof from Outer Continental Shelf Lands Act (OCSLA) claims upon which the preliminary injunction was based, and thus the district court's ruling on the OCSLA did not support fees for plaintiffs' ESA claims. Since the district court never reached plaintiffs' ESA claims in granting a preliminary injunction the appellate court determined that an award of fees under the ESA was not appropriate even though the relief granted on OCSLA grounds was substantially the same as the court would have granted had it favorably ruled on plaintiffs' ESA claims.

In *Carson-Truckee Water Conservancy District v. Watt*,[131] intervenor Pyramid Lake Paiute Tribe unsuccessfully sought attorney fees under the ESA after prevailing on the merits of their claim. The Tribe interpreted *Ruckelshaus* to *entitle* prevailing parties or partially prevailing parties to fee awards under the ESA's "when appropriate" standard. The Ninth Circuit rejected this argument, holding that parties achieving some degree of success on the merits of their ESA claims were merely eligible for, but not entitled to, attorney fees.[132]

Courts have yet to resolve the question of whether a party who successfully advances ESA claims in proceedings other than actual litigation pursuant to the citizen suit provisions of section 11 are eligible for fee awards. In *Roosevelt Campobello International*

129.   790 F.2d 965 (1986).
130.   *Id.* at 967.
131.   748 F.2d 523.
132.   *Id.* at 526-27.

Park v. United States Environmental Protection Agency,[133] the court noted that the legislative history does not indicate that Congress intended the fees provision of the ESA to apply to proceedings other than citizen suits, but the court declined to rule on the issue. The Ninth Circuit in *Carson-Truckee* similarly mentioned but refused to resolve this question.[134]

As emphasized in the *Carson-Truckee* decision, there is a distinction between eligibility for fee awards under the ESA and entitlement to such awards. Assuming a party is eligible, a court actually awards fees only upon a finding that the party's action has *substantially* furthered the purposes and goals of the ESA.[135] To make this determination, courts generally consider the importance, complexity, and novelty of issues raised in litigation, as well as whether the case in question has benefitted the public interest by aiding interpretation and implementation of the ESA.[136] Courts also may consider the costs of the litigation to the public interest in deciding whether a fee award is appropriate. In a case involving disputed offshore oil leases, the D.C. Circuit cited a $30 million government loss resulting from delays in leasing caused by litigation as a factor in its determination that a fee award to plaintiffs was not appropriate.[137]

When a court decides that a fee award is appropriate, it must determine (1) a reasonable number of compensable hours, (2) a reasonable hourly rate, (3) other reasonable expenses, and (4) any additional bonus award. The court in *Palila v. Hawaii Department of Land and Natural Resources*[138] discussed several factors relevant to the first two determinations. In *Sierra Club v. Clark*,[139] the Eighth Circuit court upheld a district court's thirty percent upward adjustment of fees awarded to plaintiffs who successfully challenged regulations allowing sport trapping of threatened timber wolves. The district court justified the bonus by citing the novelty and difficulty of the issue presented, as well as the litigation's importance for overall management of threatened species. The appellate court rejected defendant's argument that the nov-

133. 684 F.2d 1041 (1st Cir. 1982).
134. 748 F.2d at 523.
135. *See, e.g.*, Carson-Truckee, 748 F.2d 523 (1983). *See also* Village of Kaktovik v. Army Corps of Engineers, 689 F.2d 222 (D.C. Cir. 1982).
136. Village of Kaktovik, 689 F.2d 222.
137. *Id.*
138. 512 F. Supp. 1006 (D. Hawaii 1981).
139. 755 F.2d 608.

elty and complexity of the issues is not an appropriate factor upon which to base increased fee awards since litigating these issues presumably requires more hours and thus automatically results in higher fee awards. Finding that enhanced awards may be justified in some cases of exceptional success, the Eighth Circuit held that the district court did not abuse its discretion in making an such award. However, the appellate court in *Conservation Law Foundation* [140] closely scrutinized and overturned a district court's award of enhanced fees under the *when appropriate* standard contained in the OCSLA. While conceding that enhanced fee awards are equitable judgments left to court's discretion, the First Circuit held that courts must "set forth in some detail the factors underlying its decision to adjust upwards; mere conclusory statements will not suffice."

Though no court has examined the question, the availability of fee awards for proceedings other than actual litigation could prove to be an important issue in the future. For example, the availability of such fees could substantially affect interested groups' or persons' abilities to compile the information and expert opinions necessary to support a petition to list or delist a species. Since fee awards clearly provide incentive for private enforcement of the goals of the ESA through citizen suits, it would make sense for courts to extend fee awards to other proceedings involving the ESA where the statute itself explicitly invites citizens' participation, including the petition provisions of section 4.

---

140. 790 F.2d 965 (1st Cir. 1986).

Chapter 10

Conclusion

In late autumn of 1988, three endangered California gray whales became trapped in Arctic pack ice north of Barrow, Alaska when they delayed migrating to their winter habitat near Baja California. The huge mammals were forced to remain near a shrinking hole in the ice in order to breathe; the whales would have suffocated if they had attempted to swim to the nearest open water. As the whales grew increasingly battered by ice and exhausted by ocean currents, Barrow residents, including Alaska Natives, state and federal agency personnel, North Slope oil companies, and two Soviet icebreakers, worked around the clock to save the animals. The rescuers received an encouraging telephone call from President Reagan, and millions of people around the world awaited the latest news on the whales' fate. Two whales eventually succeeded in reaching open water thanks to these rescue efforts.

The attempt to free the trapped whales is analogous to efforts on a broader scale to save threatened and endangered species from the brink of extinction. Unfortunately, however, the cooperation and sense of urgency that prevailed in the frozen Arctic has infrequently characterized attempts to preserve vanishing species. For example, under President Reagan's banner of "regulatory relief," many federal environmental safeguards—including protections for endangered wildlife—were weakened or eliminated. The private sector usually shows far more concern for shareholders than for species. In addition, the American public seems terminally indifferent to the plight of many endangered species. The public took little notice, for example, when the last dusky seaside sparrow died and when a reservoir innundated the majority of remaining specimens of the furbish lousewort, an endangered plant.

Are we worse off without dusky seaside sparrows, furbish louseworts, or even whales? There are many reasons to give an affirmative response to this question. Destroying potentially valuable genetic resources before investigating their uses and disrupting ecosystems which may provide us with crucial benefits carry high opportunity costs. Eliminating species also deprives future generations of some of the aesthetic pleasures of the natural world. Lastly, many people find human-caused extinctions ethically and morally unacceptable.

These considerations originally moved Congress to enact the Endangered Species Act, still the most forceful declaration in favor of wildlife conservation made by any nation. Although lawmakers have amended the ESA four times in its fifteen-year history, they have steadfastly rejected efforts to significantly weaken its provisions. Most changes, in fact, have strengthened the statute, underscoring a continuing congressional commitment to halt and reverse the trend toward species extinctions.

Courts have often cited Congress' commitment to species conservation in construing the ESA's provisions. Following the lead of the U.S. Supreme Court, which ruled that section 7 of the ESA required a huge TVA dam to yield to snail darters' habitat needs, the federal judiciary has generally resolved disputes over interpretation of the Act by choosing to construe the Act's terms most favorably for endangered species. This trend, coupled with the ESA's broad citizen suit provision and minimal standing requirements, makes litigation by concerned private parties a significant ESA enforcement mechanism.

Public vigilance and judicial oversight will likely become even more important to ensure that listed species receive the full protections to which they are entitled. The federal bureaucracy has an increasingly spotty record of administering the ESA. During the Reagan Administration, for example, the Secretary of the Interior adopted narrow interpretations of many of the Act's provisions. Attempts to constrict the definition of "harm" within the statutory definition of "take;" interpretation of the ESA's directive to conserve species as merely an enabling clause, rather than as an affirmative mandate; and the Secretary's limited regulatory interpretation of section 7 attest to the problem that the executive branch may not always translate Congress' concern for vanishing species into forceful actions. Evidence also exists that the Secretary occasionally ignores ESA requirements. For example, a Denver newspaper reported in 1988 that Fish and Wildlife Service biologists were ordered by their superiors to issue a "no jeopardy" biological opinion for a controversial proposed dam even before completion of studies on the project's impacts and despite the fact that the reservoir would destroy up to one-third of an endangered butterfly's remaining habitat.[1]

If we seriously intend to slow the rate of human-caused species extinctions, there is no longer a margin for malfeasance, delay, or even apathy. The Endangered Species Act must be implemented and enforced with the urgency of a last-ditch rescue attempt. The stakes are high. Thousands of species face extirpation as a result of human activities. Time is short. Continued growth of the human population and skyrocketing demands for resources threaten to deepen the extinction crisis. Only genuine determination on the part of federal and state bureaucracies to conserve listed species, cooperation from the private sector, and public support and vigilance will insure the continued existence of grizzly bears and gibbons, whales and white wartyback pearly mussels, hairy rattleweeds—and humans.

---

1. The Rocky Mountain News, Apr. 14, 1988, at 6.